A Blessing
～In～
Disguise

A BLESSING ～ IN ～ DISGUISE

39 Life Lessons from Today's Greatest Teachers

ANDREA JOY COHEN, M.D.

Foreword by Thich Nhat Hanh

BERKLEY BOOKS, NEW YORK

THE BERKLEY PUBLISHING GROUP
Published by the Penguin Group
Penguin Group (USA) Inc.
375 Hudson Street, New York, New York 10014, USA
Penguin Group (Canada), 90 Eglinton Avenue East, Suite 700, Toronto, Ontario M4P 2Y3, Canada
(a division of Pearson Penguin Canada Inc.)
Penguin Books Ltd., 80 Strand, London WC2R 0RL, England
Penguin Group Ireland, 25 St. Stephen's Green, Dublin 2, Ireland (a division of Penguin Books Ltd.)
Penguin Group (Australia), 250 Camberwell Road, Camberwell, Victoria 3124, Australia
(a division of Pearson Australia Group Pty. Ltd.)
Penguin Books India Pvt. Ltd., 11 Community Centre, Panchsheel Park, New Delhi—110 017, India
Penguin Group (NZ), 67 Apollo Drive, Rosedale, North Shore 0632, New Zealand
(a division of Pearson New Zealand Ltd.)
Penguin Books (South Africa) (Pty.) Ltd., 24 Sturdee Avenue, Rosebank, Johannesburg 2196,
South Africa

Penguin Books Ltd., Registered Offices: 80 Strand, London WC2R 0RL, England

PUBLISHER'S NOTE: While the author has made every effort to provide accurate telephone numbers and Internet addresses at the time of publication, neither the publisher nor the author assumes any responsibility for errors, or for changes that occur after publication. Further, publisher does not have any control over and does not assume any responsibility for author or third-party websites or their content.

This book is an original publication of The Berkley Publishing Group.

PRINTING HISTORY
Berkley trade paperback edition / January 2008

Library of Congress Cataloging-in-Publication Data

Cohen, Andrea Joy, 1964–
    A blessing in disguise : 39 life lessons from today's greatest teachers / Andrea Joy Cohen ; foreword by Thich Nhat Hanh.—Berkley trade paperback ed.
        p. cm.
    ISBN: 978-0-425-21966-9
    1. Life.   2. Encouragement.   3. Success.   4. Conduct of life.   5. Self-actualization (Psychology).   I. Title.
    BD431.C6423 2008
    128—dc22

                                                                                2007035179

PRINTED IN THE UNITED STATES OF AMERICA

10 9 8 7 6 5 4 3 2 1

This book is dedicated to my wonderful parents,
Abe and Florence Cohen

ACKNOWLEDGMENTS

I give my sincerest thanks to everyone who made this book possible. Many people shared their story of wisdom; a tremendous thank-you to all of you.

Thank you to:

My parents, Abe and Florence, who did a fantastic job raising me—thanks for all your love, support, humor, and wisdom.

Julie Hill, my wonderful literary agent. You are more than an agent. Thank you for your hard work, special expertise, amazing insights and encouragement, and for your sincere friendship. Thank you for your commitment to making the world a better place.

The wonderful authors who wrote stories for this book. I cannot thank you enough for sharing your life and taking the time to write your story for the book.

Thich Nhat Hanh, for a beautiful foreword and for bringing more peace to the world.

Mary Cullen, for your fabulous and indispensable help with reviewing and editing the stories and the resources, and for your brilliant feedback. I couldn't have done it without you!

Julianne Murphy, for all your wonderful dedication and efficiency, and for getting me organized, providing support, and soliciting stories. You went beyond the call of duty.

Eloise Berg, for your indispensable help, love, loyalty, editing, and assistance with finishing off this book and the book proposal. You are amazing!

Anne Moutray, for keeping me organized, soliciting stories, and getting releases, and for all the help moving.

Beth Kearns, for all your dedicated assistance with the office and book details. I really appreciate it!

Claire Gerus, for your fabulous help editing the book proposal.

My fantastic editor, Denise Silvestro, for your strong faith in the book, for your support, brilliance, patience, insights, expertise, and hard work! I feel very grateful to have you as my editor.

Associate editor Katie Day, for your warmth, wisdom, hard work, dedication, and astute direction. You are fabulous!

Sheila Moody, for your copyediting expertise, Jessica McDonnell, the production editor, and Melissa Broder, my publicist.

My wonderful publishers, marketing team, publicity department, and sales team at Berkley and Penguin. I am so appreciative of your hard work and dedication.

A special thanks to the art department for the cover design. It's fantastic and I love it.

All the assistants, managers, and relatives of the contributors to this work, and permissions editors who were amazing liaisons, including my friend Luzie Mason, Alice Pierce, Karen Gerdes, Beverly Haberman, Bhikshuni True Virtue: (Annabel Laity), Sister

Chan Khong, Srinidhi Hussein, Jo-Lynne Worley, Julie Quiring, Courtney R. Miller, Katherine at Kriya Institute, Lisa Jae, Koelle Simpson, Kerri Kumasaka, Pete Sidley, Peter London, Sheri Feldman, Linda Noble Topf, and everyone else who helped.

Everyone who wrote a contribution that for space reasons did not make it into this book, or who referred a friend for the book. Thank you so much.

Those who have written and will write a review of this book, including Daphne Rose Kingma, Belleruth Naparstek, Dharma Singh Khalsa, and Stephen Levine.

Pearl Wolfson, a shining star in my life (and wild wise woman), my friend and "bubbie" who loved me unconditionally.

Anne Richter, my "sister," for your friendship, wisdom, loyalty, and phone calls. You are the best. I am lucky to have a friend like you!

Fabienne Ouaknine, for your friendship, support, advice, and lunches, and for always going beyond the call of duty.

Connie Frazer, for your friendship and support. You are a gift to the world. Thanks for being there when I need you and for your wisdom and guidance.

The Busses: David, Marcia, Zahava, Leora, Shalom, Eitan, Zack, and Raphie, for friendship and all the wonderful meals.

Joanie Borysenko, for all the shopping, travel, sisterly wisdom, and friendship!

All my teachers, past, present, and future.

My patients, for teaching me so much, and for the honor of taking care of them.

My students and workshop participants. Thank you for the inspiration to write this book.

Thank you to my friends Lisa and Moses Heguy for looking

after my house when I am out of town, and for keeping it beautiful.

To all my many wonderful friends, and also my cousins and my relatives, and their families.

I love and appreciate all of you. I feel blessed to know you all.

For specific support or help during the writing and preparation of the book, I'd like to thank Jenna Dunlop, Tamara Sofi, Linda Andrews, Lynn and Arnie Rosenthal, Peter Amato, Lucie Desmarais, Michelle Roth, Carol Mellinger, Kate Hatayama, Paula Miriani, Amy Mills, Katish Aron, Rex Bell, Dawn Mahowald, Sue Pelissier, Kurt and Julie Lear, Luisa and Dan Brodsky, Pat Madsen, Linda Moore, Boris Draznin, Carol Welsh, Shelia Brown, York Miller, Mai Lan Hyugen, Janice Richman Eisenstat and David Eisenstat, Saroch Goel and family, the Meyers, Karen Zorn, Christine and David Hibbard, Stephen and Ondrea Levine, Srinidhi and Prithima Hussein, Laurie Grant, Leonard Perlmutter, Mark Heider, Eileen Lowey, Judy Banjavic, Katherine Carol, Ilana Fishman, Mildred Lynn McDonald, Rosemary Davies-Janes, Pamela Potvin, Nicoll Stapleton, Lyndsey Hale, Elaine Arnoldy, Noreena Hertz, Ronda Loredo, Hedy Steinberg, Ildeko Toth, Shelly and Raj Bhattacharya, and Jennifer Jackson.

Also to Amma, P. Prajnana, as well as to my friends Kathleen, Bill, Sudarshan, Annelle, Raymon, Jai, Sraboni, Regina, Dorie, Viji, Tiana, Judy, S. Karuna Karma, Candice, and Maya, for your ideas or assistance while I wrote this book.

And thank you, God. I am so grateful for all the blessings in my life.

CONTENTS

SECTION FOUR: LIFE'S EVERYDAY LESSONS

SECTION FIVE: SPIRITUALITY

SECTION SIX: FAMILY, LOVE, AND RELATIONSHIPS

HOW TO USE THIS BOOK

The book is composed of 39 amazing pieces of writing, divided into six sections: Overcoming Challenges; Soul Expression; Death and Dying; Life's Everyday Lessons; Spirituality; and Family, Love, and Relationships. The book also contains original chapter-opening poems by the author.

There is not one correct way to read this book. You can read it in strict order, skip around by chapter or story, read one story a week for almost a year. You might want to form a discussion group in your neighborhood and talk over the pieces in a group setting. To help you begin conversations, I have included personal transformation discussion questions at the end of the book. I will have more information and ideas for these groups as well as book club questions on the web page DrAndreaJoyCohen.com. At the end of each section, I have included resources for books, music, company websites, and hotlines for the topic covered in the section.

I hope you will enjoy reading this book as much as I have enjoyed preparing it.

FOREWORD

Dr. Cohen and her colleagues have written this book about responding to their life experiences mindfully for self-understanding and personal transformation. By being mindful of situations that are presented in our daily lives, we are able to understand them as opportunities for learning, and can consequently develop forgiveness, heal depression, resolve jealousy, or surrender control. Our healing then begins and our heart becomes open to our birthright, which is appreciation of the peace and joy within.

In these busy times, it is difficult to be mindful and be aware of the present moment. When I am mindful, while I sit here, I don't think of somewhere else, of the future or the past. I sit here, and I know where I am. This is very important.

We tend to be alive in the future, not now. We say, "Wait until I finish school and get my Ph.D. degree, and then I will be really alive." When we have it, and it's not easy to get, we say to ourselves, "I have to wait until I have a job in order to be *really* alive." And then after the job, a car. After the car, a house. We are not capable of being alive in the present moment.

We tend to postpone being alive until the future, the distant future, we don't know when. Now is not the moment to be alive. We may never be alive at all in our entire lives. Therefore, the technique, if we must speak of a technique, is to *be* in the present moment, to be aware that we are here and now, and the only moment to be alive is the present moment.

"I know this is a wonderful moment." This is the only moment that is real. To be here and now, and enjoy the present moment, is our most important task. "Calming, Smiling, Present moment, Wonderful moment."

One wonderful seed in our store consciousness—the seed of mindfulness—once manifested, has the capacity of being aware of what is happening in the present moment. If we take one peaceful, happy step and we know that we are taking a peaceful, happy step, mindfulness is present.

Mindfulness is an important agent for our transformation and healing, but our seed of mindfulness has been buried under many layers of forgetfulness and pain for a long time. We are rarely aware that we have eyes that see clearly, a heart and liver that function well, and a non-toothache. We live in forgetfulness, looking for happiness somewhere else, ignoring and crushing the precious elements of happiness that are already in us and around us. If we breathe in and out and see that the tree is there, alive and beautiful, the seed of our mindfulness will be watered, and it will grow stronger.

We have within us a miraculous power, and if we live our daily lives in mindfulness, if we take steps mindfully, with love and care we can produce the miracle and transform our world into a miraculous place to live.

Taking steps slowly, in mindfulness, is an act of liberation. You walk and you free yourself of all worries, anxieties, projects, and attachments. One step like this has the power to liberate you from all afflictions. Just being there, you transform yourself, and your compassion will bear witness.

First, let us light the torch of our awareness and learn again how to drink tea, eat, wash dishes, walk, sit, drive, and work in awareness. We do not have to be swept along by circumstances. We are not just a leaf or a log in a rushing river. With awareness, each of our daily acts takes on a new meaning, and we discover that we are more than machines, that our activities are not just mindless repetitions. We find that life is a miracle, the universe is a miracle, and we, too, are a miracle.

The capacity to feel at peace anywhere is a positive seed. The energy to run away is not. If we practice mindfulness, whenever the energy of wanting to run away arises, we can smile at it and say, "Hello, my old friend, I recognize you." The moment we recognize any habit energy, it loses a little of its power.

It isn't necessary to run away or abandon our present home and look for an illusory home, a so-called "paradise" that is really just a shadow of happiness. When we produce faith, energy, mindfulness, concentration, and insight in our power plants, we realize that our true home is already filled with light and power.

—*Thich Nhat Hanh*

Thich Nhat Hanh has lived an extraordinary life in an extraordinary time. Since age sixteen, he has been a Buddhist monk, a peace activist, and a seeker of the way. Hanh has survived three wars, countless acts of persecution, and more than thirty years of exile. His lineage is traceable directly to the Buddha himself.

Thich Nhat Hanh has also written more than one hundred books of poetry, fiction, and philosophy, including the national bestsellers Anger *and* Living Buddha, Living Christ. *He has founded universities and social services organizations, and rescued boat people. He was nominated for the Nobel Peace Prize by the Reverend Martin Luther King, Jr.*

Love Your Soul First

Blossom my dear
Trapped in a body
The soul has no recourse
But to try to break through
The physical limitations of its host
You may hear a whisper
Or a pain
Or a song deep inside you
Free your soul to be what it must
You are here to know your soul
    first
To tumble in the deep grasses of
    summer
To rush down the river rapids
    naked with glee
Whatever you may have been told
You are not here just to collect
    televisions and CDs
Nor to gather promotions
Nor to look great in a pair of tight
    jeans
You are here to love your soul first
Nothing more, nothing less
What does this mean?
To learn the lessons of life
Joy, love, peace, strength
Betrayal, loss, jealousy, anger
To begin anew time and time
    again

To breathe every morning as if for
    the first time
To be free of the collective beliefs
    of the world
To stand up for yourself
To take good care of yourself
As if you were a newborn baby
To hear the quiet whisper of your
    soul
Or sometimes the loud roar
Sometimes it means being alone
Or finding new friends or family
Moving by yourself to faraway
    lands
Or staying where you are and
    making amends
Or doing nothing
Shhhhh
Can you hear the beat of your
    soul?
Trying to connect with you
Stop being so busy—listen
And let it be one with you
How can you love anyone else
    until you
Love your soul first
First love your soul

Andrea Joy Cohen, M.D.

INTRODUCTION

Today's world presents unique daily challenges for most people on the planet. Although you may not know it, these experiences are often meant to teach you psychological or spiritual lessons. Do you feel ready to face these challenging lessons? How many times have you wished you had more help and solutions for your problems? You may have discovered that the path of your life's journey is not well lit. Or, perhaps you've found that the lessons that you are meant to learn from your existence are not clear to you. Sometimes there is a hidden lesson or opportunity buried in your challenge, which is "a blessing in disguise."

In this book, some of the greatest teachers of our time share their incredible personal stories. As modern-day spiritual alchemists, they have digested and transformed the events of their lives. Now, by generously sharing their stories, they're transforming their lessons into healing and meaningful experiences for you. Their wisdom and humor will illuminate your learning. When great difficulties arise in your life, it is common for your faith to be shaken and to ask: "Why me? Why did this happen to me? I am a really good person." Many of the contributors to this book have visited dark times and places and reemerged stronger, with more inner peace and wisdom, strengthened faith, and a deeper understanding of life and of themselves. They have realized their life challenges are actually blessings in disguise. By reading their stories, you can learn how to do the same.

The Universe provides opportunities for soul growth through life lessons. Perhaps, as many life philosophers have suggested, our life here represents an "earth school" for our souls. Every day, we have opportunities to become more honest, kind, and patient, as well as to rid ourselves of anger, jealousy, and hate. In this life model, the lesson often presents over and over until we finally "get it." When we make that leap and understand the lesson, deep healing occurs.

How do you know if you are facing a major life lesson? Maybe you've been knocked to your knees by tragedy. Perhaps you date or marry the "same person" over and over again. Or alternatively, maybe opportunities repeatedly arise for you to realize your own power, to speak up for yourself and set boundaries, but you refuse to speak up. Perhaps you don't land the job of your dreams. Sometimes you have no idea about the meaning of the lesson. You suspect that it is only a torture experiment by your spouse or your boss. In fact, it may take years to gain some basic understanding of the situation.

It takes courage to examine your life under the microscope, to shine a light in those dark corners of your life and make the necessary adjustments. Your life may need to be pruned, fertilized, and watered to make room for new growth and love. Today you may feel that the goal of life is for everything to stay safe and stable. Furthermore, as some of the authors point out, sometimes you need to change your job, friends, spouse, and attitude to honor your soul's path.

Life lessons are all around us. Watch for them. Learn from them. You are a hero in your own hero's journey. Your lesson might be a blessing in disguise.

The real-life stories in this book were written by a diverse and amazing group of psychologists, physicians, artists, lawyers, writers, and spiritual teachers. In compiling this book, I asked the contributors to contribute a story, essay, or poem about an important or memorable personal life lesson. The luminaries are from a variety of careers, religions, countries, and philosophies, so their stories offer something for everyone. I selected these writers because of their life experiences, wisdom, honesty, and open hearts. Many were new friends, but they responded with great love, energy, and enthusiasm. I am grateful for their contributions, and know that their personal stories will inspire you.

This book is divided into six sections that deal with important issues: Overcoming Challenges; Soul Expression; Death and Dying; Life's Everyday Lessons; Spirituality; and Family, Love, and Relationships. Each section opens with a poem inspired by the topic. The inspiring essays deal with a wide range of subjects—everything from the death of a parent, forgiveness, and how to stand up for yourself to pregnancy, overcoming depression, coping with divorce, and healing from breast cancer. These wise stories provide you with a framework to interpret your own life lessons.

The stories in this book have several common themes. One is finding and expressing your unique self, despite fear, self-doubt, and the negative messages of society. The contributors have learned that they are here to express their souls and to create. They have learned that those people who find the courage to freely do so often experience fulfillment and bliss. Healing is another common theme; all of these stories are meant to help you on a healing journey. Healing means that you release the obstacles that keep you from living your authentic self and joyfully and creatively following your destiny. Healing also refers to the healing of your soul, the part of you that is eternal. Once you learn and heal from the lessons that the Universe shows you, you can feel more beauty, peace, and joy.

Wise masters say the human condition requires some type of guidance. So, consider this: we are not here only to collect material items, titles, pictures, or trophies nor are we here to work all of our waking hours. We are here to:

- Conquer fear, anger, love, and trust
- Learn about the love we have within us, as well as the darkness
- Enjoy love, beauty, and intimacy
- Make choices
- Live our dream with courage
- Manifest abundance and happiness
- Cocreate with God

However, in order to do these things, you must first learn more about your own soul. Challenges inspire your soul to grow and blossom.

As a closing thought, I want to leave you with a few suggestions from the collection of essays you're about to read. Feel free to add some of your own after you've finished your journey.

- You can cling to familiar expectations, conventions, and reasonable responses or you can listen to the sweet madness in your bones.
- Learn that real grace is not just being loved, it is learning how to love.
- I can rely on a basic inherent trust in my life.
- Anything is possible if you truly have the will to manifest your dreams into reality.
- Be grateful, compassionate, forgiving, patient, creative, and truthful.
- Hope is a skill of the heart.
- My life becomes rich and educated when I am uncomfortable.

It took me years to learn one of my greatest life lessons (patience is not one of my virtues). For years I had trouble accepting and embracing what showed up in my life. I would speculate on exactly what would transpire in my future to avoid making mistakes. I would try to second-guess situations, and I frequently made assumptions that were not correct, usually out of fear. I have come to realize that this is risky behavior, because I might miss out on the lesson that life is trying to teach me by being preoccupied with trying to control the outcome of the situation. The net result was the blockage or delay of my personal growth, or the repetition of the lesson in a bigger (and more annoying) way. Or sometimes I would manifest the very scenario I was trying to avoid in the first place! I have had to train myself to let go of this fear, and be more mindful and present in the moment, as Thich Nhat Hanh urges us to do in his wonderful foreword.

If you are having a major or minor lesson, don't forget to reach out to others to help you cope and heal. We are ultimately responsible for ourselves, but friends, relatives, and teachers can be a joy and a comfort. Get professional help if you need it. Inspiration and assistance are available—no matter what your financial means. It is possible to release your beliefs, habits, decisions, and old stories of your life and find the gift of challenge. To help you on your journey, I have included resources for further exploration at the end of each section. You might also want to form a support group to ponder the lessons, using the discussion questions at the end of the book. Remember to make the choices for yourself in the end!

This book is an invitation to lead a deeper, more meaningful life. You have the ability to deliberately create the life of your dreams. Soar as high as you can. Stretch and take that risk. Achieve the conscious choice to be healthy and happy. Let go of your old stories of yourself, and focus on what you truly want. Make every moment count. And remember that in the end, love is what really matters.

Don't wait another day. Your soul is waiting. Good luck, joy, and blessings on your journey.

—Andrea Joy Cohen, M.D.

The period of greatest gain in knowledge and experience is the most difficult period in one's life.

—THE DALAI LAMA

✌ SECTION ONE ✌
Overcoming Challenges

You gain strength, courage, and confidence in every experience in which you really stop to look fear in the face. You must do the thing you think you cannot do.

—ELEANOR ROOSEVELT

. . .

It is not easy to be a pioneer, but oh, it is so fascinating. I would not trade one moment, even the worst moment, for all the riches in the world.

—ELIZABETH BLACKWELL,

FIRST WOMAN PHYSICIAN IN THE UNITED STATES

. . .

Every blade of grass has its angel that bends over it and whispers, "Grow, grow."

—THE TALMUD

Bow at the Feet of God

We are all beggars at
the feet of God

But also his children
clamoring for his Love

His light shining from
the lighthouse of love
Finding us wherever
we are
on course
or lost.

Caught in the rocks of life
sending his lifeboat
to return us to the
right course

Bright, oh so bright
His light
Never a light so bright
has shone on me—

My eyes are almost
blinded by its intensity.
My heart gives off a flare
as if to say
Oh captain, I am
lost, please bring
me back to the
station—send help!!

And just like that→
I am back

This is grace

Bow at the feet of God.

Andrea Joy Cohen, M.D.

GETTING REAL

Rachel Naomi Remen, M.D.

I N 1972, Stanford's medical school pioneered in offering students a course on human sexuality. The first session of this course was several hours long and consisted of watching, nonstop, dozens and dozens of films on every sort of sexual practice. Some were funny, some were sad, a few were elegant, others crude, but all were graphic. By the end of the day, sexuality had become as banal as eating dinner. The idea, I suppose, was to desensitize future physicians, and help us to talk with patients about sexual issues in a way that was unembarrassed, professional, and personally neutral. Since then, physicians trained at medical schools throughout the country have told me that they have sat through such a day at the movies. Many medical schools take a similar approach even today.

When I think of what it must be like to need to speak of achingly intimate, fragile, and important things to someone who has stripped them of all meaning, I feel sad and diminished. I think that many of us could probably have served people in sexual anguish far better before this session than afterward. It took me many years to recover a sense of the power and mystery of sexuality. For a long while sex seemed absurd, if not ridiculous.

Whereas medical school taught me the banality of sex, American culture taught me that sex is only for the young and perfect, those without a hair on their bodies, a blemish on their skins, a wrinkle, or an extra ounce of fat. Many years ago, I had sat on the beach at Diamond Head in Hawaii, unwilling to take off my robe because six months before, a part of my intestine had been surgically removed and I now wore an ileostomy appliance. All around me powerful-appearing, handsome men sat in small groups, smoking cigars and presumably discussing the market with each other as slender young women many years their junior sunned themselves or played Frisbee in tiny swimsuits. Their bodies were uniformly Barbie Doll perfect, and watching them, I had been on the verge of tears. Absorbed in their own conversations, the men paid little attention to these women.

About the middle of the afternoon, the curtain of one of the cabanas was pushed aside, and a middle-aged woman with a mane of black curly hair emerged. She was wearing a white suit meant for someone perhaps fifteen or twenty pounds thinner. Very slowly and deliberately and with the utmost confidence, she sauntered across the sand and entered the ocean. By the time she reached the water, all conversation on the beach had ceased and every male eye was on her. Many of the women were looking at her, too. It was my first lesson in the difference between perfection and sexuality.

Real sexuality heals. In its presence I could begin to reclaim my own sense of possibility and wholeness, and I am grateful to this woman for inhabiting her body in this way. Without knowing me at all, she helped me to begin to inhabit my own life. Now more than thirty years later I have seen hundreds of others, people with cancer, reclaim their wholeness by reclaiming their sexuality.

Clare was one of these. In her beige linen suit and white silk blouse, she appeared flawless, competent, and totally in control. In comparison to her elegance, my waiting room looked shabby. When I said her name, she rose and shook my hand. Without another word she followed me into my office and folded herself into a chair, crossing her long, beautifully shaped legs at the ankle.

I settled myself opposite and smiled at her. Without any warning whatsoever, she burst into tears. The contrast between her tears and self-possession was so extreme that I was caught completely by surprise, and for a moment I was stunned. Then I reached forward and took her hand between my own as she sobbed. We sat like that for a long time, until she had cried enough. Turning a tear-stained face toward me, she commented, "How embarrassing. I have not cried in years."

"These are special times," I said. She nodded. "Would you tell me about it?" I asked her.

She had come because eight weeks before she had undergone surgery to remove her right breast. After much discussion, she and her doctor had made this decision together. She felt certain that it was the right choice, and she had healed nicely. "And how has this been for you?" I asked her. "I don't know," she told me.

She was in her late twenties, unmarried, and successful as a businesswoman. Until her surgery, she had worked out daily and had been very proud of her body. Men had always found her very attractive, and having a man in her life was important to her. She'd had many lovers, mostly colleagues she had met in the business world. "But that is over, now," she told me. "I could never allow anyone to see me disfigured like this." After the surgery, she had ended her relationship with the two men she was seeing. Both had accepted it gracefully and moved on.

No one at work and none of her friends even suspected that she had cancer, she told me. She had done it entirely alone. So obsessed had she been with secrecy that she told everyone that she was going on a vacation to Europe and had even made arrangements to have cards sent to them from abroad. Even her parents did not know. But she was here because the pressure of keeping this secret had become too much and she needed a place to talk and to be herself. "I can't come very often," she told me. "People would begin to suspect."

"Come whenever you need to," I told her.

For the next few years, I saw her every three or four months. On the surface her life was much as it had been, except that she lived as a celibate, putting all her energy into her work. During one of her infrequent visits I had called this to her attention and asked her if she planned to be alone for the rest of her life. "Only for five years, Rachel," she told me. Seeing my look of surprise, she explained that her oncologist was very conservative. She had picked him because she, too, was conservative. Early on, they had discussed a breast reconstruction. He had encouraged her to put off having this surgery until the fifth anniversary of her diagnosis. "And this is so that any recurrence can be easily seen?" I asked. She nodded her head. "Yes," she said. "After five years the chances are that I will be home free."

A little more than a year before this important anniversary, we had one of our sessions. During the hour, she told me that she had gone to an opening at an art gallery and had struck up a conversation with a painter who had asked her to join him for a cup of coffee. "He is a very attractive man, but obviously totally unsuitable as a lover," she told me. "So I said, 'yes.'"

"Because he is unsuitable?" I said, puzzled.

"I thought we could become friends," she had replied. Surprisingly, she had a very good time. "Will you see him again?" I asked her.

"Yes, I think so," she told me. "He is such good company."

Three months later when she returned for another session, Peter's name came up in our conversation over and over again. They had gone to the zoo. She had visited his studio and had been very impressed with his work. By now, she had met many of his friends who were artists and sculptors and found that she liked them very much. It had surprised her to discover that she fit in so well with these people and was even more comfortable with them than with people she knew from her own work. "Perhaps it's because you are creative yourself, Clare," I told her. "Business can be as much of an art form as paint or stone." She thought this over for several moments. She had never seen herself in this way before.

About two months later, she called to schedule an urgent visit. She came into the office looking somber. "It's the end," she told me. Thinking that perhaps she had suffered a recurrence, my heart jumped into my throat. But this was not what she had meant at all. "Peter left a message on my voice mail, inviting me away for the weekend. I will have to tell him now," she said. "It's over."

Relieved, I said, "Perhaps once he knows he might not feel that way about things."

"I doubt it," she replied. "He is exactly the wrong sort of man. Beauty is his whole life. He will be completely repulsed."

"When will you tell him?" I asked, my heart sinking.

"Tonight, at dinner," she said.

"Call if you need to," I told her.

I found myself thinking of her all evening, but she did not call. As the weeks went by, I continued to wonder what had happened, but I resisted calling her to see how things went. As was her way, she came in again three months later. In response to my questioning look, she laughed. "I was wrong," she said. "He still wants to be friends."

It turned out that Peter wanted to be more than friends, but Clare had refused. Her body was too ugly, too maimed. "My fifth anniversary is less than six months away and I will have my reconstruction," she told me. "Perhaps then." She went on to tell me her plans. She had scheduled the date of her reconstructive surgery more than a year ago and interviewed several surgeons and some of their patients before deciding on the surgeon she would use. She had arranged vacation time at work. As her insurance did not cover this sort of surgery, she had begun saving the money for it right after her mastectomy and over the past five years had enough money put away. It would be very expensive and difficult, but she hoped it would return her to wholeness. She looked down at her hands clasped in her lap for a few minutes. Then she looked up. "I hope it works, Rachel," she said. I was not sure, but I thought there were tears in her eyes.

I did not see her again until a few days before her fifth anniversary. She came in, looking excited and happy. I was delighted to celebrate this milestone with her, and I asked her about the upcoming surgery. She smiled and told me that she had canceled it. I looked at her in surprise. "How come?" I asked her. She returned my look for a long moment. Then slowly she unbuttoned her blouse and shrugged it off her shoulders. She was not wearing a bra, and her left breast was exquisite. But its beauty was overshadowed by the radical change in her body. Her mastectomy scar had been covered over with a mass of tiny, exquisite tattooed flowers. They looked real. In the most delicate of pastel shades, they climbed to the top of her right shoulder. As she turned away from me, I could see that they fell across it and down her back as if scattered by gravity or the wind. She stood, pulling her slacks down over her hips. Her body was beautiful. One little tattooed flower had come to rest in the small of her back, and another lay against her right buttock. Under it was a tiny initial "P." My mouth dropped open in shock, while at the same time I experienced a pang of envy. She was indescribably erotic. Men encountered women like her only in their dreams.

Shrugging back into her blouse and buttoning her slacks, she sat down again, laughing aloud at my look of astonishment. "Isn't it beautiful?" she said. "Peter painted it and we went to Amsterdam to have it done. Then we used the money I had saved for the surgery for a honeymoon. I am so happy, Rachel," she said, blushing slightly. "My husband has convinced me beyond the shadow of a doubt that anything of real beauty is one of a kind."

HEALING
EMOTIONAL PAIN

Dean Ornish, M.D.

IN my own life, and in the process of conducting research, I have learned how illness and suffering can be catalysts for transforming some fundamental issues: how we view ourselves and how we relate to the world. For my patients heart disease has been the catalyst; for me, it was emotional depression. For many years, I have struggled with many of the same issues as my patients—self-worth, self-esteem, and feelings of isolation.

I was studying at a small, extremely competitive university where most of the students acted as though academic success defined one's net worth as a person. Over half the students graduated either first or second in their high school classes, and the university had the highest percentage of National Merit scholars in the country. It also had the highest suicide rate per capita of any school in the country; I later found out why.

When I was a student there, most professors graded on a curve.

Most of the students studied almost all the time just to keep up—even bringing textbooks to parties!

I had dreamed of becoming a doctor for many years. In college, I enrolled in organic chemistry because it was required for getting into medical school—admissions committees still consider it to be the single most important course for determining entry. Although organic chemistry is relatively unimportant in the practice of medicine, the course does measure one's ability to memorize vast amounts of often-irrelevant information, which is among the most useful skills to have in medical school.

My organic chemistry teacher seemed like a cross between John Houseman in the movie *The Paper Chase* and Adolf Hitler. On the first day of school, he announced to our class, "This is a weed-out course for medical schools, and I'm going to weed you out! You don't need to know organic chemistry to be a doctor, but you'll never get to be one unless you do well in this course." Great.

I worried that I wouldn't do well enough in chemistry to be accepted to medical school. I got into a vicious cycle: the more I worried, the harder it became to study, and the harder it was to study, the more I worried. My mind was racing so fast that I couldn't sleep, even when I began taking tranquilizers and drinking some alcohol. I would lie down, watch the hands of the clock go around each hour until morning. At one point, this went on for about ten days in a row.

Becoming that sleep-deprived is enough to make anyone a little crazy, and I got to a point where I couldn't function at all. I believed that I was not going to be accepted to medical school, since I couldn't even read a newspaper headline and remember five minutes later what it said—not an ideal situation for someone trying to memorize organic chemistry equations.

I began to feel extremely stupid, that somehow I had managed to fool people into thinking that I was smart. I thought, "I just *seemed* smart in a public high school because most of the people there weren't that smart either. Now that I'm at a school with *really* smart people, they will soon find out how stupid I really am."

So I decided to see the campus psychiatrist. I walked into his office and said, "I'm really very stupid, and I feel like a fraud. I don't really know anything—somehow, I've just managed to fool people into thinking that I do. I'm impersonating a smart person."

"Of course you're not stupid. You've scored in the upper 5 percent of the standardized tests."

"The tests are wrong. Those tests don't measure intelligence—and if *you* think I'm smart, then you're stupid, too!" And I stormed out.

I wandered around the campus, trying to decide what to do. I walked up to people I didn't even know and asked them what courses I should take, what subject I should major in, what I should do with my life. At that point, I didn't feel capable of doing much of anything. Maybe I could get a menial job someday. Maybe not.

My parents very much wanted me to excel, especially in the academic arena—that's probably why they named me "Dean." I began to feel that I would never measure up and would cause them to be terribly disappointed.

And then, to make matters worse, I had a spiritual revelation in which I realized that nothing could bring me lasting happiness and self-esteem. I knew at that moment that "If only I had ____, then I'd be happy" was a lie.

I thought about what people told me would make me happy: "What if I get into medical school? What if I earn a lot of money? What if I marry a beautiful woman? What if I win a major scientific prize? What if I write a bestselling book? What if I become famous? Will that bring me *lasting* happiness?"

And I realized that I would be happy for a while—about fifteen or twenty minutes, maybe even a few days—and then I would think, "Now what?" It would never be enough. Or, "So what?" Big deal. None of these would provide the lasting meaning and self-esteem I thought they would.

It was a bad combination. I thought that I was never going to fulfill my dream of becoming a doctor. And even if I did, it wouldn't matter anyway. So I got more and more depressed.

I remember one day very clearly—I was sitting in the organic chemistry class and it suddenly occurred to me, "I'm in so much emotional pain, I'm so tired, I'll just kill myself and be done with it! I can sleep forever." It seemed so logical and clear—like, "Why didn't I think of this before?" (And in the twisted logic of the moment, part of me replied, "Because you're stupid, that's why!")

I was very depressed and getting increasingly worse. I went back to my apartment and looked around at the material possessions that were supposed to make me happy, and the idea seemed like a cruel joke. I threw my expensive stereo down a flight of stairs.

I lived in a sterile concrete apartment complex across the street from the Houston Oilers football practice field. There was a large oil derrick near the end zone, and I considered jumping off it. Too messy—and everyone would know what I'd done.

Instead, I decided to have a one-car collision—to run into the side of a bridge, as though I'd lost control of the car. That way, people would think that I just wasn't a very good driver—and if you'd ever been in a car that I'd been driving when I was eighteen, you'd know that wasn't so implausible.

I came about as close to killing myself as a person can without actually doing it. What saved me, ironically, was a physical illness—a very bad case of mononucleosis. I was so ill that I didn't even have the energy to get out of bed—which saved my life. It was my first understanding of how the mind can affect the body, in this case for the worse.

My parents finally began to understand that all was not well with their son, so I withdrew from school and went home with them to Dallas to recuperate. I felt like a complete failure. I was very anxious to get well enough to go out and kill myself. . . .

Something else happened instead. Like many college students in 1969, my sister Laurel had been searching for answers in her life, but she was dissatisfied by the easy solutions of that era. In 1970 she began studying yoga and meditation with a man named Swami Satchidananda, an eminent and ecumenical spiritual teacher who had met twice with Pope Paul VI, spoken at the National Institutes of Health, and addressed the United Nations.

She became happier and calmer. She stopped getting migraine headaches. As a gesture of support for her, my parents decided to have a cocktail party for the swami when he was lecturing in Dallas in 1972. This was considered a little strange back then, especially in Texas.

He walked in their front door, looking like a casting agent's idea of a swami: he had a long white beard, with intelligent and peaceful eyes, and he wore long saffron robes. There is an old saying, "When the student is ready, the teacher appears," and that seems to have been true for me. He agreed to give a lecture in our living room.

The swami began by saying, "Nothing will ever bring you *lasting* happiness." Well, I'd already figured that out. When I looked at him, though, he appeared very happy and content, and I thought, "This doesn't make any sense."

He went on to say what now sounds like a New Age cliché, but at that time it began to transform my life. "Nothing can *bring* us lasting happiness, but we have that already if we simply quiet down the mind and body enough to experience more of an *inner* sense of peace, self-worth, and self-esteem, one that comes not from getting or from doing but simply from *being.* And the paradox and the irony is that not being aware of this, we end up running everywhere else looking for this elusive happiness, in the process disturbing the inner joy and peace we could have if we simply quieted down the mind and body enough to experience that."

I was in so much emotional pain that I was willing to try anything. This was the first time I really understood how pain, or illness, or suffering of any kind—whether physical or emotional—could be a catalyst for real transformation. I began to practice stretching exercises, breathing techniques, meditation, relaxation techniques, and visualization. Although I grew up in Texas on cheeseburgers and steak, I began to eat a low-fat vegetarian diet. I started exercising. I found that, over time, I was able to quiet down my mind enough to experience—only fleetingly at first—an inner sense of well-being. It didn't last very long at the beginning, but I began to understand where it came from.

Stress Is Information

Once I made the connection between when I felt stressed and why, then stress became my teacher instead of my enemy. When I felt angry, upset, afraid, anxious, or depressed, this suffering and stress reminded me that I was looking in the wrong places for peace and happiness and self-esteem.

I stopped viewing pain—physical and emotional—as punishment and began seeing it as information. The experience reminded me of when I was much younger and realized when I put my hand on a hot stove that there were less painful places to put it. I wasn't being punished by the stove, and I didn't have to blame it for being hot.

In college, I experienced both extremes of a spectrum—how counterproductive it was to be outwardly defined and how empowering it was to be more inwardly defined. When I thought my self-esteem and happiness were dependent on my academic performance—that is, on getting what I thought I needed—I got to a point where I couldn't function at all and I felt like I was going to school at Hell University. I couldn't study, I couldn't sleep, and I couldn't even sit still.

When I used the lifestyle program to start quieting my chattering mind so that I could begin to experience more of an *inner* sense of peace and self-worth, I was able to perform at the peak of my abilities in the same arena. I went back to college, graduated summa cum laude, gave the commencement address, and was accepted into medical school. And I enjoyed the process, not just achieving the goals.

In short, the more inwardly defined I became, the less I needed to succeed and the less stressed I felt. The less I needed success, the easier it came. The less I *had* to get, the more I got. The less I *needed* to acquire power, the more power I realized I already had; before I realized that I used to give my power away.

These are not new ideas, but they were new to me. Listen to this verse from the *Tao Te Ching*, written over four thousand years ago:

> *Fill your bowl to the brim*
> *and it will spill.*
> *Keep sharpening your knife*
> *and it will blunt.*
> *Chase after money and security*
> *and your heart will never unclench.*
> *Care about people's approval*
> *and you will be their prisoner.*
> *Do your work, then step back.*
> *The only path to serenity.*

Choosing Life and Letting Go of Pain

When I decided not to die almost twenty years ago, I vowed to live each day fully by choice and not by default. Since then, when I wake up in the morning, I consciously choose to live. My life has been a process of learning to let go of what is unimportant—and the more I let go of, the healthier and stronger I feel. In the final analysis, all I am letting go of is the pain, like letting go of a hot stove.

Likewise, we are always making choices at every moment, even when we don't think of it in those terms. Pain can help us to examine which choices and options we have. What do we want to hold on to and what do we want to let go of? What kind of food do we want to eat? Do we want to spend time exercising or watching television? How are we defining and limiting ourselves?

Sometimes people tell me, "I know what lifestyle changes I need to make, but it's so hard to begin. What can I do?"

All changes involve some stress at first—the status quo is familiar and comfortable, even when it is killing us. When the pain of the present is worse than the stress of making changes, then it becomes easier to begin.

Illness can be the "big stick" that gets our attention, like the one a Zen meditation teacher uses to rap his students with on the back or head when their attention starts to wander. When we grow tired of being in pain—of banging our head against the wall—then our suffering can be a catalyst for making changes. We can let go of old behavior patterns more easily when we see that they are causing us problems.

Most of us are motivated to make changes either to avoid pain or to gain pleasure. Why give up anything that you like unless what you get back is more than what you give up?

It's easier to see the benefits in some arenas than in others. No one questions the reasons why a prizefighter or a swimmer or a runner spends so many hours a day in grueling training for years to prepare for competition in the Olympics. These athletes often describe the many sacrifices—what they have given up—in order to pursue this goal. Emotional and spiritual goals are more difficult to understand, but the process is also one of making choices and "giving up" or letting go of what is less important.

When the pain becomes intense enough—or when we allow ourselves to experience how much pain we have been feeling—then it becomes easier to let go. Oftentimes we ignore the earlier, minor pains, and we have to wait until we are knocked flat on our backs with a heart attack or similar crisis before we begin to make changes. Even a heart attack may not be enough to motivate some people. I have often seen patients demand a telephone in the coronary care unit "because the business just can't get by without me."

But we don't have to wait for full-blown illnesses; by then, it may be too late. It's better to pay attention to the early warning signals of distress (whether physical or emotional). When a ship is even a few degrees off course, it is easier to reset its path early on; otherwise, the ship can drift thousands of miles out to sea.

Paying Attention

So the question is: what am I not paying attention to? The function of pain, whether physical or emotional, is to get our attention. We all have an inner teacher, an inner guide, an inner voice that speaks very clearly but usually not very loudly. That information can be drowned out by the chatter of the mind and the pressure of day-to-day events. But if we quiet down the mind, we can begin to hear what we're not paying attention to. We can find out what's right for us.

The stress management techniques described in my books have several functions. First, of course, they can help us manage stress more effectively. Then, they can help to quiet the mind so we can become more aware of the early warning signs. Finally, when the mind quiets down, we can then begin to hear the information provided by our inner teacher.

Empowering Ourselves

The greatest risks for illness occur when people believe that they have a low amount of control or choice over their work or home environments.

But we always have choices. We always have options. In his book *Man's Search for Meaning*, Viktor Frankl wrote about how even in the Nazi concentration camps people responded to the same dire environment in different ways. Those who chose to give meaning to their experiences were more likely to survive. The environment was the same for all of the inmates, but the way they reacted to that situation was different.

Knowing that we always have choices can empower us. This way of looking at the world—that is, looking at pain as a teacher instead of an enemy—helps us to see new choices and new possibilities.

Where does real power come from? Where does real happiness come from? Where does inner peace come from?

Many of us believe that power and happiness come from getting more and more and more of our wants and needs fulfilled. This belief is ultimately self-defeating. Either we don't get the needs and wants fulfilled and we're disappointed and stressed and unhappy and, ultimately, sick, or we do get them fulfilled and find that they don't really bring the lasting meaning and happiness and self-worth that we thought they would.

The other way to have more power and happiness in our lives is to *decrease* our wants and needs, which is where lasting power comes from. The more we can walk away from, the more we can let go of, the more power we have.

Real power is ours already—when we stop giving it away. Real happiness is ours already—when we stop believing it's something we have to get from outside ourselves. Real peace is ours already—when we stop disturbing it. Real freedom is ours already—when we stop limiting ourselves.

We tend to think of power as something we get, not as something we already have. But everything that comes eventually goes. If we get power from outside ourselves, then we can lose it. If someone gives us power, then they can take it away.

Real power is not given to us or even created; real power is realized. It comes from realizing an inner sense of peace, self-worth, and happiness.

No one has power over us unless they have something that we think we need. If we can reduce our needs, then we increase our power. If someone says: "If you don't do what I want, I won't give you this," you can reply, "Fine, I don't need that." And then he or she has less power over you.

The more inwardly defined you are, the less you need. The less you need the more power you have.

What really frees us is letting go of the idea that these things are going to bring us lasting happiness. When we do, we can enjoy our material possessions without being bound by them.

Paradoxically, the more grounded we are in an inner sense of peace, the more we can accomplish in the external world, and with less stress, anxiety, fear, and worry. We can focus on the task instead of being too concerned with how well we are doing. We don't have to give up our jobs—we can perform them even better.

There is an old Zen proverb: "Before enlightenment, chop wood, carry water; after enlightenment, chop wood, carry water." In other words, our outward actions may not appear very different— we may still go to work every day, raise a family, etc.—but our motivations are different because our perceptions have changed.

That is, to the degree we are inwardly defined and inwardly content, then we do not need to tell ourselves, "If only I had _____, then I'd be happy." We have that already. We can act for the joy of it, not because it's essential to our happiness.

Likewise, to the degree that we perceive ourselves as *a part of* the world rather than *apart from* it—connected and intimate rather than isolated and alone—then we can begin changing the self-destructive perceptions and the resulting behavior patterns that leave us feeling even lonelier.

Of course I can't say I know how you feel, but I know how bad it is to feel alone. I know how painful it is to feel despairing. I know the darkness of feeling suicidal. I know how bleak it is to feel empty—"Is that all there is?" I've had those feelings. They may not be exactly the same as yours, but they may be similar. And in that sense we are connected.

I'm not a lot further along than I was; I still make many of the same mistakes I used to, although I catch myself sooner. I still might say to myself, "Oh, if only I can get another grant, if only the patients get better, if only I can do this or that, *then* I'll be happy." But then I start to feel stressed, anxious, worried, or depressed, and my life becomes unhappy.

That emotional stress reminds me that I'm looking in the wrong place for my happiness. I'm digging a hole and falling in it again and then blaming the world for having too many holes—which is about as useful as blaming a stove for being hot.

So it's a gradual process; it's not all or nothing. Just making the connection between when I feel stressed and why made a profound difference in my life—as important as when I realized that putting my hand on a hot stove caused pain and suffering.

But we can make different choices. We can put our hands somewhere else. It becomes easier to let go once we understand where the pain comes from.

In summary, then, chronic emotional stress can lead to heart disease and other illnesses. Stress comes not only from what we do but how we react to the external world. How we react, in turn, is based on how we perceive ourselves in relation to the world. Anything that leads to the perception of isolation causes chronic stress, and in turn, can lead to heart disease or other illnesses. Anything that enhances the perception of intimacy reduces stress, allowing our hearts to begin healing and our lives to become more joyful.

"IF I DIE BEFORE I WAKE": THE SYMPHONY WITHIN

Don Campbell

MUSIC had always been my inner and outer life. It has been the bridge to spirit, religion, occupation, and philosophy of life and entertainment. Some music moved my body, some music tortured me, some music made me so joyous that it was addictive, and some music brought me home to a core of being, a place of utter spirit.

In 1994 I suffered a mild head injury that changed my life—a mere bump to the head in my own carport. For three weeks after, I had severe headaches, blinding lights in my right eye, and an eyelid that barely opened. From the beginning, the neuro-ophthalmologist diagnosed the problem as Horner's syndrome, most probably caused by a tumor. The right eyelid could barely open, the headaches increased, and my vision was a little fuzzy. Music, imagery, and prayer were the only tools that gave me immediate clarity through those weeks of pain.

A few weeks later I had my first MRI. For an hour and fifteen minutes, the loud, pounding sounds made me feel as if some cosmic drumming group was treating me to some kind of shock symphony. As I lay in this Star Trek, tubelike capsule, I watched inner images in my mind and heard hymns over the chaotic, beating rhythms.

Immediately after they examined the scan, the doctor and the technician diagnosed a massive clot in the right carotid artery behind the right eye, and I was rushed to the emergency room. After a few hours of tests, the vascular surgeon wanted to begin procedures immediately that involved risky surgery to my face and eye. I knew I needed time to check in and sense my own inner being. Life lessons were truly right in my face. Pain was in my head, faded vision was in my eye, and my emotions were singing a rampant repertoire of hymns, chants, and prayers.

I convinced the doctor, after seven hours in the emergency room, to allow me to return home for a few days before surgery. He insisted that I watch my blood pressure with constant monitoring. With years of teaching the benefits of music to health professionals and how blood pressure could be lowered, here I was "facing the music" with my own mind and body. Needless to say, it felt strange to be racing home to meditate and let music begin to do its work.

Any noise seemed wrong; except for the simple humming of my voice, anything too bright seemed overstimulating. Soft and slow classical music felt right. Anything louder than prayer in my verbal mind seemed to have no place in the emotions that lay underneath my thoughts. So I went to bed, exhausted from a powerful and confusing day. As I drifted into a low beta-wave bed of rest, all I could remember was my Methodist, born-and-bred, childhood prayer, the only mantra to come to mind.

Now I lay me down to sleep,
Pray the Lord my soul to keep.
If I die before I wake,
I pray the Lord, my soul to take.

After many repetitions, I was jerked awake by what I was actually praying:

May I wake before I die,
May I wake before I die…

Somehow, this Buddhist infusion of spirituality became the constant repetition of my inner voice. I chanted for days on end in my mind, rather than focusing on thoughts of healing, wellness, joy, and centering. The fear of a massive stroke subsided almost instantly when I realized that the power of these moments was about life, not death. They were about consciousness and being "awake" rather than being cured.

I called my friends Larry and Barbie Dossey, who are great visionaries of complementary medicine. Over twenty years ago, we would brainstorm on the future of health, medicine, and the arts. Now the storm in my brain needed professional, personal advice. Larry's most recent book at the time was *Prayer Is Good Medicine.* Sure enough, the Methodist mantra of childhood was back in my conscious repertoire.

The following day, Jeanne Achterberg, a pioneer in imagery and health, led me through a two-hour exploration of my inner wisdom and knowledge of healing. In the beginning, I sensed water flowing through me to wash away the clot. She immediately said to let go of that image, that it might create a stroke. We went deeper and deeper, and explored image after image until there was a sound in my head. Jeanne heard it as well. Then an image appeared: a quiet lake, with a breeze blowing a cotton lace curtain next to the right side of my head as I sat in a wooden rocking chair. I felt chills, I felt spirit, I heard sound, and I knew something important was happening in my body. She suggested that I keep that image clear and repeat it five times a day.

For days, I prayed that I awaken and keep in close touch with the image. I returned to the doctor. My blood pressure was low and he suggested we have another MRI before proceeding with the surgery. He suggested that I take a baby aspirin every other day. When I returned for exhaustive tests and my second MRI, I no longer had headaches, my eyelid began to open, and I saw more clearly. Again during the MRI, I heard chants, felt drummers, and allowed my quiet imagery of the lake to hold my attention. The results were positive. The clot, which had been well over an inch in length, now was less than an eighth its original size. The danger had not passed, but the doctor felt there was no need for surgery.

The many aspects of this experience in my life will someday fill a biography, a reflection of the symphony of my inner life. I live with the power of knowing I approached this experience with the childlike hope to live, to be awake.

Every season since 1994 has created many opportunities for the realization of how much awakening I still have ahead of me. Without the urgency of having a life-threatening illness and now knowing the blessings of health and safety, I wonder if I can live consciously enough each day of my life to be truly AWAKE before I die.

FACING FINITUDE

Linda Schierse Leonard, Ph.D.

I was suffering from writer's block when Andrea Cohen contacted me to write an article on my life's lessons. In spite of this dilemma, I said I would try to write about aging. In some ways, it was a fitting obstacle. Writer's block can mask or reveal the basic human dilemma: Why are we here? What is the meaning of life? Creative block, when faced, drives us to the edge of our being and throws us before ourselves to question our existence.

I experienced the scourge of writer's block differently in younger days. Training as a journalist taught me to write for deadlines. My first professional job was as a reporter for a daily newspaper. In addition, I wrote several dissertations for various degrees. Then, in 1975, after my father died, I started to write *The Wounded Woman*. I was hoping to understand and reconcile with my father, heal my wounds, and help others on the same quest. The book took seven years to write. Finally, after forty-two rejections from publishers, *The Wounded Woman* was published and became a bestseller.

I continued to write and completed six books in twenty-five years. Passion persisted and ideas flowed. Although I fell into a "dark night of the soul" before each new book, I understood that accepting emptiness was part of the creative process, even necessary to allow space for the next vision to appear. I knew I had to work through the next theme to save myself and to grow as well as to help others. The topic of each preceding book summoned the next; and the call to create each book was so strong that my commitment and discipline persevered. I found the work hard; and I struggled as all writers do. But I wrote one book after another despite increasing personal travails and the decline of the publishing industry. During this time I passed through three decades of midlife: my thirties, forties, and fifties.

In my sixth decade, at the beginning of the twenty-first century, in the year 2000, my sixth book, *The Call to Create*, appeared in print. It was then that I decided to take a two-year break from writing to refresh and renew my psyche. I wanted more time to read, to travel, to hike with friends, and to share adventure with my longtime soul mate, Keith. After this break, I would start my next project. I planned to write two books—one on film and the unconscious, the other on the art of aging.

I moved to Santa Fe, where spirit infuses the red earth and pink-purple-orange sunrises and sunsets stir the soul. Santa Fe is a city of serpentine streets, adobe houses, concealed courtyards, shape-shifting creatures, and mystery in every corner. The potential creative community of Jungian analysts, artists, and writers within reach would inspire a romantic writer.

But instead of the peaceful, creative life I imagined, I faced the stresses of moving, finances, and other practical matters that I had postponed while writing my previous books. The collapse of my Santa Fe fantasies caused me to confront my projections about the place and stripped me of illusions.

I realized that I would never have the money to retire. I grew up in poverty. I've worked to support myself since my sixteenth birthday, when my mother marched me down to get my working papers. After fifty years of having to work, realizing that I could not retire was discouraging, especially since I was beginning to experience changes of energy brought on by the aging process. Before turning sixty, it never occurred to me that I might want to stop working one day.

Now I wanted only to write. Or so I thought. I knew that making one's living by writing alone was a wishful rarity, no longer possible for me with all of the mergers happening in the publishing business. Midlist books like mine were not profitable for firms wanting huge bestsellers and their profits. I had bought a Santa Fe house expecting to sell my Colorado condo. When the real estate market plunged suddenly, I could not sell the condo. Mortgages were due. Where would the money come from? I depleted my savings. I found security—that bourgeois aspiration I scoffed at in my bohemian period—unexpectedly attractive, but it was not to be mine.

My move to Santa Fe coincided with the economic recession, ecological and social disasters, and then the terrors of 9/11. Like many people horrified by this atrocity, I was depressed and disheartened over the declining state of the planet. Worries plagued me. Internal tyrants tormented me. Passion deserted me. Responsibilities overwhelmed me. I could neither read nor write. Something was holding me back. How ironic for an author who had just written a book on creativity.

My private dilemma seemed trivial compared to worldly events. Nevertheless, my worst fear was that I had lost the call to write. For the first time in my life, I saw neither my path of service nor of creative expression. Weren't the later years supposed to be the time of sharing elders' wisdom? What was I to do with the rest of my life?

To make matters worse, my body betrayed me: a hysterectomy at sixty and laser knee surgery at sixty-three forced me to face my finitude. Twenty years earlier, I had confronted death. Powerless over alcohol, I knelt down in humility and surrender. I learned to walk step by step the way of recovery: a spiritual practice embodied outwardly by my writing and my mountain ascents. Just as I learned to negotiate the muddy bogs, boulder fields, and icy glaciers of the peaks I climbed and to abandon myself to the bliss of the blooming mountain meadows, so I learned to accept, traverse, and appreciate the conundrum of human existence. Although I continued to walk this paradoxical path and to write about it, vicissitudes of growing old visited with a vengeance. I read how arthritis held Colette a hostage in her house so she could hardly write in her seventies, how Emily Carr became physically unable to paint, and how pain afflicted May Sarton.

Stories of Georgia O'Keeffe and Matisse, who worked even into their nineties, helped. But weren't they the exception? Just as the deep hole of addiction summoned me twenty years earlier, now the abyss of aging demanded that I descend into its void to experience and witness what was there.

Aging can bring wisdom and freedom. Consciously accepting the process can free a person from the expectations of others, from one's own projections, and from illusion. Maturing with age is life's challenge. But we cannot mature if we do not choose to confront *all* that aging brings. To mature we must see and embrace both light and shadow.

My sixties bid me to embark upon a new adventure even though it was not one that my ego-self desired—the adventure of aging. I have never shied away from adventure, which seems to be in my blood. Adventure called me to be a newspaper reporter, to teach philosophy, to explore the world of the unconscious as a Jungian analyst, and to write. Adventures in nature were part of this process. Keith challenged me to climb Mount Kilimanjaro in my forties, to trek in the Tasmanian and Patagonian wilderness, and to journey to Siberia to meet with nomadic reindeer tribes in the arctic tundra in my fifties. Although these trips were difficult and dangerous, I learned to travel the terrain of inner and outer wilderness. Learning to discover Nature's ways prepared me to accept and encounter struggles that would help me on this new journey.

A major fear blocked my way, a new kind of writer's block, whose precise form I did not recognize. I agonized over the worry that I had nothing more to say. Would I only be repeating myself if I wrote another book? Did I really want to jump so quickly and consciously into the abyss of aging? Writing a book on aging would require that descent.

While I was worrying about these concerns, Andrea contacted me again. My deadline for the article was approaching and she needed to know when I would have it ready. As chance would have it, she called just as I was leaving for a surgical appointment to remove a bothersome minor skin cancer. I told her I would try to get the article to her as soon as possible. Secretly I questioned my ability to write something worthwhile, indeed, anything at all.

The skin cancer turned out to be a mass of squamous cells. The surgeon cut out the tumor, but the pathology report was ominous. A baffling condition called perineural invasion complicated total eradication. The surgeon said it was serious—a life-or-death matter—not something I could ignore or delay. Scattered cells had escaped removal of the mass and I would have to undergo radiation. My chance of survival was better than average at 75 percent.

Cancer was the last thing on my mind. Now it superceded everything. I could not avoid seeing the mark of death, just as I could not escape the elongated scarlet scar that blemished my face where the tumor had been. Would it be the end of me, the demise of "Linda Leonard"? Disbelief! Shock! Anxiety! Terror! Anger! Grief! Fear of physical pain. Emotions I knew well from former times struck all at once like the rapid fire of lightning bolts.

That night I had a dream. Keith and I were walking along the coast of a long peninsula in South Africa where undiscovered exotic creatures were said to roam. Across the sea we could see a huge cave carved in the rocky cliffs. Suddenly scores of bright luminous giant furry baby birds emerged from the cave two by two as from Noah's Ark. Duos of white-feathered birds came out first, followed by fluffy black ones. Holding hands, we were awestruck before such beauty. Wondrous images from a strange new world inspired me with a feeling of the holy.

When I awoke, I experienced a sudden sense of relief. I felt released from the multitude of agonizing worries that plagued me. Death, or the possibility that I might die, had brought me back to life.

Yes, my worries had been real. Now they seemed trivial. I knew that the pattern of worry was addictive and I had been praying for help. The serenity prayer was my daily ritual:

Please help me to accept the things I cannot change, have the courage to change the things I can, and have the wisdom to know the difference.

I had always found the last part of the prayer, to "have the wisdom to know the difference," perplexing.

The answer to our prayers sometimes takes bewildering and uncanny forms. Strangely, the cancer diagnosis brought me peace. So what if I did not have enough money to retire or to live comfortably in old age. So what if I did not write another book or even another article. So what if…ad infinitum. I realized that even if I were to die soon, I had experienced a rich and exciting life. I had written six books that hopefully helped others, and that was good enough. Even the dark experiences—the traumas of childhood, adolescence, and later of addiction—contributed to my ability to understand and have compassion for others and myself. What really mattered now was how I faced death and how I lived each moment of my life.

I tackled the challenge of radiation, a treatment that previously I had vowed never to undergo. Five days a week Keith accompanies me to the Cancer Center at St. Vincent's Hospital in Santa Fe. I appreciate the philosophy of this nonprofit healing facility in which the uninsured poor receive treatment along with the privileged, honoring St. Vincent's vow to help the poor. As we enter, the nurses, doctors, radiation therapists, and staff greet us with care and humor.

When it is my turn I enter the radiation room, lie down on the table, and put on the mesh mask specially designed and decorated with a drawing to direct the rays to the area around the scar on my face. The wax insert placed in my cheek and underneath my lips to protect my teeth hurts the sores that now engulf the inside of my mouth, but the soreness is temporary and bearable—no worse than the aches and pains suffered willingly from an arduous mountain climb. The mask is fastened down so that I cannot move; I am positioned under the machine; and the treatment begins. The procedure itself is short and lasts only thirty seconds.

When the technicians release me from the mask I get up and we joke and laugh together. They come out and say hello to Keith.

The cancer experience is not the surreal nightmare scene I imagined. I do not feel trapped in the jaws of a demonic machine and system I was dreading. Instead I feel gifted to be with such warm, humane, compassionate people in an atmosphere of healing.

The daily routine of treatments brings an external structure to the life of this introverted author. People are so kind. The program directors for lectures that I apprehensively canceled to undergo radiation therapy support my decision and will reschedule. Andrea has extended my deadline so that I can write this article. Friends, colleagues, and others call and write notes that sustain me. I feel love and nourishment from them and my local friends who are present to hike with me in the Sangre de Cristo (Blood of Christ) mountains each day.

Every morning, when I awake, I see the Sangre de Cristos from my bedroom window and sense their sacred spirit. The aspen tree graces my patio along with the birds, squirrels, chipmunk, and rabbit that visit to eat seeds and bathe in the water that Keith puts out for them. Keith and I have become even closer through participating together in the process. He also suffered from skin cancer, surviving melanoma. He appreciates and listens to me and I understand his experience better. Just as we have taken inner and outer wilderness treks together, so we are soul mates on this adventure, too. I have rediscovered that the world is a much friendlier place and I try to live fully every moment, every day.

And I am writing, too. Learning I had cancer paradoxically broke through my block and brought creative energy. Facing death brings life. I am emerging into the sunlight like the glowing, glistening giant white and black baby birds came out of the cavelike Noah's Ark in my dream to remind me that all of existence—the light and the dark—has beauty and meaning. Whatever happens, I am in the process of rebirth—engrossed in the adventure of creation.

SAYING "YES!" TO BREAST CANCER

Susan Jeffers, Ph.D.

Y ES! *is* more than a word. *It is an attitude of Spiritual fullness,* the essence of Higher Self thinking. The word YES! says to me that "No matter what happens in my life, I'll make something wonderful out of it." I know this sounds difficult when one thinks about the possible losses and disappointments life often brings. But saying YES! is the antidote to the fear that more often than not accompanies these losses and disappointments. I speak from experience.

Many years ago I had a mastectomy and experienced firsthand the many fears involved in having breast cancer. But my choice (and it is a choice!) to say YES! to breast cancer, instead of NO, turned this potentially devastating experience into an enriching one. I talk about my positive experience of breast cancer in all my books and talks, hoping it will bring comfort, not only to others in the same situation, but also to those who live in fear of this very prevalent disease. Because of this, I received an award from the Associates of

Breast Cancer Studies, a wonderful organization that raises money for the John Wayne Cancer Institute in Santa Monica, California.

I'd like to share with you part of my acceptance speech. It demonstrates how the attitude of YES! can exist even with something as potentially devastating as breast cancer. It demonstrates that the beauty is always there *if you look for it*. That's the key. If you don't look for it, you remain stuck in a victim mentality…a very powerless and frightening place to be stuck. And you miss out on so many of the opportunities that even a disease such as cancer can bring. Also in this speech, you will notice the humor. We take things much too seriously in our present-day world. Laughter can bring a lot of joy where only sadness once prevailed. With these thoughts in mind, here is my acceptance speech:

Tonight I am being honored with the Spirit of Discovery award. This is such an apropos award for me, because, impossible as it may seem, breast cancer has indeed offered me a great opportunity for discovery. In fact, I can go so far as to say that breast cancer has been one of the most enriching experiences of my life. Now don't look at me like I'm crazy. Let me explain.

For many years before my illness, I was teaching my students how to say YES! to life…how to say YES! to whatever life hands them and to find the beauty no matter how difficult a situation may be. I had learned this philosophy of life after reading and re-reading *Man's Search for Meaning* by Viktor Frankl, a book which, as many of you know, describes his experience in a concentration camp. He had seen and experienced the worst life had to offer and yet, he learned that one thing no one could ever take away from him was his *reaction* to whatever life handed him. And his choice was to react to his horrible experiences in a way that brought much enrichment to his life and to the world.

After the first reading of this inspiring book, I said to myself, "If he can say YES! to something as horrible as a concentration camp, which included the worst kind of treatment one can imagine and the loss of his loved ones, then I can say YES! to anything." And I've tried to live my life with a great big YES! in my heart ever since.

So there I was lying in my hospital bed thirteen years ago and saying to myself, "OK, Susan, you have a choice now. Are you going to see yourself as a victim, or are you going to say YES! and find the blessing in something as frightening as breast cancer." With my YES! philosophy, I thankfully chose the latter. Trust me when I tell you I didn't understand immediately what possible blessings there could be in breast cancer, but when I set my sights on looking for the blessings instead of the negatives, I found so many. And I am still counting.

Let me share some of these blessings with you.

1. I was dating my present husband, Mark, at the time. I wasn't quite sure where I wanted this relationship to go. I was the "no-need" woman, incredibly independent. He was the workaholic, work coming before everything. When I was diagnosed with breast cancer, he was able to see my vulnerability and dropped everything to be with me. I was able to see the incredible nurturer that emerged from deep within his Soul...and I let myself take in all the gifts of love and caring he was giving. This experience was so meaningful to the both of us that we decided we wanted to spend the rest of our lives together. So Mark and I got married...and so many years later it remains a marriage made in Heaven.

2. What else did I learn? This is for you women out there. I learned that sexuality had nothing to do with a breast. I have never

had a breast reconstruction after my mastectomy simply because I did not want to incur any more trauma to my body. And when I look in the mirror, I do not feel mutilated as some magazine articles suggest I should be feeling. Rather I look at that scar and breathe a sigh of relief and gratitude knowing I've conquered a disease. I celebrate the fact that I am now healthy. And I feel just as sexual as I did before the mastectomy. I learned that sexuality is an attitude, a way of being. It has nothing to do with a breast. In fact, my husband Mark says I look like a sexy pirate!

3. Another blessing. When Mark used to travel a lot on business, as a joke, I would often put my spare prosthesis in his suitcase with a love note. He often bragged that he was the only man he knew who could take his wife's breast with him whenever he goes away! Dare I reveal it, but he calls me his "titless wonder"! And I never cease to be thrilled by my title. I feel special.

4. At the time, I also asked myself if there were any negative emotions I was holding within that could cause disease in my body. As I looked, I couldn't help but notice I was still holding on to a lot of old anger, like many women still hold today. While I liked being angry (It was a very pseudo-powerful feeling!) I decided it was time to let it go…to deal with the fear and pain that was lurking behind the anger. I learned that anger can be a cop-out for not taking responsibility for my actions and reactions in life. I stopped casting blame; I took charge of my life; I honored who I was; and I learned how to open my heart. Wow! What a difference an open heart makes in your life! It lets in the sunshine instead of the gloom. My letting go of my anger was also my impetus to writing my second book, *Opening Our Hearts to Men*.

5. Then there was the time I went for a mammogram. As I was paying my bill, the cashier said it was 120 dollars. She looked again and said, "Wait. It's only one side. That's 60 dollars." And I shouted, "YES! I even get to save some money!"

6. And then there's my teaching. Often when I talk about saying YES! to life, a student will say: "That's easy with the little things. But what about the big things, such as cancer?" It's here that I can say, "You sure can say YES! to cancer. I did!" And I tell my story.

7. And then there's the issue of aging. Someone asked me recently if aging bothered me. I said, "Are you kidding?! Once you've had cancer, you celebrate every birthday with much greater joy than you ever did before. And so do the many people who love you."

8. In many ways, cancer is like a wake-up call. It says one never knows how much time one has left in life. So we should stop focusing so much on the future and pay more attention to the simple pleasures of everyday life. And that's what I have learned to do. That first cup of coffee in the morning. YES! The hot shower on the back. YES! The purr of the engine when the key is turned in my car. YES! The beautiful sun warming the very depths of my being. Heaven! I discovered that it's not the grand splashes of brilliance that define a beautiful life. It's the simple pleasures of the NOW. A beautiful lesson indeed. And it was this discovery that eventually led to my book *End the Struggle and Dance with Life.* You see, it's all grist for the mill!

9. And then there was the day I received a phone call from the ABCs asking if I would accept the Spirit of Discovery award. Would I accept it! YES!!!

I hope this acceptance speech conveys in a meaningful way the enormous power in saying YES! to life...in *looking for the good* in any situation we find ourselves...even one as potentially devastating as breast cancer. If we focus only on the negative, that's what we will get—the negative. If we focus on the positive, that's what we will get—the positive.

I know it's very easy to say YES! when things go right for us. But the trick is saying YES! when things *seem* to be going badly. We can only do this when we realize there are blessings inherent in all things and our task is to find these blessings. I promise you that this attitude of YES! makes all the difference between a life filled with misery and scarcity or a life filled with joy and abundance. I am forever thankful that I learned I had a choice...as we all do.

RESOURCES: OVERCOMING CHALLENGES

Books

EMOTIONAL HEALTH

Attracting Abundance with EFT, by Carol Look (AuthorHouse, 2006)

End the Struggle and Dance with Life, by Susan Jeffers (St. Martin's Press, 1996)

Minding the Body, Mending the Mind, by Joan Borysenko (Bantam, 1988, 2007)

PHYSICAL HEALTH

The Best Alternative Medicine, by Dr. Kenneth R. Pelletier (Simon & Schuster, 2000)

Breast Cancer beyond Convention, by Isaac Cohen, O.M.D., L.Ac., and Debu Tripathy, M.D. (Atria, 2002)

The Breast Cancer Prevention Diet, by Dr. Bob Arnot (Little, Brown, 1998)

Dr. Dean Ornish's Program for Reversing Heart Disease: The Only System Scientifically Proven to Reverse Heart Disease without Drugs or Surgery, by Dean Ornish, M.D. (Ivy, 1995)

Endometriosis: One Woman's Journey, by Jennifer Marie Lewis (Griffin, 1998)

Food as Medicine, by Dharma Singh Khalsa, M.D. (Atria, 2004)

How to Live between Office Visits, by Bernie Siegel, M.D. (HarperCollins, 1993)

A Pace of Grace: The Virtues of a Sustainable Life, by Linda Kavelin Popov (Plume, 2004)

The Wisdom of Menopause, by Christiane Northrup, M.D. (Bantam, 2006)

Women's Bodies, Women's Minds, by Christiane Northrup, M.D. (Bantam, 2006)

You Are Not Your Illness, by Linda Noble Topf (Simon & Schuster, 1995)

INSPIRATION

My Grandfather's Blessings, by Rachel Naomi Remen, M.D. (Riverhead, 2000)

The Power of Intention, by Wayne Dyer (Hay House, 2004)

The Power of Positive Thinking, by Norman Vincent Peale (Running Press, 2002)

Take Time for Your Life, by Cheryl Richardson (Free Press, 2002)

Who Moved My Cheese? by Spencer Johnson (G. P. Putnam's Sons, 1998)

AUDIO

Health Journeys for People Managing Pain, by Belleruth Naparstek (Time Warner, 1995)

The Wisdom and Power of Music, by Don Campbell (Quest, 2006)

Websites

American Cancer Society
www.cancer.org
800-ACS-2345

National Cancer Institute
www.NCI.org

Anxiety Disorders Association of America
www.adaa.org

Disabled Sports USA
451 Hungerford Drive, Suite 100

Rockville, MD 20850
www.dsusa.org

Eating Disorders Awareness and Prevention
www.nationaleatingdisorders.org

Support for kids with a parent with cancer:
Kids Konnected
P.O. Box 603
Trabuco Canyon, CA 92687
www.kidskonnected.org
800-899-2866

National Depressive and Manic-Depressive Association
www.nmda.org

Basics of EFT (emotional freedom technique):
www.emofree.com

Adventure-based wilderness programs:
Outward Bound
www.outwardbound.com
888-882-6863

Help Lines

24-Hour National Depression Hotline
800-242-2211

24-Hour Suicide Hotline
www.suicidehotlines.com
800-SUICIDE
800-784-2433

SECTION TWO

Soul Expression

And the day came when the risk to remain tight in a bud was more painful than the risk it took to blossom.

—ANAÏS NIN

. . .

How wonderful it is that nobody need wait a single moment before beginning to improve the world.

—ANNE FRANK

What Is It You Came Here to Do?

You were sent with a
mission
Although you may not
remember

Among the many things
you have to do
is your soul's purpose

Sometimes clear
Sometimes cryptic
Always truth

Illuminate the niches inside
and see the truth

Wipe away the cobwebs
if you need to
and hang on
Let it shine through you
and don't let fear stop you
from what you came here to do

Andrea Joy Cohen, M.D.

WHAT EINSTEIN KNEW

Elizabeth Lesser

No problem can be solved from the same consciousness that created it.

—ALBERT EINSTEIN

WHEN Route 25 leaves the mountains of northern New Mexico, the city of Albuquerque appears suddenly like a mirage—a slice of strip-mall America shimmering on a flat shelf of ancient desert. In all my years of visiting friends in New Mexico, I had not ventured into Albuquerque. I had passed by it many times, on my way to and from the airport, but never had a reason to turn off the highway until one afternoon, when I went looking for a psychic whose card had been given to me by a friend in Santa Fe. This was during the first difficult days of being separated from my husband of fourteen years, a time when people who tried to help me would eventually give up, too frustrated to continue following me around a maze with no exit. The day before I left my friend's house, she handed me the business card of a psychic and said, "Don't ask. Just go."

The front side of the card read,

Name: The Mouthpiece of Spirit
Location: The Road of Truth

I found more helpful directions on the other side, where three rules were printed:

1. *Pay Only in Cash.*

2. *Bring a Blank Tape.*

3. *Do Not Hold Me Responsible for Your Life.*

And then the address, which led me through dusty, treeless streets, past a few warehouses and truck lots, to a trailer park on a forlorn road a couple of miles from the airport. The place looked like a bad movie set—several old trailers and dilapidated outbuildings, discarded automobiles, and a dog tied to a clothesline. At a dead end I came upon the last trailer in the park, set off under a gnarled tree strung with flashing Christmas lights. Rechecking the directions, I was alarmed to discover that this indeed was the Road of Truth, the home of the Mouthpiece of Spirit.

On the steps of the trailer things got even weirder. The psychic met me at the door. She had the most hair I had ever seen— piles of bleached blond tresses arranged in a beehive on top of her head. She was wearing a red-and-white-checked cowgirl shirt, white stretch pants, and high-heeled sandals. Her eyes were clear and blue, and her nails were painted bright red to match her dangling, heart-shaped earrings. She seemed surprised to see me, as if I hadn't called earlier in the morning to confirm the appointment, as if she wasn't a psychic at all. After I established what I was doing on the steps of her trailer, she invited me in, asking me to excuse the mess. We stepped over boxes, books, magazines, and bags of pet food and potato chips. On the couch, watching TV, was a man—perhaps the psychic's husband—and a big white poodle with plastic barrettes in its hair. Neither seemed to notice me as the psychic led us to her bedroom.

The psychic sat on a king-size bed that took up most of the space in the room. She motioned to me to sit on a folding chair in the corner. I could still get out of this, I thought, as I squeezed behind the bed to sit on the chair. But before I could say anything, the psychic announced in a no-nonsense tone, "You have something in your purse for me. Something from your husband. A letter." Her voice was husky—a smoker's voice—but it also had a regional twang, making her sound like a Texas Mae West. In fact she reminded me of Mae West, and I wondered what the hell I was doing, in a trailer near the Albuquerque airport, asking for life direction from Mae West.

"So, do you have a letter in your purse or not?" demanded the psychic.

"No, I don't," I stammered, defensively. "I don't usually carry letters in my purse."

"I am quite sure you have something, something from your husband, in your purse." Her voice softened some, and I suddenly realized that I *did* have a letter from my husband in my purse—a letter that spelled out the sad jumble of our marriage and revealed to me all the reasons for staying in it, as well as all the reasons for leaving. I had brought the letter with me to show my friend, to see if she could interpret it in a more definitive way, but I had forgotten all about it and never showed it to her. Instead, I had spent my time in Santa Fe doing exactly what Albert Einstein warns people with problems not to do. *No problem can be solved from the same consciousness that created it,* he writes. In other words, don't try to solve a problem using the same mixed-up thinking that got you into the mess in the first place. You will just keep swimming around in tight little circles of indecision and fear.

I had been in a state of indecision about my marriage for so long that my ability to move in either direction had atrophied. I had recalculated the reasons for staying and the reasons for leaving over and over, like Einstein struggling with an equation that never quite added up. Something told me I would not find my way out of this quandary using the same old arguments, but I didn't know where to look for a new perspective. It was as if I was underwater, swimming around and around in darkness. Far above me, beyond the weight of an ocean of worries, a ray of light was pointing in a luminous, new direction, but I was too distracted to notice. I was caught in waves of conflicting questions: Would I ruin my children's lives by getting divorced? Or was it worse for them to live with unhappy parents? Was I a dreamer, looking for an elusive happiness that real life could never deliver? Or were we meant to know the rapture of being alive, even at the cost of breaking the rules? The questions ebbed and flowed, back and forth, an endless exchange with no answers, no winners, just a worn-out swimmer.

How was I to break out of my tight circle of fear into a new consciousness? How did Einstein do it? How did he quiet the admonishing, skeptical voices in his head—the ones barking bad directions—long enough to hear the steady whispers of the universe? How was he able to peer beyond himself and follow the light to the more lucid answers?

I opened my purse, and there was the letter. I leaned over the bed and gave it to the psychic. She held on to it with her eyes closed, not even opening the envelope. After a few moments she asked, "Would you like to tape the session, dear?" sounding no longer like Mae West but more like a kindly waitress at a diner. I took the blank tape out of my jacket pocket, leaned across the bed again, and gave the psychic the tape. She popped it into a tape recorder that had seen better days, pushed the record button, and the session began—an hour-long mix of wacky chatter, astute philosophy, and unexplainably accurate information about me, my husband, my children, my whole mixed-up life. She jumped around from epoch to epoch: a past life with my husband in China; the destiny of my youngest son; the next man I would marry; and the eventual "last days" of earth time.

Sitting in the corner, I felt as if I had left my body and the Mouthpiece of Spirit had taken up residence. This was the only way I could explain her sudden knowledge of my life. Otherwise, how would she have known that I had a letter from my husband in my purse? How, just from holding on to that letter, did she know that my marriage was crumbling? She sat cross-legged on the bed, squeezing her eyes shut, clutching the letter, mumbling to herself: "*He* wanted to leave, but now he's changed his mind. Hmmm." She fluttered her eyelids, then shut them tight again. "He's desperate to come back, but now *she* wants to leave. She feels guilty; he is angry. Okay, okay," she whispered, as she opened her eyes and studied the return address.

"Rick-shaw, Rick-shaw," she drawled, mispronouncing my husband's last name in her Texas twang. Closing her eyes again, she said, "I see you pulling a rickshaw. I see you serving your husband in China. He is a nobleman; you are his servant girl. You have served him in many lifetimes. You served him then, and you hid yourself. You serve him now, and still you hide yourself. Still you do not claim your power. Do you understand?"

I nodded my head. Regardless of her dubious methodology of determining past lives, I did understand how I gave away power to my husband, how I resented him for steering our marriage, how I had so little trust in my own voice.

"Well, it is time to break the cycle. For you and for him. But you must be the one to do it. You must take back your power. Do you understand?"

"It's complex," I complained. "It's not his fault that I lack confidence and he doesn't."

She looked at me hard. "Write this down," she said, tossing me a pen and a pad of paper with a border of little bluebirds and flowers. "Those with power never willingly concede their control. Do you understand? Your husband will never, ever be able to let you grow into who you are supposed to be. It is not in your karmic contract. It's not a matter of fault. The truth is that, in order to find yourself, you must leave him. This is your quest. And in order for your husband to find himself, he must lose you. Y'all have lessons to learn—lessons that are more important than the marriage itself. The soul comes to earth to learn lessons, not to get married, or stay married, or to take this job or that job. You have been asking the wrong question. It's not whether or not to stay married. *The question*," she said, leaning closer to me, "*is what lesson does your soul want to learn? Do you know?*"

What lesson did my soul want to learn? I liked this question. It was new. Right then and there I felt it pointing me in a different direction. I felt it leading me up toward the light.

"Well, I'll tell you then," the psychic said when I didn't answer. "Your lesson in this lifetime is to find and trust your own precious voice. Your husband has his own lessons to learn. You cannot help each other on your quests anymore as husband and wife. Write that down. His grief at your leaving is also his fear of losing the power he has had for lifetimes. Those days are over for him, and he is in turmoil. But if you are to help him on his soul's quest, you will leave him. It is your job—your sacred contract—to free him, and to free yourself. Write that down too."

She sat patiently as I scrawled her astonishing speech on the little pad of paper. When I was done, she explained that human beings were coming into "the last days." This period of earth time could extend for a decade, or a century, or more. She didn't know; but things were speeding up and people were finally learning that only those who love themselves can love others, that only people who claim their own voice can hear the true song of another.

"It is time for you to answer the call of your soul," the psychic said emphatically. "It's calling, but you're too scared to listen. You think you know what's important, but you don't. You think it's important to keep things safe, but that's neither here nor there. What's important in this life is to learn the soul lessons.

"My dear," she said with great tenderness, "what feels like such a painful loss now will become something beautiful later on. You cannot escape your destiny. You can certainly try. People do so every day. They hold on tight, and the river just dries up.

"Now, I have more things to tell you," she said, handing back my husband's letter.

"But wait," I said. "Can I ask you another question?"

"Just one," she answered, looking at her watch.

"What about my children? I don't want to ruin their lives. Don't kids need a stable family and a safe—"

The psychic interrupted me with a wave of her hand and said,

"Phooey. You're not listening. Your children are *fine*. They are telling me that if you are strong, then they are safe. If you are sure-footed, they are stable. That is all. We're moving on now." I wanted to ask her more about my husband, my kids, my fear, my grief, but she was done with that subject. "Just look at your notes," she said. "That's all you need to know. You married your husband for soul reasons then; you're leaving him for soul reasons now. You're on the Road of Truth, my dear. You've put the truck in forward, but you're looking out of the rearview mirror. It's a dangerous way to drive, you know. If you choose to stay with your husband, you will be living in dead time. Dead time. If you leave, you'll be born again. As my mother said, 'Things may get worse before they get better, but they'll only get better if you let them get worse.'" She chuckled and closed her eyes.

Quite suddenly, she sat up straight on the bed and shook her head so that her earrings made a tinkling sound. "Now I am getting a name vibration," she announced. "Yes, I am getting a name vibration, and it is T-O-M," she said, spelling out the name. "The name vibration is Tom. Do you have a Tom in your life?"

I almost fell off the chair. I certainly did have a T-O-M in my life; in fact, I had three Toms in my life. In the past year, I had gone from being a most serious and principled wife and mother to being the kind of woman who had three other men in her life, all of them named Tom! The first was a man with whom I was having a doomed love affair. The second was a novelist I had never met but whose letters and phone calls were sources of mirth and sweetness in an otherwise desperate life. And the third was a man I had recently met. Although we had talked to each other only a few times, this new Tom seemed to know me, to see me, all of me—the part of me that was a big mess, and the part that was beginning to come out from behind the shadows. He wasn't frightened by my messy self, or my liberated self. I had never before met anyone quite like him. His personality was less dense than those of most people I knew. Perhaps this was because he had been born in a little town in West Texas, where the sky is a lot less confining than in New York, or maybe it was due to the fact that he was several steps ahead of me on the divorce path. His wife had left him a few years previously, taking his wealth and his young son. He had lost everything. Now he was emerging, like a phoenix from the ashes, with new wings and an open heart.

I didn't know what to think about this new T-O-M. I didn't know what was in store for us.

"Do you have a Tom in your life?" the psychic asked again.

"I have three." I laughed, smiling for the first time since our conversation began. "But I had never really noticed that they were all named Tom." I described my relationship with each of them to her, and she nodded her head as if she knew them quite well, waving me on with an impatient hand when she had heard enough.

"You are finished with the first T-O-M, your lover, but you will remain indebted to him, throughout all of your lifetimes," she said. "He gave you back your body, your heart, your voice. Do you understand? When you found him, you found your own precious voice. This is the contract you had with him; he has had this contract with many others. He freed the song of your soul. He comes with fire to awaken the dead. And yet he burns himself with his own heat. You cannot stay with him or you will burn yourself as well. I know you love this man, so write this down: Tom, throughout all eternity, I am grateful to you for the gift of my soul's voice."

I wrote that down, and then asked, "But, why does he—"

She waved her hand again, and said, "Don't worry about this

man. He is learning his soul lessons too. He will find the peace that his soul is searching for. You have given him the key to this. You have fulfilled your contract with each other." Her eyes closed, and her earrings tinkled. "The next T-O-M is not yours," she said, shaking her finger at me. "He belongs to someone else, and that is all you need to know. Stop writing him letters." She paused and tipped her head back, as if basking in the sunlight. "But this new Tom—the one with the light above his head. Yes, this is him, the name vibration, T-O-M. You will marry this man. His light will guide you. You will help each other become your True Selves, capital *T*, capital *S*. This is the contract you signed long ago. You have been looking for each other through many lifetimes. The name vibration T-O-M has led you to him."

Now the psychic leaned over and took my hands in hers. "My dear, karma is over with your husband. You must leave your marriage in harmony, because you will continue to work with the man who once was your husband. You missed nothing by marrying young. You were true to your soul's destiny in finding your first karmic mate, and now you have more years to give to your second karmic mate, Tom. So you are on the Road of Truth. Do not waver. May all be released without any negative karma. May friendship and brotherly love prevail."

That's where the tape ends. I do not remember leaving the trailer, or driving back down the dusty road, or flying to New York. Funny the way the mind can forget so much, yet retrieve a white poodle wearing barrettes and a blue-eyed psychic whose ruby red nails matched her heart-shaped earrings.

Almost twenty years later, I came across the tape and the psychic's business card when I was going through a box of old letters and photographs. Now that I knew how the story turned out, the psychic's predictions, in retrospect, were astonishingly uncanny. So I sent her a note, using the street address on the card and the only name I had: "The Mouthpiece of Spirit." I told her that my first husband and I had divorced, and that we continue to work together to this day. I told her that we had parented our children together and well. And that, amazingly, I had married the T-O-M with the light above his head, and when I paid attention, I could sense his light guiding us toward our True Selves, capital *T*, capital *S*.

But my letter never reached the psychic. It was returned from the post office with a message stamped across the envelope: "Person moved. No forwarding address provided."

Who was the Mouthpiece of Spirit? If there is one thing the psychic taught me, it's that people and events are rarely who and what we think they are. They are more meaningful, more worth our attention—part of some finely choreographed, eternal dance that we would be wise to bow down before in gratitude and humility. For all we know, an eccentric-woman living in a trailer on a dusty road near the Albuquerque airport may know more about the workings of the world than a professor or a poet or a president.

The philosopher Friedrich Nietzsche wrote, "If our senses were fine enough, we would perceive the slumbering cliff as a dancing chaos." He meant that literally: A rocky cliff is indeed a mass of dancing atomic particles, spinning and vibrating at tremendous speeds. This book you are holding, the chair you are sitting on, your own body—none are what they seem to be. Book, chair, body—everything is circling in a cosmic dance, appearing to us as solid form, yet if our senses were fine enough, we would stand around with our mouths hanging open at the glory and grace of it all. We would sense the presence of mystery everywhere: the angels keeping us safe as we drive home from work; the spirits hovering around our children; the thin waft of light pointing us in the direction of the Road of Truth. All we can do is try to refine our senses. We can try to quiet the noise in our minds, listen for deeper instructions, and leap without fear beyond what we think is so.

In his published journals, Einstein wrote about his life in Princeton, New Jersey, where—despite criticism from his contemporaries and years of unsuccessful research—he struggled to find a grand unifying theory of physics. "I have locked myself into quite hopeless scientific problems," he wrote, "the more so since, as an elderly man, I have estranged myself from the society here." I can just imagine Einstein, perplexed and lonely, walking in the prim neighborhoods of Princeton, engaged in impossible, circular dialogues with himself. Perhaps when he reached a low point, hopeless about ever resolving his scientific problems, he confided in a young student. Perhaps that student suggested that the old professor visit a tarot card reader who lived somewhere down the New Jersey Turnpike, beyond the closed orbit of the university. And Einstein said, "What the hell? I could use a change of scenery."

I imagine him driving out of Princeton on a blustery day, his hair blowing wildly as he speeds south, past scruffy pine forests and cultivated fields. I can see him squinting at the directions, exiting at a little town, and pulling into the driveway of a ramshackle farmhouse. No one is around. The wind whips through the trees and sings a strange and melancholy song. Einstein wonders what he's doing out in the boondocks. What will a tarot card reader know about the laws of physics? But he feels he has nothing to lose, nowhere else to turn. His mind is cluttered with the voices of other people. He hears his mother's voice warning him to stay out of trouble; his father's voice doubting his practical ability; his colleagues' voices questioning his judgment; the rest of the world telling him to think like everyone else. He senses that, somewhere beyond the noise, he will find his soul's voice, which will lead him to unravel the mysteries of the universe. Perhaps the tarot cards will point the way.

He enters the little house and spends an hour with a strange, barefooted gypsy whose head is wrapped in a sequined scarf. She spreads the cards out on her bed, studies them carefully, and tells Einstein all about himself—about his parents, his first sweetheart, the Nazis, the theory of relativity, his failed marriage, his children, his nagging guilt about the atomic bomb. She asks him probing questions that bypass his troubled mind and soften the tightness he feels in his heart. He lets down his defenses, and once again he remembers that it is his soul that has always unlocked the most hopeless scientific problems. He feels the fresh wind of the universe stirring his creativity. He prays that he will live long enough to discover what the gypsy woman says is hovering close by.

Before he departs, the gypsy serves Einstein sweet tea and then reads the leaves left at the bottom of the cracked white cup. She looks directly into his eyes and says, "No problem can be solved from the same consciousness that created it. Do you understand? Write that down."

TO DIE IN ONE LIFE IS TO BLOSSOM IN ANOTHER

Tama J. Kieves

I don't know if you have ever died while still breathing, but I have. Picasso said that every act of creation begins with an act of destruction. Jesus said you must lose your life to find your life. Dying is in all the great teachings, but none of that matters when you are trying desperately to hold on to the last few fibers of all *you* know—and all you've ever been.

I was only twenty-five years old when I died, died to one life, one trembling identity, and arose in another. I had been leading this absolutely "perfect" existence. I had graduated from Harvard Law School with honors and worked for probably the most prestigious law firm in the city where I lived. Not only that, I was squarely on partnership track, a hot, rising star. I was young and ambitious and bright and accomplished. I was well paid and lauded and destined for great things and good jewelry.

But I had this dirty little secret. I was cold inside. I felt trapped by my success, trapped on the track and by the dreaded realization that I didn't seem to *connect* with my work, enjoy it, or care about it other than the paycheck and the praise.

I lived in a shadow world, hungry, orphaned, feeling as though I didn't belong in this expensive wool suit, in this plush hallway, in this lavish office, in this life. I didn't know where I belonged and increasingly I didn't know *if* I belonged.

I told a therapist that I fantasized about being on the express bus in the morning and having the bus explode. It was the perfect out. I could still be perfect on the way to my perfect job; only I wouldn't ever have to get there. What a perfect plan. Thankfully, my soul had a better one.

Listening to my job woes, a friend of mine convinced me to leave the office and take a vacation. So I flew to California, sped down the coastline, and sat on a beach, staring into the glittering sweep of ocean. I watched the waves endlessly crash—rolling in, rolling back. Spitting bubbles and foam, wild water unfurling as thick and gracious as a lion's mane.

It was in the presence of the natural that I could no longer remain unnatural. Breathing in that environment of salt air, slapping waves, silver gleams, and maddened gulls, something in me broke free and refused to be restrained. The ocean had turned rocks and shells into raw bits of sand and it was working its brute magic on me.

I did not want to come undone. I did not want to cave in on myself, admit the unbearable truth to myself of my core unhappiness. I didn't want to recognize the lies I'd been telling myself, about how it would all get better, how it was reasonable to stay in my powerful career.

Before this moment, I had held my life together with willpower, the approval of others, exhaustion, relentless work, and deadlines, shoving my feelings down and somehow holding my breath. But suddenly I couldn't hold my breath anymore. I couldn't hold back my tears anymore. I couldn't hold back *desire* anymore—this simple raw instinct to just let go and be alive, to just let go and let a dying life *die*. I felt then how much energy it had taken, how much will-power, self-control, and misspent strength it took to make myself stay where I did not want to stay.

But I did not go down without a fight. I kept thinking, "Just hold on. Relax, rest. Go back and do your job, maybe just a few more years. Save some money. It'll all get better. You'll see."

However, this time the words weren't working. They came from an old self, and she suddenly seemed so very far away and wistful. Barking orders at myself didn't work, either. Even my fool-proof willpower could not damp down the wildness.

The wildness was taking over. Instinct eclipsed intellect. My soul's pure, clear emotion overrode my father's dominating voice, society's cautioning voice, my own voice of control pleading for its life. Something shimmied within me. And I let go of the well-worn, wretched reins of control, and laughed and cried, and died.

And here is the biggest thing I learned from that terrifying, mystifying, and holy experience. My inner needs are not self-destructive, are not bad and shameful, are not something naughty, irresponsible, and frivolous.

My inner need saved my life. My pain saved me from a life of suffocating comfort and took me into a life of leaping, plunging, and living. My pain busted the myths I'd been handed since childhood. All along, the voice I was fighting back, the one that questioned and wanted more, the one that told me to walk on the beach for a thousand miles with the sea wind in my hair—that voice was not crazy, but crazed for life.

This self was pure and healthy and instinctive and self-loving.

And now I knew what it meant to "love myself." It meant to listen to myself and to listen to my pain. It meant to honor my desires and dreams and let go of what I thought I was "supposed" to do.

My pain was the only part of me that had told the truth. It was like the voice that says the emperor has no clothes. My pain was not bewitched by money, status, approval, or Prada. My pain would not fall asleep. I was withering inside while others said how wonderful I was doing. My pain underscored the withering.

I stayed at that beach for as long as the light would bear. I cried and journaled and listened to my feelings, maybe for the first time. A storm raged up from within and I could not stop the wind.

Some deep inner voice said with certainty and compassion, "You cannot go back to the firm. You cannot go back to that life. You can pretend you don't know, but you *know*. You *know*. And now, *you know, you know*."

I felt panic-stricken. This was forbidden, ridiculous, impetuous, obscene. This was not in my five-year plan. It wouldn't look good on my résumé. And my parents wouldn't want to brag about this event at the synagogue.

What would it be like to just quit? To give up the appearance and the investment? What would I do, how would I live? What if I was throwing away a prestigious career just because I'd sat in the sun too long and had a meltdown, a ragged flash of insanity?

However, the insanity didn't care. It seemed to announce, "You can't go back. You can't hold your breath. You've breathed already. You've crossed over to the other side."

There is a freedom that comes when you let go of the struggle and slide headlong into whatever life has to offer, when you stop holding back the relentless pull of your own mystical instincts. The lack of "real life" was killing me, but real life meant stepping off the track. Real life was wild life, making up steps based on my fledgling instincts and desires.

I was born that day on the beach in every one of those tears and sobs and shudders. The waves crashed with the perennial knowing of the ages, letting go and rolling, letting go and rolling, letting go and rolling.

I did not give my notice the day I returned, but I did shortly after. I stepped off the track and onto a thousand-mile beach in my life where I became a free person extraordinaire, a poet who wrote with purple pens, an impassioned speaker, a creativity and life/work coach. But most of all, I became myself.

These days, I still find myself listening to the wild and unconventional wisdom that ambushes me periodically. And I am equally amazed at where this self-love leads me. Most recently, I felt propelled to self-publish the book I had written for twelve years that revealed my personal journey of career transformation. That book would become *This Time I Dance! Trusting the Journey of Creating the Work You Love.*

Of course I knew nothing about the publishing process, how to design a book or distribute and promote it, but I decided to follow the pull that seemed to indicate this direction. Soon after, a well-known author read the book and suggested I show it to her agent and get it published by traditional means.

This is every writer's dream. I should have been ecstatic. But something in me felt frozen and stiff. I did not feel moved to go this way. The logical part of me screamed, "This is a once-in-a-lifetime opportunity." But every time I thought about doing it, I felt heavy, sad, unmotivated, and petulant.

I prayed and scribbled wildly in my journal, questioning my feelings up one side and down the other. And finally, I sighed deeply, dialed the author's number, and reluctantly honored myself, turning down her generous offer.

Then, in just a few weeks, I received an e-mail that changed my life. It came on a Saturday afternoon and read, "Your Fairy Godmother Has Arrived." I read the e-mail with my natural New York skepticism, but soon my chain-link fence dissolved into hot tears of gratitude.

A former vice president of publicity and marketing from a major publisher had somehow discovered my self-published book on Amazon.com, read it, loved it, sung its praises over and over, and insisted on showing it to a New York publisher for me. This time the opportunity felt delicious and holy. And it turned out that "my fairy godmother" had a good friend who happened to be the president of Tarcher/Putnam, the very publishing company I had always secretly fantasized about.

Tarcher/Putnam not only decided to publish my book, but they decided to publish my *exact* book, my design and words as is, an event as likely as an e-mail out of the blue from a New York "fairy godmother."

And this is what I continue to learn from dying to "safe" choices, a dying that began many years ago on a gleaming California beach. You can live a life of either trusting your inner voice or distrusting your inner voice. You can cling to familiar expectations, conventions, and "reasonable" responses or you can listen to the sweet madness in your bones.

Yet, nothing but the madness knows your unique way home. I'm not sure that it gets any easier to listen to our own wisdom, since wisdom will often cost us the lives we live in. I guess letting go is simply the amazing way we transform ourselves. But at least I know now that what feels like dying is probably *birthing*. Because to crash in one life is to recognize, stir, and blossom in another.

THE SUN

David Whyte

This morning on the desk,
facing up,
a poem of Kavanagh's
celebrating a lost love.

"She was the sun," he said,
and now she still
lives in the fibre
of his arms,
her warmth
through all the years
folding the old man's hand
in hers
of a Sunday
Dublin morning.

Sometimes reading
Kavanagh I look out

at everything
growing so wild
and faithfully beneath
the sky
and wonder
why we are the one
terrible
part of creation
privileged
to refuse our flowering.

I know
in the text of the heart
the flower is our death
and the first opening
of the new life
we have yet to imagine,

But Kavanagh's line
reminds me
how I want to know
that sun,
and how I want to flower
and how I want to claim
my happiness
and how I want to walk
through life
amazed and inarticulate
with thanks.

And how I want to
know that warmth
through
love itself,
and
through the sun itself.

I want to know
that sun
of happiness
when I wake
and see through
my window
the morning color
on the far mountain.

I want to know
when I lean down to the lilies
by the water
and feel their small and
perfect reflection
on my face.

I want to know
that gift
when I walk
innocent through the trees
burning with life
and the green

passion
of the pasture's
first growth,

and I want to know
as lazily
as the cows
that tear at the grass
with their
soft mouths.

I want to know
what I am
and what I am
involved with by loving
this world
as I do.

And I want time
to think of all
the unlived lives:

those that fail to notice
until it is too late,

those with eyes staring
with bitterness,

and those
met on the deathbed
whose mouths are wide
with
unspoken love.

Every year
they keep me faithful
and help me
realize there is more
to lose
than I thought
and more at stake
than the mere
possibility
of a recognized
heroism.

They remind me
why
I want to be found by love,
why I want to come alive
in the holiness
of that belonging
and like Kavanagh

I want to be courageous
in my terrors.

I want to know
in life or death
all the ways
the warmth of that
great rose fire
sun
in its heaven
has made me.

And everything
that made me
has been
a sun to my growing,
that is the article
of my faith,
even the darkness
of that soil that went
before the time of light
was another
kind of sun.

What I am
is what I have
been grown by,
the sun,
that great love,
all the many small loves
and that one love too
who waited so long

to find me and
who has always
walked by my side
folding my
remembering
hand in hers.

REFLECTIONS

Dani Noble

A mirror shows the reflection of anything that stands before it. We stand in front of a mirror and look to the mirror for answers. But what if we turned to *ourselves* for the answers instead?

This article, which I title "Reflections," outlines an important life lesson that I have come to understand in my thirteen years here on earth. I hope that you may find some new knowledge in this piece to go forth and learn more about who you are.

Who Am I?

Isn't it strange that everyone forms an idea on who you will become or where you're going; yet, the only person that is clueless is you? From the time you were a child, it seems that everyone sees your future through a crystal clear window. You are confused, however, while you struggle to peer through the foggy glass hung on the wall. Countless times you look hesitantly into the mirror, not sure whose face you will see today, because you are constantly redefining who you are; but then it's the same face.

Discovering who you are is a lifelong journey. But in the early stages of your life, you already have the foundation for this elusive concept. You know many of your likes and dislikes; you know the things that brighten your day or the things that make you upset. Even just looking at the environment that you live in can say a lot about you. When you look at the types of people around you or the mood of the atmosphere you've created in your personal space, this can portray a clear image of who you are.

Embracing Who I Am

You're in awe of this person who stands before you in the mirror. Your eyes are full of determination; your face is serious and sure; and your lips form into a slight smile of satisfaction. This is you, in all of your glory. This is you for the rest of your life.

I cannot tell you how many times I have been surprised by the face that stares back at me in the mirror. I cannot tell you how many times I have been startled by the gap between who I was and who I am. I cannot count the times where I have simply smiled back at the face and said quietly, "This is me; this is who I am." Satisfaction fills my body, blocking any doubt from crossing my mind. It's such a feeling of peace and harmony; like nothing could ever touch me or carry me down from where I float. I'm not joyful or depressed; I'm just *me*.

Embracing who you are is another way of *understanding* who you are; it's the process in which information becomes knowledge.

When you embrace this information, you are inhaling the data so that it may become a part of you as a whole person.

Becoming Your Best Friend

It has taken me many years to catch up with myself. But, with much practice, I have learned to live from day to day, not knowing who I will become tomorrow, but living with the confidence that I will love whoever I will become. I look into the mirror with the knowledge that tomorrow I may bloom into someone slightly different from who I am today. But I see past me, present me, and future me; and I love it all with such a deep passion.

I call this section "Becoming Your Best Friend" because I believe that the love that I have for myself is that of a close companion. This love is the most important affection one can have. Friends may come and go, but this friend will *always* be there with you. This friend is your best support and best caretaker, your best role model and best motivator. Others can influence, but only *you* can make it happen.

I didn't always have this outlook, though. I'm not exactly sure when this new beginning actually happened, but I do know that there was a large, dividing line between one half of my childhood and the other.

Discovering Your Mission

There have been points in my life where I felt like I have been immersed in such beauty and splendor that I break down and cry. It's at these moments that I am surrounded with such a deep understanding of my purpose here on this earth; it's at these moments that I know why God made me the way I am. And it's at these moments that I love myself more than ever. Sometimes these occurrences will be during an untouched encounter with nature— something that brings out the organic and natural aspects of the soul. Sometimes it will be a total release of all thought and tension; and the gained feeling of total freedom. Or sometimes it's just a good time with the people I love most.

In 2001, I took a short vacation with my mom to Florida. We traveled to Key Largo to swim with dolphins in a center for dolphin research. It was one of the most amazing experiences of my life. I remember being underwater with these magnificent creatures swimming around me; these beautiful animals that swam about without a care in the world. It seemed as if time stood still in that natural tank. I thought of nothing but the world that I was surrounded by, this perfect, harmonious world. I looked at these animals that had built such a perfect society. And I thought that if the entire world could look to these dolphins as role models, all of our problems would be solved.

That was a new awakening for me. I wanted to be the person to bring this sort of peace to the world. I felt so confident and sure that I could fulfill this task that (it felt as if) God had placed into my very hands that day. The seawater washed away all of my fears and doubt, and stripped me to my soul. That day I was glowing; that day I was the purest me I have ever been.

It takes some people a lifetime to find out who they are and then another lifetime to love that person. But sometimes the answers to all of our deepest and hardest questions are right within our reach. If we just take some time to look around us, look at the love that surrounds us, the environment that cradles us. That is the time when we will find out who we are; and that is the time when we will love that person with all of our mind, body, spirit, and soul.

UNCOVERING
A GIRL'S AMBITION

Belleruth Naparstek, L.I.S.W., B.C.D.

I first discovered I was flat-out ambitious when I was thirty-four years old, and, truth be told, it was a bit of a shock. Up until that time, I'd been coddling the notion that I disdained competition and had no desire whatsoever for an unseemly and unladylike climb up the organizational ladder.

On the contrary, I believed that what made me happy at my job was *influence*, not power. A bleeding-heart clinical social worker from the get-go, professionally molded in the steroidally idealistic sixties, I'd always aimed to leave the world a better place and make good things happen, particularly but not exclusively for the downtrodden and suffering—still do, in fact. But in those days, I also believed that it didn't matter whether it was I or somebody else who was officially piloting the Engines of Change, as long as I could help chart their course and maybe navigate some. This was how women born in 1942 were taught, and, sadly, it's not all that different for a lot of women born in 1972.

I was my mother's daughter, even if I didn't know it growing up. (My father was much more fun.) She'd been a brainy executive secretary who had once hoped to become a lawyer. Instead, she basked with reasonable contentment in the glow of having produced three achieving kids, programmed—indeed, required—to do better than their parents. She gave mixed reviews to the traditional woman's role, and had allowed me considerably more latitude and attitude than she'd ever given herself. But when all was said and done, I'd absorbed her belief that a woman was far more attractive, feminine, virtuous, and valuable when supporting and empowering the Grand Fromage, rather than *being* the Grand Fromage.

Indeed, it was my contention in the early days of my career that it was actually *preferable* for someone else to shoulder the burdensome mantle of Boss and absorb the aggravation, deal with the politics, and sail my edgy new ideas through the dangerous straits of bureaucratic infighting. Of course, this was only so because they *were* my ideas. I had the boss's devoted ear, and he (and it was always a "he" in those days) deemed me his trusted confidante, idea generator, sounding board, ethical muse, fingers-on-the-pulse-of-the-organization informant, and all-round pal—all of which I was. Like the wily wife in a fifties sitcom, I fluffed my guy up, knotted his tie, packed his briefcase, and sent him off to fight the good fight at senior staff meetings, while I stayed behind and fretted over possible outcomes.

For ten years, spanning three different jobs, working for three very different men in three different mental health settings, I made what to me was the ideal trade: I helped make my boss look even better than he was, supplied him with what we would today call "content," and lent my energy and skill toward advancing his career.

In return, he adored me, deferred to me, and implemented my notions of good programs, all the while protecting me and taking the heat from the opposition.

What's more, I could remain one of the gang and stay popular with my peers, because I hadn't been contaminated by a promotion up the heinous chain of command. Indeed, in my position as Supreme Insider, I could grease the wheels for my pals and lob their worthier suggestions into the net for them. Better yet, my special status as Go-To Gal with the line staff and Invaluable Sidekick to the boss gave me, a mother of three, leeway to work at home or leave early when one of my kids got sick. I was proud and grateful for what I'd managed to pull off.

So for about a decade, this felicitous arrangement was supremely satisfactory to me. In my handcrafted role as unofficial Queen Consort, I balanced each of my bosses' quirks and maintained my indispensability. I coached one to tone down his confrontational style when his argumentative ways ran the risk of blowing our agenda, and pressed another to show some backbone and get off the fence when his tendency toward obsessive worry paralyzed him.

Then, when I was thirty-four, my then boss got promoted. The CEO of our mental health center, a dazzlingly charismatic African American woman named Myra Wesley, who suffered none of the compunctions that burdened me and who possessed enough heart, brains, humor, pizzazz, and integrity for me to make her my very first ever professional role model, revamped the place and wisely made my boss her chief of operations. So now his position was open, as were several other new department chief slots.

Major jockeying for position ensued, rocking the hallways, perturbing staff meetings, and producing indigestion in the cafeteria. Many of my peers eagerly tossed their hats into the ring. Names were floated. Bottoms were kissed. Backs were bitten. Alliances were made and broken. The buzz of gossip reached record levels. Tension, worry, and excitement suffused the air.

I tried to maintain my amused, above-it-all detachment and keep my distance from what I saw as unseemly, tasteless, competitive scrambling. Weeks passed and a few of the open positions were filled by some of my colleagues. Indeed, several peers, some a bit on the mediocre side, had, one by one, shot past me on the organizational chart. They were now *Management.* I was reeling from the whiplash of watching them whiz by me.

To my immense chagrin, and in spite of my best efforts to feel otherwise, I discovered I was preoccupied with feeling left behind. I found myself increasingly distressed, losing sleep, and, truth be told, just plain eating my heart out. I could not help but notice I was waking up at three in the morning, feeling overlooked, hurt, angry, jealous, resentful, and wildly competitive—all the emotions I'd convinced myself I didn't have. In a nutshell, I'd been taught, like so many women of my generation, to succeed without caring about success. And here I was, busted. Evidently I cared *a lot*...about power, recognition, status, being a big shot, and everything else I presumably disdained.

Many predawn discussions ensued with my baffled but sympathetic husband, who couldn't quite grasp what the problem was, having been brought up, boy-fashion, to succeed *precisely* because he cared about success and went after it. With his help, I decided I'd best bite the bullet, swallow my pride, and tell the truth, first (and hardest) of all to myself, and next to my beloved CEO, Myra.

The truth was, I wanted the damn job my boss had vacated. And I was hurt and insulted that I hadn't been offered it.

It's hard to describe the exquisite discomfort and squirmy sense of embarrassment I felt when I approached her and confessed that I wanted to be considered for unit chief.

Myra did one of her famous double takes, one eyebrow cocked, and then let loose her inimitable, raucous guffaw. *"YOU want the job? I thought you would never consider taking that job! We've been racking our [expletive] brains trying to figure out what to do with that job! HAW!!"*

I told her I hadn't known I wanted it until the great shuffle began and I started feeling psycho on a regular basis at three a.m. My face was hot. I dearly wanted to be elsewhere.

"HAW!"

More squirming.

She started grinning and shaking her head. Then I started grinning.

She said, *"Honey, you got it. The job is yours. HAW!"*

That conversation—indeed, the whole process of self-discovery and resolution—was alchemical and transformative. The ruse was over. The jig was up. There was nothing else for it but to step out of an ill-fitting and inauthentic conceit I'd been cloaking myself in for thirty-four years, and instead take on the taboo mantle of direct power and authority. Claiming it was exhilarating, scary, and liberating.

I of course made my share of mistakes in the months that followed, especially given my girlie attitudes and biases about power. But it was a fascinating ride, and one I wouldn't have traded for the world. I learned a lot and became a decent manager. Eventually I discovered that administration wasn't my favorite thing to do. Unlike Myra, I wasn't a natural at it. Managing well was a strain for me, where writing, designing programs, and practicing psychotherapy were a pleasure. So eventually, after a few years, when I'd learned what I wanted to learn and accomplished some things that mattered to me, I went back to doing what I loved best, only this time for the right reasons.

But I'll never forget that moment when I finally owned my ambition and asked for what I wanted. That was the time—marriage and motherhood notwithstanding—when I indeed got myself promoted: from girl to woman.

RESOURCES:
SOUL EXPRESSION

Books

Art and Healing: Using Expressive Art to Heal Your Body, Mind, and Spirit, by Barbara Ganim (Three Rivers Press, 1999)

The Artist's Way: An Artist's Guide to Higher Creativity, by Julia Cameron (Jeremy P. Tarcher, 2002)

Broken Open, by Elizabeth Lesser (Villard, 2004)

Callings: Finding and Following an Authentic Life, by Gregg Levoy (Random House, 1997)

Finding Your Own North Star, by Martha Beck (Three Rivers Press, 2001)

The House of Belonging, by David Whyte (Many Rivers Press, 2002)

The Joy Diet, by Martha Beck (Crown, 2003)

Life Makeovers, by Cheryl Richardson (Broadway, 2000)

Life Strategies, by Phillip C. McGraw (Hyperion, 1999)

The Mozart Effect: Tapping the Power of Music to Heal the Body, Strengthen the Mind, and Unlock Creative Spirit, by Don Campbell (Quill, 2002)

New and Selected Poems, by Mary Oliver (Beacon Press, 1992)

The Nine Modern Day Muses, by Jill Badonsky, M.Ed. (Gotham, 2001)

Poetic Medicine: The Healing Art of Poem-Making, by John Fox (Jeremy P. Tarcher, 1997)

The 7 Habits of Highly Effective People, by Stephen R. Covey (Fireside, 1990)

Simple Abundance: A Daybook of Comfort and Joy, by Sarah Ban Breathnach
    (Warner, 1995)
Staying Well with Guided Imagery, by Belleruth Naparstek (Warner, 1995)
Ten Poems to Change Your Life, by Roger Housden (Crown, 2001)
This Time I Dance, by Tama J. Kieves (Jeremy P. Tarcher, 2004)
The 12 Secrets of Highly Creative Women, by Gail McMeekin (Conari Press,
    2000)
Who Are You? 101 Ways of Seeing Yourself, by Malcolm Godwin (Penguin,
    2000)
Writing to Heal the Soul: Transforming Grief and Loss through Writing,
    by Susan Zimmerman (Three Rivers Press, 2002)
Your Heart's Desire: Instructions for Creating the Life You Really Want,
    by Sonia Choquette (Three Rivers Press, 1997)

AUDIO

Health Journeys: A Meditation to Ease Grief, by Belleruth Naparstek,
    (Image Paths, 1992)
Inner Peace for Busy People, by Joan Borysenko (Hay House, 2001)

Websites

Journals and stationery:
Brush Dance
100 Ebbtide Ave. #1
Sausalito, CA 94965
www.brushdance.com
800-531-7445

O, The Oprah Magazine
For subscription information, contact:
P.O. Box 7831
Red Oak, IA 51591
www.oprah.com

Academy of American Poets
www.poets.org

Music

The Andrew Lloyd Webber Collection, by Sarah Brightman (The Really
Useful Group, 1997)

Bach: The Complete Brandenburg Concertos, by Boston Baroque;
Martin Pearlman, director (Telarc, 1996)

Eden, by Sarah Brightman (Nemo Studios, 1998)

Josh Groban, by Josh Groban (Reprise, 2003)

The Mozart Effect, Volumes 1–5, by Don Campbell (Spring Hill, 1998 and
2000)

Ocean Dreams, by Dean Evenson (Soundings of the Planet, 1989–1999)

Time to Say Goodbye, by Sarah Brightman (Nemo Studios, 1997)

SECTION THREE

Death and Dying

Nothing is impossible unless you think it is.

—PARAMAHANSA YOGANANDA

• • •

When you use life's experiences as your teacher and learn from them the true nature of the world and your part in it, those experiences become valuable guides to eternal fulfillment and happiness.

—PARAMAHANSA YOGANANDA

Light

Light
Light so bright
It burns my eyes
I turn away
for fear
I will be burned
not knowing the truth
That light is love
and cannot burn
can only heal
that light is God

and can only bless
That light is gold
precious, so precious
That light is eternal
can only grow
find your light
let it be love
eternal love
can only love

Andrea Joy Cohen, M.D.

THE SECRET THAT GLOWS IN THE DARK

Stephen Fulder, Ph.D.

THOSE suffering from chronic disease or disability, and those close to them, are often overwhelmed by the tragedy or sadness of the situation. It is sometimes hard to see the blessing in diseases and the changes that they bring. Yet we have the opportunity to use all events, good or bad, as a vehicle for the growth of wisdom and inner freedom, especially those that are significant. Disease can be the gateway to a deep letting go, a surrender to the power of life that is so much more than our attitude toward it.

I wrote the poem below to my mother, Marlies, when she was in an advanced stage of Alzheimer's disease. She was a warm, compassionate, lively, and capable person, with a certain level of underlying anxiety as a refugee from the Holocaust. When the disease began, she went through three years of real difficulty and suffering—fear, insecurity, confusion, and guilt. But after that period, she let herself go, and for nine more years lived with ever-decreasing abilities with equanimity, love, and a deep inner peace that was never apparent in her ordinary life previously. For the last few years, she was completely bedridden, and couldn't talk, move, or look after herself in any way. Yet she radiated a powerful inner peace and goodness that touched everyone who had contact with her—her family, friends, and medical professionals. More than once we would find the nursing staff just sitting by her bed, in silence, doing nothing, just resting and being bathed in her inner peace. Here is the poem.

The Secret That Glows in the Dark

I want to share a secret,
For those who can listen
About the gentle radiance
Of these last years
So clear, so soft, so good,
That even the doctors
And the visitors who come and go,
Stop to take a breath
And will never forget you.
You are not ill
Illness is our label
Inscribed by our fears.
You know neither illness nor wellness
Just thereness.
No fear of death
No anxieties of what the future may bring,
Or may not bring
No pain, no blame,
No loss, no regret

No anger at those who abandoned you,
When you were no longer useful
No time, no purpose
But the gentle kiss of life itself
The grace that comes when all else goes
To what do you listen to, so intently?
Is it the music of your heartbeat,
Tapping celestial rhythms
On the gates of your soul?
Or is it the humming of bees
On that summer's day?
Or the barking of your dogs,
That only you can quiet,
Or your fingers in their thick fur?
Or long dreams of play and play of dreams
The past kaleidoscoped into present
Uninterrupted by our harsh reality
As I lie next to you,
And feel this life flow through
And watch your face,
No frown, no wrinkles, no burden of the past,
Just open presence,
Then, like the moon that shines between passing clouds,
Beams a joyous smile,
That vanishes so fast,
That I do not know if I really saw it
And now, again, you teach me,
About a life without fear, without walls, without end,
Just as you did when I was born
And, like then, share your happiest years

A Family's Journey from Mourning to Celebration

Peter L. Sheras, Ph.D., and Phyllis R. Koch-Sheras, Ph.D.

W E live on the East Coast now, but we are both originally from the Midwest. My name is Peter. I met my wife, Phyllis, right after graduate school and discovered that we had a lot in common: we were both born and raised in Chicago; we each had one same-sex sibling; we both enjoyed photography; and we shared a not-so-secret addiction to chocolate. Soon after moving together to a small city in the Southeast to take jobs at the same university, we married and began our family.

Phyllis's parents and my mother stayed in Chicago when we moved. After my parents divorced, my dad had moved back to the small town in Michigan where he grew up. There he married a second time. His new wife was named Phyllis as well.

"My" Phyllis and I have been happily married for more than twenty-five years now; and "Grandma" Phyllis and my dad were married nearly as long. As our children grew up, we continued to be in touch frequently with our folks about their lives and our own. This story is about how we faced one of life's saddest yet most meaningful moments as a family several years ago.

One summer afternoon a call came from Grandma Phyllis in Michigan. She said the doctor had told her that Dad had taken a serious turn for the worse and would likely die soon. If we wanted to see him, the doctor said when we called, "You need to come here soon."

Dad had prostate cancer; he had been diagnosed four years before but had been in remission until the previous Thanksgiving, when he was in an automobile accident and began to lose ground.

The logistics of getting there in a hurry were difficult—clearing our own heavy work schedules for the week and retrieving Dan, age fourteen, and Sarah, eleven, from camp. What we dreaded most of all was telling them the reason for our hastily planned trip to the Midwest. We would have to say that "Paw-pa" was dying and that we wanted to go and say good-bye. We would have to confront his imminent departure in our role as parents, as well as son and daughter-in-law. Overcome with sadness, fear, anxiety, and anticipatory emotional exhaustion, we wondered how we could deal with the kids' grief—and Dad's feelings as well.

Dad had always been a solid, quiet, noncommunicative type. Once we did talk for an hour about how funny it was that both he and I had married women with the same name and how our kids knew they had a mother Phyllis and a "grandma" Phyllis, too. For us that was a long conversation.

Nevertheless, our family knew he loved us and that he was very sensitive to our needs. If he didn't call us, it was because he didn't want us to worry about anything. Dad was generous to a fault.

During an earlier hospitalization, his nurses told us that he always apologized when asking for pain medication or even the most routine help; he didn't want to be a burden on anyone. When he first became ill, he said he didn't want any presents as he didn't want me to be inconvenienced in any way. "It is no trouble," I said.

We agreed that a box of Frango Mints, his favorite chocolate, would be the right thing to bring. Our family had inherited our passion for chocolate from him, and there was no more famous or delicious chocolate confection, sold since 1929 exclusively at Marshall Field & Company in Chicago. At a loss as to how best to show my love, I bought him the biggest box they had: five pounds, more than a hundred pieces.

Knowing him as we did, we sensed that Dad would be upset that we had troubled ourselves and the kids to come see him, just to cheer him up. We foresaw our sadness, the kids' fear and worry, our desire to give emotional comfort to Grandma Phyllis, and Dad's upset, all rolled up into a long and tiring five-day trip.

The next evening, Phyllis and I sat down to share our feelings. Did the trip have to be the way we imagined it would be? What was our goal and deepest desire in going to see Dad? Surely there must be a way for our trip to be memorable in a more positive way. So we asked ourselves, "What would the best trip we can imagine look like?" We decided to visualize the possibilities of our journey from the ideal, not from the ordeal.

The ultimate goal of our ideal trip would be for Dad to recover from his cancer as a result of our visit, or at least for it to prolong his life a while. A second positive outcome would be for Dad to be happy to see us and for us to be happy to be with him—joyful, laughing, and definitely not sad or morose. What if we decided to have fun traveling to see him and Grandma Phyllis, not in a funeral cortege, but on a real vacation, like the road trips we had made in earlier years? And how about a visit that gave our kids a sense of the history of the generations of their ancestors? All of that would be too much to hope for—or would it?

How might we make such a trip come about? As a family, we began to create a vision for the trip. The first challenge would be getting there. How about a big car, perhaps a convertible? We always rushed to get to the house from the airport. What if we took a bit of time and saw the sights along the way? We agreed that would be more fun. Arriving in a better mood, we thought—not looking like we were responding to an emergency, rather like we were on vacation—would be more agreeable to Dad. Plans were made to get there when he was most alert, spending a few hours only the first day, maybe a few more the next.

We put our heads together as a family to talk about how we wanted to be when we were with him. We wanted to be talkative, engaging, and upbeat without being in complete denial about what was happening. All the while, we wanted to make sure that Grandma Phyllis was there as much as possible to help guide and participate in the conversations and tell Paw-pa how much we loved him. Reminiscing about our great times together, looking at family photos together, and hugging him often would be the most helpful, we thought.

Armed with these goals, we set off on our trip, committed to making our vision a profound expression of love and fun for all of us. We landed at the airport at noon and picked up our rental car, a Lincoln Town Car. Then we cruised up along the shore of Lake Michigan, stopping at various stores and outlet malls on the way. We arrived before dinner, checked into the nicest motel we could find, with the best swimming pool, and then went to see Dad and Grandma Phyllis. We were laughing and smiling when we first saw him. He appeared pale and weak, sitting by the hospital bed that had been moved into the living room of their sprawling ranch house. His eyes sparkled and his face lit up when he saw his grandchildren. The children recounted our day to him, telling how much they had missed him.

We had a short visit then went to dinner and had a swim at the motel. The next day we spent the morning at the house. Then my Phyllis and I took Grandma Phyllis out to lunch, while Dad told his grandchildren the history of our family. They were wide-eyed with wonder and excitement when they told us the stories later on our way back to the motel. We spent that day and the next visiting and taking the kids to swim at the nearby beach.

During the days, we spent time talking with Paw-pa while he sat up in bed or in a nearby chair. He shared his Frango Mints with us every evening and he would eat one a day before he went to bed, he told us.

On our last morning there with him, the four of us stood at the foot of his bed and handed him a Polaroid camera and Dad took a picture of us laughing and smiling at him. We had sent him many pictures of us, but we all knew this one would be special. Dad loved taking pictures. We all did (in fact, my brother Michael is a professional photographer). When the picture developed a few minutes later, we left it at the foot of his bed where he could see it (and us) looking back at him. After kissing him good-bye, we were on our way in the Lincoln Town Car.

It was only as we headed home that we began to feel the sadness of potentially losing this wonderful man. At first, we were all silent in the car. Then we began to tell stories of the meaningful time we had spent with him. We laughed a lot, cried a little, and shared how good we felt about going to visit him. I spoke of my childhood memories of my dad when my brother and I would go to visit him in Michigan. Knowing he would likely die soon, none of us mentioned it; we didn't need to just then.

When we got home, we took out the birthday card Dad had sent to my Phyllis just a month before. She had saved it, because the words had moved her so much. Tears came then as we read the message that also fit *him* so well: "We use the word 'wonderful' so much that sometimes it loses its meaning. We should save it for the best parts of life—for celebrating special events, for times that bring us true happiness, for special people who stand out from the rest. You really are a wonderful person, a person worth celebrating. You bring joy in so many ways, and you deserve a day as wonderful as you."

That "wonderful person" had to have been in him, too, in order to see it in Phyllis and select this special message for her.

That family trip was in July. The doctors had said he would likely pass away by the end of that month. We called him every few days to support him and recollect the good time we had just had on our visit. Dad was very lively and talkative; he rallied physically. After our visit, he felt much better and got up from his bed. He and Grandma Phyllis were able to go for a walk every afternoon for an hour or so, and they sat and talked for hours. In the evening before bed, he would have his Frango Mint.

Despite earlier predictions, Dad lived through July and August. He was still feeling fine in September, but began to fail in mid-October. He died at the end of the month. Grandma Phyllis said those last few months were the happiest they had ever had together. We talked about our trip with him frequently, and our children spoke to him on the phone with a special warmth that we had never heard before.

I had the chance to visit him two more times before he died. The whole family, however, returned only for his funeral. Our kids were not frightened, but remembered what fun we had had with him; they helped us all celebrate his life. Dan and Sarah felt as if they knew him well after that visit and shared something unique and loving with him. It was a bittersweet ending for us.

After the funeral, we returned to the house. Grandma Phyllis called us over to the large box of Frango Mints. It must have had more than a hundred and fifty candies in it at one time. When she opened it there were six left. Together his beloved wife, my brother, the two of us, and our two kids—Dad's closest family—ate the last of the Frango Mints. The bittersweet ending was sweet at the last.

Our family plan, the one we had envisioned and made up together, was fulfilled. The Polaroid photo still sits in their house on the dresser in the bedroom. Grandma Phyllis sees it every day; we look at it when we visit her, and we would all like to think Dad's spirit watches over it.

THE FINAL GIFT: HONESTY

Barry Neil Kaufman

A sequoia can live two thousand years. A squid has a four-year life span. A mayfly, born with the dawn, is gone by dusk. Each life is a whole life, complete in itself. The quality of that life has nothing to do with its longevity, but everything to do with how it is lived. For me, the greatest tragedy in dying would be to have been known and loved for who I am *not*, rather than to be assessed, judged, embraced, or even discarded for who I *am*. Saying what's on our minds and in our hearts, being authentic, is ultimately easier than dying with our omissions and lies.

I learned many lessons from the experience of supporting my father during the last two years of his life as he was challenged with cancer. As we faced his death together, my father, with whom I'd had a difficult relationship, finally allowed himself to be emotionally naked in my presence as I had learned to be with him. Our letting go allowed us, in the end, to discover each other anew and create nurturing legends about each other. Two glorious years reversed decades of misunderstandings and emotional distance. The catalyst: approaching death.

Isn't it ironic that in our culture many of us might believe that the way to make it easier for someone facing a difficult illness or impending death is to say *nice* things rather than what is in our hearts? No wonder people can live and die in the midst of caring and concerned family members, and yet, in the deepest sense, die alone (never really heard, never really known).

How could this happen? Most of us have been systematically groomed to be inauthentic in order to either take care of ourselves or to take care of others. We do it for the best of reasons—kindness, love. However, withholding our *real* thoughts and *real* feelings builds an invisible wall of separation. "Tell your sister you think her prom dress is attractive even though you think it looks like a relic from another century." "Tell your grandma you really like her soup even though you wouldn't feed it to your dog." It begins innocently—and, for many of us, *reasonably*. Unfortunately, such withholding escalates. In the end, we hold the hand of someone we love who is facing a critical life-threatening challenge and say, "Everything will be okay," when we know it won't. We go further by sharing, "You look great," when we think you look very sick. Our apparent kindness leaves the person we address isolated and alone. Worse, the person we seek to comfort often chooses to reflect inauthenticity back to us to save us from our own discomforts about their illness or situation.

This was my life twenty-five years ago. When my mother was in the hospital, having just had a mastectomy, I remember leaving her bedside in order to go to the bathroom. As I stood in front of the mirror washing my hands, I heard a man in one of the stalls sobbing intensely; in fact, he seemed to choke on his own emotions.

The depth of pain expressed by that man sent chills through my body. I didn't know what to do. I thought about trying to comfort him, but he had locked the door to the stall, apparently wanting privacy. I considered getting a hospital attendant or priest, but here again, I didn't want to intrude on his space with misguided Good Samaritan impulses. I had been taught to stay away from the private zones in people's lives. Ironically, my entire profession now puts me squarely in the middle of those tender and, at times, turbulent private zones in thousands of people's lives. But back then, I couldn't make sense of my mom's life-threatening condition or the despair and anguish expressed by the man in the toilet stall. As I turned to exit the restroom, I lingered uncomfortably, listening to the gut-wrenching sounds that continued unabated. I could see the top of the man's head visible above the gray partition. Obviously, he stood alone, leaning against the metal cubicle that had become both his refuge and his prison. Finally, I decided to leave him, to avoid intruding on his privacy and his grief. But as I walked to the door, I stopped again, disturbed by my own unwillingness to become involved. I looked back toward the toilet stalls. Something about the top of this man's head seemed suddenly and oddly familiar. I tiptoed toward the cubicles to get a closer look. I then realized, this man sobbing in the stall was my father.

I backed away, stunned, experiencing my own emotional meltdown. I had never seen my father cry or display any pain whatsoever. I wanted to reach out to help him or hold him, but I couldn't. My father taught me to stand alone, as he stood alone in the bathroom stall. Be strong. Be a man! I didn't know how to make sense of what I was seeing. Silly as it might sound, I hadn't known my father had emotions, at least not the kind that erupted from his throat that day.

I left the bathroom without acknowledging what I had witnessed, an action I believed he would have wanted me to take. At the same time, I berated myself for being a compliant fool. I felt physically sick and nauseated when I returned to my mother's room. I smiled as if nothing had happened, but everything inside seemed poised to explode. Then, some time later, my father returned to my mother's bedside, smiling at her, me, and the others in the room. I smiled back at him, never betraying that I knew where he had been and what he had been doing.

It was in that moment that I first began to hate the lies that separated us from each other: the lies that left my father without any comfort or caring from others in the face of his grief, the lies that left me confused and angry with myself and with him, the lies that left my mom dangling in a sea of formula smiles. Nevertheless, I played the family game for at least a few more years, certainly until after my mother had died. It wasn't until later that I broke the mandate to lie politely, either by design or omission, and opened my heart and inner world to everyone.

Years later, when my father called me to help him, as now he faced invasive cancer, I vowed to open the doors wide to complete honesty (even though it violated the family ethic of polite smiles and withholding of feelings). My desire was not to challenge him but to truly love him. For the very first time, we started to talk about what we really felt about each other and ourselves... and, for the very first time, we built bridges of warmth and intimacy. This allowed us to have experiences together that previously would have been unthinkable.

My father lived in my home during the last two months of his life. On one particular morning, as I passed by his room to say hi, he stopped me and asked, "Could you help me with something?"

I said, "Sure, what can I do?" He then said, "I want to go to the bathroom." He had not been out of bed for three days, using a bottle to relieve himself.

I eagerly said yes and began to guide his legs to the floor. I then slipped the blanket off his body and noticed that his weight loss continued to take a significant toll. Not only had his legs narrowed, but the muscles of his thighs and calves had shrunk noticeably. The skin encasing them draped loosely over the bony portions of his legs, the elasticity now gone. It was hard to believe that just weeks earlier, he had been pumping iron at the gym. I had him put his arms around my neck, and I pulled him up. Then I moved around his back, put my arms around his upper torso, and slid my feet beneath his. We then began to shuffle towards the bathroom, which was just across the hall from his room. Each time I picked up one foot, he did the same.

"One step at a time," I said. "We're doing great." Slowly, we made our way across the six-foot expanse separating us from our destination. It felt as if we were climbing Mt. Everest, and it was such a privilege to join him on the ascent. "Two more feet and we're there," I announced proudly. "You're doing it. You are one amazing guy... or, as Raun" (my son) "might say, 'one amazing dude.' "

"Some dude," he said, amused by the reference.

"Now, I'm going to turn you around by the toilet. Do you want to do this standing or sitting?"

"Standing," he said.

We stood together and waited, and waited, and waited, but he did not urinate.

"Okay," I said with conviction. "How about both of us just stare at the water in the bowl and imagine a steady stream of liquid coming out of your body and cascading into the pool below, like a glorious fountain somewhere in Europe? Just keep visualizing this easy flow and the graceful splashing…"

"Wait, I have a better idea," he said, turning his head and peering mischievously at me out of the corner of his eye. "How about you just shut up and let me pee?" We both laughed, and sure enough, he started to urinate.

I then realized that the man who hid in the toilet, decades ago, behind a closed door, was now fully available to open his heart to love and be loved…now available to be self-revealing and playful even in what most people would consider one of life's delicate moments. What an inspiration for me to be able to live with that kind of openness and willingness to change and grow.

What might appear to be areas of discomfort dissolve in the face of authentically shared moments and authentically shared experience. Inauthenticity is a lonely road to travel—to be known (and valued) for who we are not rather than loved and appreciated for who we are. My father and I found the safest place to be with each other—no more secrets, no more hidden corners. We said the *best* and the *worst* of what we had thought about each other, and in the end, we came to adore what was left—two men, father and son, flawed, imperfect, sometimes locking heads together, but now open and honest and totally adoring these new and very precious moments together. When my father died in my arms, I felt we had built a bridge of honesty all the way to heaven.

WAKING UP WITHIN LIFE'S MASHUGANA DREAM

Joel Levey, Ph.D., and Michelle Levey, M.A.

IN most traditional cultures of our world, the day begins and ends with some time of meditation, prayer, worship, or communion and thanksgiving that affirms a life of balance in relation to the larger Whole. For those of us who make the time for such attunement on a daily basis, life takes on a different tone as we establish a reference point of deep balance to access throughout the turbulence of the day.

Joel remembers, as a child growing up, his grandfather's practice. "Each morning before work, my grandfather, who was Jewish, would take time with his prayer book and skull cap to *davin*—say his prayers. I think he started this on a daily basis after his own father had died. While he was praying, I'd often play in the kitchen at dawn with the sun streaming through the windows as it rose majestically over the Cascade Mountains to the east of our home.

When he'd finish, we'd talk and have breakfast together, often oatmeal, or eggs and toast, and then he'd set out with his pickup truck to his shop and junkyard. Then again in the evening before bed, Gramps would read the Psalms and take some time in prayer. Though he never pressured me to follow in his example, in his wise and gentle way Gramps succeeded in transmitting an important message through his disciplined, reverent example: there is a larger reality worthy of my reverent supplication, and making time to commune with it on a daily basis is a wise way to begin and end each day.

"Years later, sitting on his deathbed together as we weathered the last raging storms of his life, we took refuge in his faith and the confidence that he had indeed lived a good life. When I first arrived at the hospital, he looked at me, saying in a serious tone, 'Son, something is really wrong, and I think I'm going to die. And I'm just not sure what to do.' After being with Gramps in the hospital more than a dozen times before, I took his tone to heart. 'Well, I'll be here with you and we'll make this journey together, at least as far as I can go with you. And you know, you just can't do it wrong.' For days, his condition worsened until, writhing and moaning in pain, Gramps started pulling out his intravenous tubes. He seemed like a woman ten months pregnant—trying to give birth to himself. Weak and exhausted, he finally drifted off to sleep resting in my lap, and I sat with him on his bed. A deep quiet and peace seemed to radiate from his frail body, so unlike the unbearable turbulence and struggle of the previous three days.

"Then after about a half hour, Gramps opened his eyes and looked at me from a place of profound peace. He looked transformed, renewed, perhaps even resurrected, with a clear gaze like a young child waking from a peaceful nap. His eyes were deep and steady, and he seemed to gaze out from a clear, deep, loving pool. His presence was radiantly peaceful and I felt like I was looking into the eyes of someone very close to the Mystery. 'Son,' he said, bemused and with a tone of discovery, 'my whole life has been a crazy *mashugana* dream!'" (*Mashugana* is Yiddish for "crazy.") "Surprised by Gramps's radical transformation, I laughed and replied, 'It took you eighty-nine years to figure that out, old man!' 'Yeah, I guess so!' He chuckled as he continued, 'My whole life has been a crazy dream, and ya know what?' 'What?' I asked, leaning closer. 'I'm going to dream a happier dream next time!' And then, with a twinkle in his eye of absolute wonder and amazement, he explained how he had just died and come back, and died and come back again and again, and that he was not afraid to die now and felt that he knew the way.

"Then, looking around the room, he said, 'You know, son, I know there is only you and me here in this room, but I've got to tell you there are so many others here with me. My ma, and my dad, and Molly, and all my brothers and sisters.'" (All had been dead for many years.) "'They're all here with me and I can see them so clearly. Can you see them, too?' I absolutely believed what he was saying, and looked hopefully around the room. With some disappointment I had to admit that I was unable to discern any angelic presences. 'No, I can't see them,' I admitted, 'but I absolutely believe that you are close enough to the threshold and the door is open wide enough for you that you can see through.'

"The impact of Gramps's close encounter had a profound effect. After three days of unbearable pain, his agony vanished, his fear evaporated, and the radiance of his peacefulness and joyfulness became a blessing for all who entered the room. Everyone who came into his presence left feeling more buoyant and balanced. The doctors were amazed at his transformation and thought he actually might live, but it became clear that his body was beyond repair. Two days later, on the last Sabbath of his life, when he was too weak to say any formal prayers, I played some Jewish music for him. He began to hum along. 'Gramps, do you know any Jewish songs?' I asked. He laughed and said, 'Oh, sure I do. I know lots of songs,' and then he started singing. 'On Friday afternoon'—he began in Yiddish, and then translated to English—'we clean the whole house and everything is clear, bright, and beautiful, and when the Sabbath begins the whole house is happy!' he sang. 'Yeah, it goes just like that,' he laughed. As death approached, his peace, love, and joy deepened. The intense suffering and turbulence of the days before never returned. His strength and his breath gradually waned. At dawn on Memorial Day, his breath became more and more subtle until at last only his radiant smile remained. As the sun rose over Mount Rainier to the east and flooded the room, Michelle and I sat quietly and peacefully in meditation and prayer. What a beautiful conclusion for Gramps's 'crazy *mashugana* dream,' and perhaps what a beautiful beginning to his next one!"

As we pause to reflect on life's lessons from this sacred time with Gramps's ordeal, transfiguration, and death, a number of insights arise that inspire our own lives. First, we learned lessons about how to sit in the most intense fire that burns in this world— the fire of being with a loved one who is in tremendous pain and not being able to "do" anything tangible to take it away. In finding the peace and presence of mind we needed to just *be* with Gramps as he rode the waves of his pain—and to at the same time ride our own waves of helplessness in the face of it—our hearts and minds were broken open to a profound quality of compassionate presence and peace. To simply be present and not deny, deflect, or need to do something was the greatest offering we could make to him at that time. This openness also allowed us to be sensitive to his needs, and to do or say those little things that were helpful and comforting to him during this difficult time. From this quality of deep compassionate presence we were all able to source a quality of abundant grace that offered the greatest healing possible given the circumstances. Sitting through the fire, letting it burn through flesh, bone, concepts, identities, hopes, fears, expectations—clean and clear through to our hearts and souls—we each discovered a quality of love and freedom of spirit seldom glimpsed in our lifetimes: a quality of being that is truly omnidimensional and profoundly sacred in its nature.

Reflections on Grace and the Truths That Bring Tears to Our Eyes

Grace is found in both intense peace and activity. Polls tell us that fully a third of us—your friends, family, and coworkers—have had a profound or life-altering religious or mystical experience. In reality, this unnameable mystery is as close to us as water is to waves. Even if we don't talk about it, even if we don't have the vocabulary to discuss it, there have been moments in most of our lives when, for a timeless moment, the fabric of the story we tell ourselves has dissolved to reveal that, in truth, we are both particle and wave, wave and ocean. As Saul demonstrated on the road to Damascus, and as countless others have experienced giving birth, playing sports, in nature, in love, or driving down the road on the way to work, we are utterly unable to protect ourselves from spontaneous moments of grace.

Can you remember those precious moments in your life when you glimpsed a vaster, more profound, multidimensional, and universal view, or felt so ecstatically whole and alive that it brought tears to your eyes? The mystic poet Kabir says:

Between the conscious and unconscious, the mind has put up a swing; all earth creatures, even supernovas, sway between these two trees, and it never winds down. Angels, animals, humans, insects by the million, also the wheeling sun and moon; ages go by, and it goes on. Everything is swinging: heaven, earth, water, fire, and the secret one is slowly growing a body.

Kabir saw this for fifteen seconds, and it made him a servant for life.

At rare and precious times in each of our lives, we catch a glimpse of the exquisite balance we call grace. If you are an athlete, you might describe this experience as being in the zone. For others, such an event is regarded as a peak experience. And for those with a more spiritual orientation, such rapturous moments of unity and wholeness may be reverently regarded as moments of grace or as spontaneous communion with the sacred Source—by whatever name you call it. These are times when balance is realized in its fullness across all dimensions of our being.

Can you remember a time when your tiny bubble of your ordinary self cracked open, dissolved, or expanded, when the illusory boundary between your inner and outer worlds touched, communicated, and unified? Can you remember the exquisite moments of love, peace, and wholeness when boundaries dissolved, and you beheld yourself and your world as radiant and alive with a sacred Presence?

Often when we lecture on this topic, we will conduct an informal poll. We'll ask, "How many of you have experienced moments

of grace?" Our poll has made it crystal clear that anytime, any-
place, with the next step, or the next breath, we may tumble out of
the chaos and confusion into the spiritual balance of grace.

In these precious and timeless moments, it is as though a key
is turned, unlocking and opening a quality of being and experience that is both profoundly familiar and wondrously liberating.
Something inside of us releases, lets go, and says "yes" to belonging to the Mystery. These moments of grace have much to teach
us about the true nature of balance. We learn about living more
effortlessly, with a sense of flow and a joy that at times may be profoundly peaceful, though often intense beyond imagination. What
emerges is an exhilarating sense that whatever this larger reality is,
it is here in its wholeness with us in every moment.

What is unusual is not these moments of grace themselves—
we are multidimensional beings, who live mostly unaware of the
totality of ourselves. What *is* unusual is that we seem to live in a
culture that, until recently, has been very shy about speaking
openly of experiences that lie beyond the stifling confines of our
status quo reality. Yet as the stress and pressures in our busy lives
increase, and more and more people are feeling unbalanced, in ill
health, or out of control, and as we watch our children and parents
growing older, these instances are signposts reminding us of our
deep belonging and the sense of profound inner peace that is only
a breath away.

Moments of grace deepen our faith that it truly is possible to
live in balance with the spirit of wholeness that is the source of
all life. And they strengthen our aspiration to live our lives in a
way that is likely to bring more balance into our turbulent world.
As Brother David Steindl-Rast reminds us, "To those among us
who have entered into this mystery through faith it need not be

explained; to others it cannot be explained.... But to the extent to which we have given room in our hearts to gratitude, we all have a share in this reality, by whatever name we may call it.... All that matters is that we enter into that passage of gratitude and sacrifice, the passage which leads us to integrity within ourselves, to concord with one another, and to union with the very Source of Life."

When we touch times of profound balance we are given a glimpse of who and how we are at the core of our being. Even if only glimpsed for a few seconds, they may guide and inspire a lifetime that seeks to bring wholeness alive. "Everything is swinging: heaven, earth, water, fire, and the secret one is slowly growing a body." When we find ourselves in balance and see this, like Kabir, it makes us a servant for life.

DEATH AND DYING

Thich Nhat Hanh

YESTERDAY, a six-year-old boy asked me where his daddy is now because his father committed suicide not very long ago. Knowing that his father is dead, the boy wanted to know how to get in touch with him. The boy was also afraid that he was going to lose his mother, and he is living in fear and sorrow.

I will try to answer his question. We know that according to the Buddha, according to our practice, it is possible to live happily. The answer is yes, it is possible to live happily in the present moment; and it is our practice.

The other question is whether we can die peacefully and happily also. The answer is yes. It is possible to die happily and peacefully if you have insight learned from your practice of meditation. Many people are very afraid of dying; their fear is based on their ignorance. That is why it is very important to look deeply into our true nature in order to get the insight about life, about reality, and to remove fear in us. With no fear, you can die with a smile, happily.

When a cloud is about to become rain, if the cloud knows it

is not going to die, it is going to be transformed into rain, then it
would not be afraid at all. To be a cloud in the sky is very beautiful. But to be the rain, falling on the grass, is also very beautiful.
And with that kind of knowledge, a cloud is not afraid of dying. It
is impossible for a cloud to die. A cloud can only become the rain,
the snow, or the ice. A cloud can never die, and become nothing.

   Referring to the boy I mentioned earlier, I told him: "Your
father is like that. Your father has transformed himself into other
forms. He is always there, maybe very deep inside of you. If you
know how to touch him, then you feel he is with you twenty-four
hours a day. And not only is he within you, he is all around you.
And if you have the eye of the Buddha, you can touch him and
recognize him."

   Those of us who have lost our loved ones should practice the
teaching of the Buddha to get free from grief. Our beloved one
is still there. He or she is like a cloud. If a cloud cannot die, then
neither can your loved one. From something, you cannot become
nothing. From someone, you cannot become no one. And that is
the teaching of the Buddha—to look deeply into our true nature in
order to overcome fear.

   Many people ask the question, "What shall I become after I
die?" Many people ask, "What happens to me when I die? What
shall I become after I die?" This question seems to be difficult,
but to me it is not difficult at all. Everyone can answer that question if she or he knows how to ask another question. That question
is, "What happened in this moment when I am still alive? What
do I become in this moment that I am still alive?" This is a very
important question. If you can answer that question, then you can
answer the question, "What happens when I die?"

   In this very moment, what happens to me? What happens to

you? In this very moment, I am producing thoughts; I am produc-ing speech; I am producing physical action. And all of these things come from me, they are a continuation of me. In Buddhism, we speak of "right thinking." Right thinking means the kind of thing that goes along with understanding and compassion. That kind of thinking will never bring you suffering and will never bring suffer-ing to other people.

That is why it is very important to produce right thinking. And in this moment I am producing thinking. I want it to be right thinking. In this very moment, you are producing thinking. I hope you are producing right thinking. This is the thinking that goes along with reality, with understanding, and with compassion, because every thought is our continuation and bears our signature.

When you have produced a thought, that thought penetrates into you and into the cosmos. It bears your signature; you have to be responsible for that thought. You cannot deny that thought, say-ing, "That's not my thought. No, that's not true." You produced that thought and if it is a thought produced in the line of right thinking, then it is a good continuation of you. In my daily life, I produce a lot of thoughts. I want all of my thoughts to be in the line of right thinking...that is my continuation.

When you look for me, you should look not only for this physi-cal body. I am in my thinking. The nectar of my being can be found in my thinking and my practice to try to produce only right thinking that will bear my signature. You may like to produce right speech. Right speech is words that can inspire confidence, under-standing, love, and consideration.

If your speech is characterized by anger, discrimination, de-spair, or violence, then that's not right speech. That is why I very much care that the speech I produce is right speech. There is no anger, no discrimination, no fear, and no violence. I know that all of my speech bears my signature and I cannot deny that those aren't my words. I am responsible for all of my thinking and all of my speech.

If you say something not beautiful, you will be continued not beautifully. This is because your speech is your continuation. When you look for me, you should look for my speech. You should not only look for my physical body, you should look for my speech because my speech is truly me.

And in your daily practice, you want to make sure you only produce right speech, the kind of speech that inspires confidence, hope, joy, and reconciliation. In every moment of my daily life, I want to produce right action. Right action is the kind of action that expresses love, understanding, help, or service. The kind of action that is motivated by violence, hate, and fear is not right action. Every action of mine, physically speaking, bears my signature. After I have produced an action, I cannot deny that it was not my action because it bears my signature in it. That is why your thinking, your speech, and your actions are your true continuation.

Suppose I light this candle. This candle is not very different from a human being. The first question you ask is what happened to the candle after it died, after it came to the point where it was lit. And the new question is, "What happened to the candle in this very moment?" If you answer the second question, then you can also answer the first question.

What happens in this very moment to the candle? What is the candle becoming in this very moment? It is not difficult to see. In this very moment, the candle is producing many, many things. The first thing that is easy to see is that the candle is producing light. The candle is producing heat; the candle is producing smoke and water.

The candle may produce a fragrance. There are many types of fragrant candles. In this moment, the candle is producing many things and all of these things should be recognized as continuations of the candle. You have to see the candle and what it produces. You should not see only the candle as in the wax.

I have told my friend that you should not recognize me through this physical body; the physical body is like the wax. I am my thinking, my speech, my actions, and if you recognize me as these three items, then you really recognize ME.

So if you think of me as this physical body, you miss most of it, most of ME. So the teaching of Buddha provides us with the methods, helping us to handle the present moment the best way we can. It is in the present moment that we are offering ourselves. We are producing our thoughts, our speech, our actions, and that is our continuation.

I cannot die. I can never die. I can only be transformed into my thoughts, my speech, and my actions. And my thoughts, my speech, and my actions are not only here, they are also in you. Don't look for me in that direction. Look for me in the other direction. Look for me in yourself, because I am partly in each of my friends. It is like when you look into your left hand you can see your mother; when you look into your left hand you can see your father. You do not have to look very hard to see your father; he is right here, very concrete.

Let us do our meditation together. This piece of paper is the object of our meditation. When you look deeply into this sheet of paper, you can see a tree, a forest. Because you know very well without trees, without forests, you can't make paper. They cut the trees and they make the paste and with that paste they make paper, all kinds of paper including toilet paper and Kleenex and so on.

If you are a true practitioner, look into this sheet of white paper and you can see the green color of the trees and the forest. When I touch this sheet of paper, I touch the trees and the forest. And then you can see a cloud floating in the sheet of paper. Can you see the cloud? You don't have to be a poet to see a cloud floating in the sheet of paper. You know very well that without clouds, there would be no trees, and no paper. That is why, when I touch the piece of paper, I touch the cloud.

And I can touch the sunshine, because without the sunshine, no trees can grow. That is why looking deeply you see many, many things in a sheet of paper; and we have mentioned a few: a tree, rain, forest, and the sunshine. You can touch many more things in the paper too. You can touch the earth, the soil, and the minerals in the earth, because without them the trees cannot grow.

You can touch the mill worker, because without him the forest, the trees, sunshine, could not have become the sheet of paper. So I can touch the mill worker in the paper.

You may like to ask, "Dear little sheet of paper, where have you come from? Have you come from nothing? Can you tell me your birth date?" Do you think that the sheet of paper has a birth date? The birth date is that moment when the sheet of paper took this form. But the sheet of paper has not come from nothing.

But in your mind, you *can* become something from nothing. From nothing, you do become something. From no one, you all of a sudden become someone. That is the way our minds function.

In our mind we think that to "be born" means that from no one, you suddenly become someone. That is the moment that you call birth. And you make a birth certificate. If you were born on February 1, 2000, and you think that before that moment you did not exist, you are wrong. You were already in the womb of your mother before that. That day of your birth is only the day that you were out, here on the earth.

So to say that you did not exist before that date, that is not correct. So the date on your birth certificate is not correct. Before that moment, you had been there, inside of your mother; she had carried you at least nine months. We can't say that during these nine months you did not exist, that is not true. You already existed before your birth date. You were the object of love of your mommy and your daddy. That is why you have to put the date back nine months.

That date is also not correct. The moment of conception in the womb of your mother is not really the beginning of your existence. You think that before that you did not exist, and that is not true. You had been there, half in your mother and half in your father. That date is not correct either. It is not possible for us to establish the date of the birth certificate, because our true nature is nature of no birth. We have always been there, in other forms. That moment of your birth is only a moment of a new manifestation, not the moment of your birth, but the moment of your continuation in another form.

Suppose we burn this sheet of paper. We want the sheet of paper to die and become nothing, is that possible? You already know that it is impossible for a cloud to die; it is the same with a sheet of paper. A sheet of paper can never die; it can only be transformed and continue in other forms.

If I burn the sheet of paper and if you are watching carefully, with mindfulness, then you will see the processes of transformation. You see the sheet of paper being transformed into smoke, going up to the sky and joining a cloud. You see the heat produced by the burning of the paper. You see it penetrate into me, into all of you, and into the cosmos. You see the ashes falling down. Those are only three things that I have mentioned.

That is why the moment of the so-called death of the sheet of paper is only a moment of continuation. After I burn the sheet of paper, a part of the sheet of paper becomes a cloud. I can look up there and say, "My little sheet of paper, I know you are up there, and maybe tomorrow you will drop down on my forehead as a drop of rain and we will meet each other again soon." Therefore, it is impossible for a sheet of paper to die. *Birth and dying are only ideas that we have in our heads.*

The French scientist Lavoisier said, *"Rien ne se crée, rien ne se pesdi!"* which means, "Nothing is born; nothing dies." He declared that as a scientist. He was not a Buddhist, but he practiced looking deeply into the nature of energy and matter. He found out that nature is also the nature of no birth and no death. Nothing is created, nothing dies, and becomes nothing.

The nature of a cloud is the nature of no birth and no death. Before being a cloud floating in the sky, the cloud has been water, heat fog, vapor—all of that. The cloud has not come from nothing; it has come from many things. The birth of the cloud is only the continuation of the cloud in the cloud form. You know that a cloud can never die because you have learned to look with the eyes of the Buddha. When you drink some tea, drink in mindfulness and you will see that you are drinking a cloud. I am practically drinking a cloud.

Thank you, cloud, you have made yourself available to us in the form of water, in the form of rain. Look at it through the eyes of Buddha. Then you can get in touch with a cloud, not in the sky, but right in your cup. When you eat your ice cream, smile at the ice cream and recognize the cloud in ice cream. Say, "Thank you, cloud. Now I am in touch with you in the form of my wonderful ice cream. Because ice is water; ice is cloud." We are caught in forms; that is why we suffer. If you have the ice of formlessness and silence, you don't have to suffer anymore.

If you are attached to a particular cloud, all of us, all of you have been attached to a particular cloud, and when a cloud is no longer in the sky you suffer, but your cloud is always there, it is now just in another form. Your cloud is in the rain, and the rain is calling you—"Darling, darling, I am here, don't you see me? I am here. Don't cry." And you keep crying, because you don't recognize your beloved one in his new form.

So with the eyes of Buddha, you can get out of your grief and smile. Smile to yourself. Smile to your cloud. Smile to your loved one. He is no longer in his usual form and it is possible to recognize him or her in other forms.

Your father is always there, within you and around you. You can smile at him, touch him, and recognize him at any moment.

RESOURCES:
DEATH AND DYING

Kids

How I Feel: A Coloring Book for Grieving Children, by Alan D. Wolfelt
  (Companion Press, 1996)
Living with Grief: Children, Adolescents, and Loss, by Kenneth J. Doka, ed.
  (Hospice Foundation of America, 2000)

For books related to children and grief:
Center for Loss and Life Transition
Fort Collins, CO
www.centerforloss.com
970-226-6050

Books and Audio

GRIEF

Awakening from Grief, by John E. Welshons (Open Heart, 2000)
Creating Meaningful Funeral Ceremonies, by Alan D. Wolfelt (Companion
  Press, 2000)
The Grief Process: Meditation for Healing, by Stephen and Ondrea Levine,
  audio CD (Sounds True, 2000)

Health Journeys for People Experiencing Grief, by Belleruth Naparstek,
   audio cassette (Time Warner Audiobooks, 1993)
The Journey through Grief: Reflections on Healing, by Alan D. Wolfelt
   (Companion Press, 1997)

DYING

Conscious Dying, by Benito Reyes (World University of America, 1987)
Death and Spirituality, by Kenneth J. Doka with John D. Morgan (Baywood,
   1993)
The Dream Sharing Sourcebook, by Phyllis Koch-Sheras and Peter Sheras
   (Lowell House, 1999)
Dying Well, by Ira Byock, M.D. (Riverhead, 1998)
From Victim to Victor, by Harold Benjamin (Jeremy P. Tarcher, 1987)
Handbook for Mortals: Guidance for People Facing Serious Illness,
   by Joanne Lynn, M.D., and Joan Harrold, M.D. (Oxford
   University Press, 1999)
How to Know God: The Soul's Journey into the Mystery of Mysteries, by
   Deepak Chopra (Three Rivers Press, 2000)
*Living in Balance: A Dynamic Approach for Creative Harmony and
   Wholeness in a Chaotic World*, by Joel Levey and Michelle Levey
   (Gift, 2007)
No Death, No Fear, by Thich Nhat Hanh (Riverhead, 2002)
No Regrets, by Barry Neil Kaufman (H. J. Kramer, 2003)
On Death and Dying, by Elisabeth Kübler-Ross, M.D.
   (Scribner, 1997)
Peaceful Dying, by Daniel R. Tobin, M.D. (Perseus, 1998)
A Sacred Dying, by Barry Neil Kaufman (Epic Century, 1996)
Still Here: Embracing Aging, Changing, and Dying, by Ram Dass
   (Riverhead, 2000)
When Bad Things Happen to Good People, by Harold Kushner
   (Anchor, 2004)
Who Dies? An Investigation of Conscious Living and Conscious Dying, by
   Stephen and Ondrea Levine (Anchor, 1989)

Websites

Grief Recovery Institute
www.grief-recovery.com
323-650-1234
Help line: 800-445-4808

National Hospice and Palliative Care Organization
www.nhpco.org
800-658-8898

‏❧ SECTION FOUR ☙

Life's Everyday Lessons

Patience, patience, patience is what the sea teaches. Patience and Faith. One should lie empty, open, choiceless as a beach, waiting for a gift from the sea.

—ANNE MORROW LINDBERGH

Jewel

A brightly colored
exquisite jewel

Sits in my heart

Sometimes marred by
daily existence
But brilliant all the same

I might add to some
it seems an unlikely
place for such a jewel
but I'm not surprised
is it the only place?
for such a shining star

Oh oh oh
my heart is bursting
with the gift of this
explosion of life
words cannot describe
only a soul knows
and the knowingness
goes so deep

Where is the rest of
the soul?

Seek seek seek
within you

The fireworks are never
ending to the seeker
of truth

Look inside
my friend

today, not tomorrow,
as you will quickly
"see" the truth that
lives within you is so
like a baby
swaddled by its
mother
in a blanket filled
with such love, it's
ineffable

The soul knows all
directs all
translates all to
mankind—in a form
he can understand

It's not too late to mine
your soul

Look inside my friend
It's there
Find it under the layers
Peel them away
Pray for help (if you need it)
Layer after layer
deep within

And finally the jewel itself appears
Oh "Atma"
exquisite, yes?

Sitting there in your heart
Touch it

Andrea Joy Cohen, M.D.

UNDERSTANDING WHY

Bernie Siegel, M.D.

MANY years ago my great-grandfather told me of the persecution he experienced in Russia that led him to come to this country. He said the Cossacks would pursue him at night, when he was out teaching, and slash him with their sabers. One night he was on the hill above his village with his rabbi, the Baal Shem Tov. As they looked down they could see the Cossacks riding down and killing their Jewish brethren. They might have felt the same had they seen their loved ones being taken away to become slaves in a foreign land.

My great-grandfather heard the rabbi say, "I wish I were God." He asked, "Do you want to be God so you can change the bad into the good?"

"No, I wouldn't change anything. I want to be God so I can understand."

It's important to remember our present problems are not new to mankind. Ninety percent of the natives of South America died when the explorers brought to their continent infectious diseases to which they had no immunity, and forty percent of Europeans died during plagues of the past. Manmade wars and holocausts have taken millions of lives, and with today's destructive weapons, we are more of a threat to each other than are infectious diseases, which we can learn to resist. The question is not, will there be difficulties and threats to our existence, but rather, how will we deal with them and what can we learn from them? How can they become blessings to society, as a life-threatening disease is to an individual, by teaching us about the meaning of our life and existence?

When I was a young boy several of my friends became seriously ill and another was hit by a car while bicycling to my house. When they all died I asked my father, "Why did God make a world where terrible things happen? Why didn't God make a world free of diseases, accidents, and problems?" He said, "To learn lessons." I didn't like that answer and asked my rabbi, teacher, and others. They said things like, God knows. Why not? Who knows? That's life. To bring you closer to God. Some were honest enough to just say, "I don't know." This didn't leave me feeling satisfied or enlightened. When I told my mother what they said she answered, "Nature contains the wisdom you seek. Perhaps a walk in the woods would help you to find out why. Go and ask the old lady on the hill, that some call a witch. She is wise in the ways of the world."

As I walked up the hill I saw a holly tree had fallen onto the path. As I tried to pull it aside, the sharp leaves cut my hands. So I put on my gloves and was able to move it and clear the path. A little further along the path I heard a noise in the bushes and saw a duck caught in the plastic from a six-pack. I went over and freed the duck and watched him fly off. None of this seemed enlightening.

Further up the hill I saw five boys lying in a tangled heap in the snow. I asked them if they were playing a game and warned them the cold weather could lead to frostbite if they didn't move. They said they were not playing but were so tangled they didn't know which part belonged to whom and were afraid they'd break something if they moved. I removed one of the boy's shoes, then took a stick and jabbed it into his foot.

He yelled, "Ow."

I said, "That's your foot, now move it." I continued to jab until all the boys were separated, but still no enlightenment.

As I reached the top of the hill I saw, in front of the old woman's cabin, a deer sprawled on the ice of a frozen pond. She kept slipping and sliding and couldn't stand up. I went out, calmed her, and then helped her off the ice by holding her up and guiding her to the shore. I expected her to run away, but instead she and several other deer followed me to the house. I wasn't sure why they were following me so I ran toward the house. When I reached the porch and felt safe, I turned and the deer and I looked into each other's eyes before I went into the house. The old woman came to the door. I told the woman why I had come and she said, "I have been watching you walk up the hill and I think you have your answer."

"What answer?"

"Many things happened on your walk to teach you the lessons you needed to learn. One is that emotional and physical pains are necessary—we cannot protect ourselves and our bodies. Think of why you put on gloves to move that holly tree and how you helped those boys. Pain helps us to know and define ourselves and respond to our needs and the needs of our loved ones. You did what made sense. You helped those in front of you by doing what they needed when they needed it.

"The deer followed you to thank you; their eyes said it all, thanking you for being compassionate in their time of trouble.

What you have learned is that we are here to continue God's work. If God had made a perfect world it would be a magic trick, not creation, with no meaning or place for us to learn and create. Creation is work. We are the ones who will have to create the world you are hoping for. A world where "evil" means not responding to a person with disease or pain, whether it be emotional or physical. God has given us work to do. We will still grieve when we experience losses, but we will also use our pain to help us know ourselves and respond to the needs of others. That is our work as our Creator intended it to be. God wants us to know that life is a series of beginnings, not endings. Just as graduations are not terminations but commencements."

Let me tell you about people who have been my teachers. The first, a teenager sexually abused by his parents who now has AIDS. When he was about to commit suicide by jumping in front of a subway train I asked him why he didn't kill his parents instead. He said, "I never wanted to be like them." Love has sustained him and he is alive today.

Another young man with a life-threatening illness said, "What is evil is not the disease. Many great creative works will come from individual suffering, but what is evil is to not respond with compassion to the person with the illness."

An example is parents I know who, because they had a child who died young, are working to improve the lives of other children and raising funds to find a cure for the disease that took their child so other children will not have to die as theirs did.

How do we turn our afflictions into blessings? How do we use them to help us complete ourselves and our work and understand the place for love, tolerance, and kindness? How can we learn as Jacob did from his experience of wrestling with an angel? Justice and mercy must both be a part of how we treat those who terrorize, because when you understand you can forgive and when you can forgive you do not hate and when you do not hate you are capable of loving—and love is the most powerful weapon known to man. It is not an accident that we say, kill with kindness, love thine enemies, and torment with tenderness.

As Golda Meir said, "The only way to eliminate war is to love our children more than we hate our enemies." When we raise a generation of children with compassion, when parents let their children know they are loved, teachers truly educate them and not just inform them, and the clergy let them know they are children of God, we will have a planet made up of the family of man, where our differences are used for recognition and not persecution. Words and experts cannot be our Lord. Abraham did not bargain or refuse his Lord's request, and Jesus, who was capable of performing miracles, did not jump down off the cross to impress everyone with who he was. Our Creator must be who we have faith in so we can live as Abraham and Jesus did, fearing only separation from our Lord.

In closing let me say that as a surgeon, I know something you may not: that we are all the same color inside and members of one family. To paraphrase Rabbi Carlebach, let us hope that someday all the Cains will realize what they have done and ask for forgiveness of the Abels they have killed. In that moment, we will all rise and become one family, accepting that we are here to love and be loved. Until that moment, may you accept and learn from your mortality what is truly important in the time of your life.

YOU ARE THE GIFT

Daphne Rose Kingma, M.A.

THINKING of what I might share from a life now quite rich in its many beautiful teachings, I found it not entirely surprising that the lesson I want to share was delivered by my father. During his life, my father, a college professor, taught me many things—an appreciation of beauty, of the natural universe, and especially of plants. He taught me about the remarkable complexities of life, how all our experiences gather, collect like spring rain in the cistern, to give us the well from which we drink. He was a brilliant student of human nature. I can still remember standing beside him, noticing the way he could cradle the spirit, the contradictions, and the talents of another human being in the words he offered them. But it is a learning from his dying that for me remains most profound.

I was twenty-seven when it all started. He was dying of cancer, colon cancer to be exact, and when he found out, when he had been delivered the diagnosis, he said rather poignantly from his hospital bed, where his body was now embroidered with a latticework of scars, "One hopes always for good news; this isn't the news I had hoped for." Then he wept, unabashedly, like a child;

and then he proceeded to go through all the terrible and beautiful stages the dying pass through, while I, in its midst, was privileged to witness him.

It was winter when the journey began. Gray skies thudded into the roofs of buildings; without a moment's notice, the word went out that he would no longer be teaching. I watched as his students, stunned by the news of his imminent departure, came in solitude, in clumps, in streams to visit him. They were always bringing him gifts, a plant, some flowers, a box of candy, poems, a raft of beautiful cards. His room was scattered, adorned with these gifts, like a Christmas tree in the woods hung with tinsel and balls and suet and popcorn to entrance and enchant the wild birds. It was filled with these testaments to his love—the love that he had always given and that now, day by day in these homely gifts, was being returned to him.

I often sat with him in his room, watching the mysterious unwinding of his body from his soul. One afternoon as I sat there, one of his favorite students showed up, a young man who'd been like a son to him, so dear that he'd often joined us at our family's dinner table. My father had been like a father to him, had loved him with an intelligence of the heart that his own father, a different kind of man, had always been unable to give him. This young man was torn to pieces to learn that my father was dying.

On this particular day, as I sat by the window, I watched as this young man walked—I should say fairly raced—into my father's hospital room. He greeted my father; then, suddenly realizing he had forgotten the gift he had meant to bring, he started wildly scraping his pockets for his gift or trinket, the offering he hadn't remembered. He went over to my father's bed and, suddenly in anguish, tears flying down his cheeks, said, "I wanted to bring you a gift, but I forgot it! I haven't brought you anything!"

He was beside himself with disappointment. I knew he'd wanted to please my father, to bring some delight to the afternoon; but I realized, too, from his wailing, that he had wanted also to bring the charm that could keep my father from dying, the antidote, whatever it was, to my father's imminent death, the hex that could trick the gods and stay the execution.

It was already late in the game. My father was in a lot of pain and not looking as good as he had for most of his sixty-five years, looking no longer like a living person, but clearly like a man who was dying. His eyes had gone yellow with jaundice, and his hands, which had never been particularly beautiful, by now had obtained a strange pale elegance as they lay in surrender across the folds of his blankets. He looked up at the tearful young man and said in a solid voice of steady grace, a voice filled with love and conviction: "You have brought yourself. You are the gift."

I watched then as the young man, amazed at first by the simple statement, was gradually moved by increments from shame to relaxation, from guilt about his carelessness in having forgotten the gift, to finally having arrived at the tranquil and beautiful state of knowing that he himself was the gift. From where I sat on the ghastly plastic orange chair that counterpointed the pale green walls of the hospital room, I realized that I myself had finally arrived in my father's classroom—not the rooms where he taught Camus and Shakespeare and Hellenistic culture, but the real classroom, the cathedral of life, the temple of wisdom.

"You have brought yourself," my father said. Yes. Yes, of course. "You have brought your self." How perfect. What a beautiful thing to say. How real. How true. What better gift could anyone bring? You and I—yes, of course, we are always the gift, I was thinking. And if we are the gift, then it behooves us to craft that gift as fine and true as we can, to make ourselves as deep and real, as filled with light, as beating with love, as grand and generous of spirit as our own struggles—our own spirit-honing cups of anguish— will allow.

It has been an exquisite, and at times excruciating, journey in my own life to know, to believe, and to feel that indeed, the one real gift I can bring is myself. That learning has been a work of the soul; and it continues still; for the lesson of that afternoon was stilettoed into my heart with a sharpness I choose to never forget. Ever since then, in one form or another I keep asking myself, "Who is the self I am bringing? What is the finest, the most loving self I can bring when I show up as myself?"

My father told his student that he had brought himself, that his self was the gift. In so doing, he chimed the news about the infinite value of a single human being, the preciousness of a single person who authentically presents himself. In so saying, he soothed a young man's heart, and rescued an afternoon. He told this young man, in effect, that although there may be no talisman, no way of staying the execution, the moments in which we stand exactly and only as ourselves in the presence of one another are far stronger than death.

I learned that day the power of simply being myself, of being real, whatever that means in any given moment. I learned that when you are real, there is room for real love; that when you are real, the souls of your brothers and sisters rejoice; when you are real, the consciousness of the world expands. And when you bring your true self, the self you have worked with and wrought, you become the vessel in which all other selves can find room and home.

PATIENCE PAYS—WAIT: LIFE LESSONS LEARNED FROM BEING A MEDICAL PIONEER

Dharma Singh Khalsa, M.D.

THE surgeon general of the United States of America, Vice Admiral Richard Carmona, M.D., M.P.H., turned to me and said, "Your work should now be considered mainstream." With that one sentence from Dr. Carmona, I felt vindicated. It was as if all my hard work of the past decade had finally received the recognition it deserved.

The surgeon general's spacious office is in the Health and Human Services Building, overlooking an expansive park in front of the Capitol Building in Washington, D.C. I had been invited there to testify before Congress about my work utilizing an integrative medical approach to prevent and reverse Alzheimer's disease. This program is now known as the Brain Longevity Platform.

I was in our nation's capital representing the Alzheimer's Prevention Foundation International, of which I am the founding president and medical director.

It had been an arduous journey to get here. More than a decade before this sunny May day, I had had the realization that Alzheimer's is, in large measure, a disease of lifestyle. I was then the director of the Acupuncture, Stress Medicine, and Chronic Pain Program in the Department of Anesthesiology at the University of Arizona's teaching hospital in Phoenix, Maricopa Medical Center. There, I was very happy to have one day a week for academic duties, such as reviewing the medical literature, writing, and planning research activities. During the second half of 1992, I was busy reviewing the field of stress medicine. I had last done so a year earlier, when I was a participant in Harvard Medical School's Mind/Body Medical Program, led by the illustrious Herbert Benson, M.D. At that time, I had furthered my knowledge of the effects of stress on physical, mental, and emotional health. I knew that chronic, unbalanced stress was instrumental in leading to heart disease and other problems, including perhaps even playing a role in cancer. But what was new to me there and then was the work of noted neurobiologist Robert Sapolsky, Ph.D., of Stanford University, who was showing that chronic stress led to cognitive decline.

"Okay," I thought, "we know that stress raises the level of cortisol in the blood, and cortisol can affect our brain negatively." Cortisol, I recalled, is a hormone released from our adrenal glands, which sit on top of the kidneys. In normal amounts, it aids the body's metabolism, but when elevated by chronic stress, cortisol can be toxic to our memory center, killing brain cells by the thousands. And I knew from my study of the research on the regular elicitation of the relaxation response that techniques such as meditation could lower cortisol and improve cognitive function. "So it stands to reason," I continued to myself, "that lowering cortisol through the regular practice of meditation, along with living a healthy lifestyle, may actually go a long way toward the prevention of Alzheimer's disease." It was as if a light went on. "I have the answer to Alzheimer's disease," I thought. "And it doesn't lie in a magic-bullet drug. Rather, the answer to Alzheimer's disease is in lifestyle measures we can do for ourselves." On that basis my wife, Kirti, the former director of regulatory affairs for a large international company, and I formed the Alzheimer's Prevention Foundation.

Soon afterward we moved to Tucson, Arizona, to begin our work. As conventional wisdom of the time said that there was virtually nothing that could be done for the brain, it wasn't long before the news spread that there was someone who was using a holistic program called "the four pillars of brain longevity"— nutrition, stress management, exercise, and various types of medication, including hormone replacement therapy—to help people slow down the ravages of time on their mind. I also began to help people with age-associated memory impairment and Alzheimer's disease as well.

Why did I think I could help people maximize their cognitive function? Because as I've said so often, and continue to say today, the brain is flesh and blood, just like the rest of the body. Because the brain is flesh and blood, just like your heart, for example, it should respond to the type of program I've outlined above. And respond it did. The word spread, and many people who were told by their conventional doctor that nothing could be done for them began coming to see me. And my program worked to help them slow down their Alzheimer's and reverse some of its symptoms. It was also at that time that I wrote my first book, *Brain Longevity*, and began sharing my theories and the results of my work in the United States and around the world.

Well, let me tell you. It was as if I said the world was round to people who, for all of their lives, believed it was flat! They couldn't line up fast enough to dismiss my work. Not being a thick-skinned politician, but rather a sensitive physician, the criticism hurt. To be more precise, it was frustrating, because I knew my program worked, my patients knew it worked, and all I wanted to do was to help people by sharing this information.

One bright spring day, we were at home packing for a trip when a television news station came knocking at the door. The news team, ready with questions while the cameras were running, wanted some quick answers to their skeptical queries about my work on Alzheimer's disease. There was an underlying sentiment of suspicion and a suggestion that perhaps, in my zealousness in helping those afflicted, I might be too quick to take their money before a real approach was formulated to understand and stave off Alzheimer's disease. Ironically, I was heading out the door to go to an international Alzheimer's conference in Europe, where I'd been invited to present a paper on my work.

I was persuaded to sit and talk with them right then and there about my findings and work to enable better cognitive functioning through one's later years. I spoke from my heart for this television piece, and the response was positive. In fact, it was so good that a few years later, when the same station was running a series, entitled "Aging Well," they asked to interview me for the section on brain health.

As they came up my driveway for the second time, I noticed that the cameraman was the same, while the others were different.

"Don't I know you?" he asked me in all seriousness.

"Yeah, we've met once before" was all I said. "And since then," I thought to myself, "it looks like we've come full circle."

And come full circle we have, as today much of my work has been adopted by many academic institutions and major organizations. Moreover, I'm now asked to present my ideas on the integrative medical approach to Alzheimer's disease at important medical conferences.

So, what life lessons did I learn that allowed me to keep at it, when very few people believed in what we were doing and, beyond that, wanted to discredit our work?

The first is faith. The second is forgiveness. And the third is patience.

According to the sages of India, the law of faith states, "It already exists, and it is already written. We just have to see it now." Faith comes from the inner knowledge that you're doing the right thing. I believe it also comes from the confidence that you know your work. Having faith in my work allowed me to keep going when another person might have folded in under the pressure of outside condemnation. I had faith in my work because I had taken the time to research the literature and formulate an excellent program based on good science and good sense. Moreover, I had seen my program work.

Beyond that, I had faith in my higher power. After over a decade of meditation practice at that time, I had faith my actions were correct and coming from the depths of my soul. I did not feel God would steer me wrong.

Although it wasn't easy, over time I have come to forgive those who I felt were unsupportive of my work. I'm very happy I have been able to forgive them, for the opposite of forgiveness is anger, resentment, and unresolved conflict, none of which is good for your health, your relationships, or your work. Practicing forgiveness has allowed me to do more for people than if I had remained stuck in my feelings of pain and anger. Because I have forgiven those I felt wronged me, out of their own lack of knowledge about the subject and their own insecurities, I have experienced the joy of knowing my work has risen to such a high level that I am now able to testify before Congress and meet the surgeon general.

Because of my faith, and because I practiced forgiveness, I developed patience, although I must admit I never thought of myself as being patient. Rather, I saw myself as someone who was just plugging away, putting one foot in front of the other to get the job done. But I was blessed to become more and more patient as time went on.

The law of patience tells us to trust. It tells us to wait and see what is in store for us as we allow the hand of God to work for us. Patience is really tied very closely to faith, especially in God. After all, isn't it a powerful Creator who has the birds fly south in the winter and has the flowers open at exactly the right time in the spring? I have come to learn that if I can just let go and get out of the way, this same power will take care of me, and grant me His protection in the same way He takes care of all of His incredible creation.

Recently, at a summer retreat at which I was a participant, many other attendees came up to me and thanked me for my work and books. They told me how much their lives have been touched by my efforts. For that I am extremely grateful and offer my own gratitude very humbly to my spiritual teacher, Yogi Bhajan, for always telling me: "Patience pays. Wait."

WE ARE NEVER TOO YOUNG FOR LIFE'S LESSONS

Anne Wilson Schaef, Ph.D.

IN 1938, I was four and one-half years old and lived with my parents in Fayetteville, Arkansas. One of the highlights of my young life was the daily walk my mother and I took up to the town square. The town square was where everything happened. It was the center of commerce, community, and conversation. The post office was smack in the middle of the square. At the post office, letters that connected us with the world outside Fayetteville came and went. For me, the outside world was a vague idea except for my grandparents and uncles who lived about thirty miles away. We visited them often.

Our daily walks combined many elements of our life. We would stop to visit with friends and neighbors on our way to the square. These "visits" often resulted in a "treat" in the form of a cookie or a flower for me while the adults talked.

My mother and I would window shop. We didn't have much money and "It didn't cost a cent to window shop," my mother always said.

We would send and pick up our mail, chatting with the postmaster, who almost always commented on how much I had grown since the last time he had seen me—which was usually yesterday!

After stopping at the post office, we would walk around the square to see what was going on in town, again visiting and greeting people.

Often we would walk an extra block and visit my dad at Montgomery Wards, where he worked. Everyone there knew me and most of them called me "Blondie."

Then, we would call in at the grocer's and/or the butcher's. From there we usually headed on home to start dinner.

All in all, our walks were peaceful and fun. They broke up our day and gave both my mother and me an opportunity to "get out," get some exercise, and interact with the community. Thus were business and life conducted in a small, Southern university town.

This particular day started out much like any other. I played around in the yard most of the morning while Mother did what she usually did in the house. Around noon, she called me in to get cleaned up for lunch. We ate lunch together and then "took our little rest." Mother seemed to enjoy this little rest time much more than I did. I was more interested in the excitement of our walk and wanted to get on with it. However, nap time was imposed and I complied. Try as I might to stay awake and convince myself I didn't want or need to rest—I often fell asleep for a while.

After our rest, we headed for town. We lived two blocks from the square. Since these blocks went up a hill, we always took our time climbing them. The hill blocked our view of the square until we had almost reached the top. So, we had no idea of what was going on around the square until we were there.

On this day, there seemed to be a bit of a commotion on the corner of the square at the top of the hill so we quickened our pace.

That particular corner was always occupied by a boy we referred to as "the crippled boy" who sold pencils. (Mother always called him a "boy" although he looked pretty big to me. His body was all twisted and he couldn't talk very well.) I don't remember his name and I am sure Mother knew it. He was one of our "regulars." We always stopped to have a chat with him and Mother would drop a few pennies in his cup. He sold pencils for a nickel apiece. We rarely had a whole nickel to spare but Mother always gave him something. We never took a pencil. Mother said that we didn't need the pencil and besides he could then sell it to someone else. Mother always said that no matter how little we had there was always enough to share with someone who needed it more.

On this particular day, three big teenage boys had decided to tease and harass the boy who sold the pencils. They had scattered his pencils all over the sidewalk, spilled his coins, had kicked the pencils and coins around, and were poking him. I had never seen anyone behave like this before.

Nor had I seen my mother behave as she did when she reacted to the situation. Now, I need to say here that my mother was a small woman. She was thin (with big breasts!) and about five feet tall. Suddenly, right there before my eyes, my mother got taller. I swear she did. She became about eight feet tall—bigger than any of those boys. She grabbed the two biggest ones—one by the nape of his neck and the other by the ear, took a swing at the third with her foot, and let out a shriek like a banshee. I'll bet the entire town square stopped, paralyzed, when Mother swung into action.

"You stop that!" she screamed. "Pick up those pencils—every one of them. Haven't you had any proper teaching? Didn't anyone ever show you how to behave? Shame on you! Put those pencils back in that cup. Check to see if any are damaged. You'll pay for any damage you've done. Pick up that money and put it back in the cup. All three of you get down on your knees and apologize. And, don't you ever let me see you doing anything like this again. Now get out of here."

Believe you me—those boys scooted fast. All during Mother's monologue "the crippled boy" was mumbling, "That's all right, Miss Manilla. They don't mean anything by it. They're just cuttin' up."

"It's not all right," said my mother. "Now are you hurt? Are your pencils okay?"

He nodded with tears in his eyes.

My mother dropped our few pennies in his cup. She automatically reached out her hand and I slid mine into it. Meanwhile she had returned to her normal size and quiet personality. I was proud of my mother.

The town square went back to its routine as my mother quietly said to me, "Remember, Elizabeth Anne, we have been given so much that it is always our responsibility to take care of those less fortunate than ourselves."

Those lessons learned that sunny, summer day on the Fayetteville town square have never left me and continue to inform my life.

1. Regardless of what we have, we always have something to share.

2. If we don't speak up for what is right, who will?

3. We can never let the strong abuse the weak.

4. When we need the power, we have it.

5. Regardless of how little we have, we have been given much.

6. It is always our responsibility to care for those less fortunate than ourselves.

7. How much a parent can teach a child by her/his actions!

8. How good we feel about ourselves when we do what is right for us!

9. Never believe that others have a right to torture or harass you or anyone else.

10. No one is better than anyone else.

THE POWER OF GENUINE APOLOGY: A SHAPE-SHIFTING TOOL

Angeles Arrien, Ph.D.

ONE afternoon I was waiting for the shuttle to take me to the airport. Sitting next to me was a woman reading her newspaper. But my eyes were on a fourteen-year-old boy who was on his skateboard. He wore his baseball cap turned around with the bill in the back, the cool look, you know.

He buzzed us once. He buzzed us twice. Then he came around a third time for what turned out to be his grand finale, and he inadvertently knocked the newspaper out of the woman's hand.

She immediately started yelling, "Oh, you teenagers! No wonder the world is going to pot, because you're in it! I can't stand it!" And so on.

The boy went down to the corner to talk to his buddy, and they turned to look at us. Then they talked together some more.

In the meantime, the woman began to gather up her newspaper

and get it all back together. She put it under her arm, walked to the middle of the block, and motioned the boy to come to her.

Very slowly and reluctantly, he came on his skateboard, and almost as an act of defiance, he turned the baseball cap around, put the bill straight up in front, and said, "Yeah?"

She responded by saying: "What I meant to say is that I was afraid I would get hurt, and my comments were totally inappropriate and out of line. I hope you will accept my apology."

The boy's face has been a source of inspiration for me ever since. He looked at her and smiled, then he said, "How cool." I was deeply moved and touched by that moment.

In Latin America, in some of the Hispanic societies of the world, that moment would be seen as a healing moment, as a holy moment. They would call that moment a *milagro pequeño. Milagro* means miracle; *pequeño* means small. I had witnessed a *milagro pequeño*, a small miracle.

Within ten minutes' time, through a conscious intention and action of genuine apology, this woman made a choice. She made a life-affirming choice to create a life-changing moment between herself and the boy; a *milagro pequeño*. He will never forget that moment. I will never forget that moment. And she who shapeshifted that moment, through genuine apology, will not forget that moment!

RESOURCES:
LIFE'S EVERYDAY LESSONS

Anger: Wisdom for Cooling the Flames, by Thich Nhat Hanh (Riverhead, 2002)

The Book of Love, by Daphne Rose Kingma (Conari Press, 2001)

The Four-Fold Way: Walking the Paths of Warrior, Teacher, Healer, and Visionary, by Angeles Arrien (HarperSanFrancisco, 1993)

Gift from the Sea, by Anne Morrow Lindbergh (Pantheon, 1997)

Kitchen Table Wisdom, by Rachel Naomi Remen, M.D. (Riverhead, 1996)

Love, Medicine and Miracles: Lessons Learned about Self-Healing from a Surgeon's Experience with Exceptional Patients, by Bernie Siegel, M.D. (Harper, 1998)

Meditations for People Who (May) Worry Too Much, by Anne Wilson Schaef (Ballantine, 1996)

On the Way to the Wedding: Transforming the Love Relationship, by Linda Schierse Leonard (Shambhala, 2001)

The Wounded Woman, by Linda Schierse Leonard (Shambhala, 1998)

You Can Heal Your Life, by Louise L. Hay (Hay House, 1999)

Your Child: Bully or Victim? by Peter L. Sheras (Fireside, 2002)

ભ SECTION FIVE ભ

Spirituality

I believe in the absolute oneness of God and therefore also of humanity. What though we have many bodies? We have but one soul.

—MAHATMA GANDHI

Earth and Sky

Touch the earth
Touch the place
your heart meets
God

Touch the sky
Touch the place
your soul meets
God

Sit on the earth
Praise the place
your body meets
God

Reach the sky
Touch the place
your soul is God

Andrea Joy Cohen, M.D.

TO BE HAPPY

Peter Amato

IT took me thirty years to realize that not only had I not lived, but also that I was slowly dying. I was living in a very tiny, self-centered, self-seeking world, which oddly enough was totally empty. What a paradox!

My journey began forty-seven years ago, when I was born the fourth child of hardworking, lower-middle-class parents, who, driven and proud, struggled to grind out the American dream. By thirteen, I was working seven days a week after school and on weekends in the family business selling automotive parts.

I was living life like a fly on the wall of your typical Italian American family. I was the baby, and my given directive in life was to go to school, get an education, and take the family business to the next level. During the regular growing-pain/motivational discussions that Dad would have with the older boys, the plastic fruit would literally fly from the basket that was always on the table. "What were you thinking?" he would bellow if they had a bad day in sales.

My career as a partner building the family business of distributing automotive parts worldwide—both wholesale and retail—evolved from mopping floors and cleaning glass cases to retail sales, warehouse work, phone sales, road sales, purchasing, marketing, advertising, and finally, business administration. As the business thrived, I began to explore the material realms of success. Love for high-performance automobiles and motor sports was my passion as well as the family livelihood.

I began drag racing professionally and collecting exotic sports cars, such as Porsches, Mercedes-Benzes, Ferraris, and Lamborghinis. My hero was my oldest brother, who went on to become a five-time world champion in NHRA drag racing and was recognized as having won the most championships in the history of the sport, until his record was finally beaten in the mid-nineties.

As the business expanded worldwide, we had our private jet in the hangar and two full-time pilots on standby. Wearing custom-made ten-thousand-dollar suits and handmade shoes, I believed I was feeling powerful, proud, and enjoying the fruits of success and good fortune.

However, in time, life became a mess. I was all shined up on the outside, but felt desperate and hopeless on the *inside*. I had realized that material success was not enough to sustain any form of happiness or wholeness. I knew something was missing in my life.

I began drinking daily and using drugs to celebrate my achievements. I became a slave to drugs and alcohol. My skin became jaundiced. I pushed everyone away while I isolated myself with my drug of choice, cocaine.

Visine and handkerchiefs became my best friends, and I pretended I had a head cold for twenty years. Feeling homicidal and suicidal, I glazed over in disbelief at where life had taken me. I had become paranoid, living a life of seclusion. I was alone and afraid.

At one point, as I was destroying my marriage to my high school sweetheart, I began to do the afternoon and evening bar circuit. As my drinking progressed, I spiraled down, losing touch with reality, finding myself in very low-class bars. At some level, I felt I fit in and belonged there; these places felt like home.

After a few years passed, bodily scars, blackouts, and deep unseen emotional scars became the cloak of my disease. Our local district attorney called my family and recommended either rehabilitation or incarceration. I chose rehab.

A few days after I began detoxification, I realized I was in rehab to save my life. I had been suffering from a fatal disease called alcoholism. Untreated, my prognosis was jail, or worse, death. I recall my counselor in treatment saying, "You are emotionally and spiritually bankrupt. You have lost the ability to feel, as well as identify, your feelings." This notion had profound ramifications.

For the very first time in my life, I was glimpsing the realization that I could surrender to a higher power, be real, and touch peace.

Today, I understand that my addiction was an underground search for God. I thought that with my power, success, and drugs, I was invisible and invincible. However, as time went on, it became clear that Superman was dying on the inside as he continued to destroy vehicles, hurt people, and end up in emergency rooms receiving stitches from bar fights.

My therapists showed me that I was removed not only from my community, but from my essence and from my spirit. The only way out for me was to reconnect with my spiritual self and look inward.

Regaining my physical health, I began the daily practice of meditation. A friend in recovery told me that the only way I could rediscover who I really am was to sit still and breathe in and out, therefore eventually realizing that there is a difference between the self-image and the Self. Every time a thought would arise, I was to continuously come back to my breath, to observe my own breathing.

I recall my sponsor, Tom, saying, "If you sit still for thirty days, you will develop a relationship with a power greater than yourself and truly understand that recovery is the result of a spiritual condition—and this, my friend, is an inside job." Although I had no idea what he was talking about, somewhere deep within me, I knew that this was an ultimate truth.

This practice, or level of discipline, put me in touch with my internal/eternal witness or observer. My meditation practice became my path to sanity and humility. In discovering who I truly am, I have been able to realize a peace that surpasses all understanding.

My sponsor also said, "This experience of yourself will define a remembrance of a reality long forgotten." The timeliness of his wisdom has quantum-leaped my evolution. To *remember* has been a beautiful gift...I know that now my life's work is about one candle lighting another.

I reentered the mainstream world and began serving in various capacities of societal healing—locally, regionally, and international-ally—as a voice to help create change and eliminate human suf-fering. Through volunteerism and a reconnection with the Self, I eventually learned that I could love myself. Through loving others I was able to transcend my ego and realize that we are all intercon-nected. I realized I had a much higher calling in life than collect-ing money, possessions, and accomplishments.

I was overflowing with a newfound inner bliss and I wanted to understand it. I began to study, teach, and travel in the name of "spirituality"; I could not absorb enough of these teachings. I met with some of the greatest masters alive—enlightened men of India, seers and sages. There, I basked in the energies of holy people who had left their bodies.

I realized then that the peace I ultimately found was not "out there," but had been inside of me all along.

I learned that the root cause of addiction was a lack of "spirituality," meaning I had no relationship with my heart, spirit, or soul. The symptoms were living a life ruled by delusion, headed by an alter ego rooted in fear and false pride, owned by a small, limited view of reality.

I have been practicing and teaching spiritual practice for ten years now, having traveled the world to study the teachings and traditions of the world religions and philosophies. My hope is to put together a universal spiritual system and language for all people.

In addition, I am doing pioneering work in the field of integrative medicine. This medicine form treats the whole person in mind and physical body, as well as in the spirit. I call it "whole person, relationship-based, patient-centered medicine." Age-old healing arts combined with modern medicine, engaged spirituality, and emotional freedom is very healing.

I find my life now is filled beyond my wildest dreams with doing what I truly love—teaching in workshops, the health-care field, corporations, prisons, and drug courts, and working with adolescents. I am ecstatic with passion and a boundless zeal for living.

My story is one of hope. Only when I reached for help did I realize I had a problem that in turn became a blessing. So you see, at the end of the day this "car guy" is no different from who I've ever been. For me, this has been an opportunity to cleanse the veil of perception. To see with clarity the reality of what it truly means to be a spiritual being having a human experience.

Everyone has a story. And that's all it is...just a story...just an illusion. Mine is really no different from yours. The hypnosis of social conditioning plays itself out in each of our lives. The melodrama that we experience leads us to believe that *that* is the reality...when in fact it is the illusion.

Only when we are able to distance our inner Self from the sometimes wonderful illusion and sometimes awful illusion of the content of our story can we experience a glimpse of who we truly are; and only then do we know what to do. (Sometimes we even think we are real!)

The vision is to keep the lights on, and the only way to mirror present-moment reality on an ongoing basis is to continuously arrive there. Now that I realize that I *am* the vehicle, my Soul gets washed, waxed, and buffed daily, keeping the glimmer and gleam in showroom condition.

As I train to drive in this race of life, present-moment awareness sustains me, fueled by intention and led by Spirit to always *be* my final destination. Therefore, winning is inevitable.

This gift puts me in touch with who I am and why I am here. My purpose now is to continue to tell my story, and to pass on the knowledge and healing I have found. At forty-seven, I am doing just that. Understanding that we each have a mind, body, and spirit to develop and nurture is the message I want to spread to the world.

A MOTHER'S LAST GIFT: OF LOVE AND FORGIVENESS

Joan Borysenko, Ph.D.

M Y mother was a formidable woman. This story is her legacy, and a lesson about the spiritual art of forgiveness. Whenever I tell it, deep gratitude for the gift of her life takes me by surprise, as if I'm experiencing her soul face-to-face for the very first time. Part of the magic of the forgiveness we shared together is that it's always new for me, no matter how many times I tell her story. In that newness, a bit of grace often gets transmitted to those who hear or read it.

The morning of her death, in the late 1980s, my mother was transported to the basement of the hospital where I worked as a medical scientist and psychologist. She was bleeding internally, and they'd sent her down to radiology to get a fix on the source. She was gone for hours. My worried family, who had gathered in her room to say good-bye, finally sent me to search for her. I found her alone, lying on a gurney, in the hospital corridor. She'd been waiting her turn for an X-ray there, with nothing but the bare wall as a companion for several hours.

I found the doctor in charge and asked if I could take her back to her room. He shook his head from side to side in the negative, frowning. "I'm sorry, but she's bleeding," he said. "We need a diagnosis."

My mother, as pale as the sheet she was lying on, colored up a little and raised an eyebrow. "A diagnosis? Is that all you need? You mean to tell me that I've been lying here all day just because you needed a diagnosis? Why didn't you ask me?"

The doctor, who looked as if he'd just seen a ghost, was speechless for a bit. He finally stammered out a weak, "What do you mean?"

"I'm dying, that's your diagnosis," my mother replied with her usual acerbic humor. To his credit, the doctor saw her point, and I was able to talk him into letting me take her back to her room. We were supposed to wait for an orderly to do the transport, but she begged me to go AWOL and speed her back to the family before anyone else could grab her. We were finally alone together in the elevator, riding back up to her floor. She looked up at me from the gurney, transparent in the way that small children and elderly people often are. There was no artifice—she was who she was. She reached for my hand, looked into my eyes, and said very simply that she'd made a lot of mistakes as a mother, and could I forgive her? The pain of a lifetime evaporated in that brief journey between floors.

I kissed her hand and then her clammy cheek. "Of course I forgive you," I whispered through a throat swollen with tears. "Can you forgive me for all the times I've judged you, for all the times I wasn't there for you? I've made a lot of mistakes as a daughter, too." She smiled and nodded at me as tears welled up in her rheumy eyes, once a striking cobalt blue more beautiful than a clear mountain sky. Love built a bridge across a lifetime of guilt, hurt, and shame.

When we returned to her room, each family member had a few minutes alone with her to say good-bye. Then, as day disappeared into long shadows, and the early spring night fell like a curtain around us, everyone left except my brother, Alan, my son Justin, and me. We three were the vigil keepers.

Justin was a young man of twenty, and fiercely devoted to the grandmother who'd always been his champion. He seemed to know intuitively what a dying person needs to hear—that her life had had meaning, and that she had left the world a little bit better off by her presence. He told her stories of their good times together, stories of how her love had sustained him. Justin held his dying grandmother in his arms, sang to her, prayed for her, and read to her for much of her last night with us. I was so proud of him.

Unusual things can happen at births and deaths. The veil between this world and the next is thin at these gateways, as souls enter and leave. Around midnight, Mom fell into a final morphine-assisted sleep. Justin and I were alone with her while my brother took a break. We were meditating on either side of her bed. But I was awake, not asleep; perfectly lucid, not dreaming. The world seemed to shift on its axis, and I had a vision—if you've ever had one, you know it seems realer than real. This life appears to be the dream, and the vision a glimpse of a deeper reality.

In the vision, I was a pregnant mother, laboring to give birth. I was also the baby being born. It was an odd and yet deeply familiar experience to be one consciousness present in two bodies. With a sense of penetrating insight and certainty, I realized that there's only one consciousness in the entire universe. Despite the illusion of separateness, there's only one of us here, and that One is the Divine.

As the baby moved down the birth canal, my consciousness switched entirely into its tiny body. I felt myself moving down the dark tunnel. It was frightening, a death of sorts, as I left the watery darkness of the womb to travel through this unknown territory. I emerged quite suddenly into a place of perfect peace, complete comfort, and ineffable Light of the sort that people tell about in near-death experiences.

The Light is beyond any kind of description. No words can express the total love, absolute forgiveness, tender mercy, divine bliss, complete reverence, awesome holiness, and eternal peace that the Light is. That Light of divine love seemed to penetrate my soul. I felt as though it had seen and known my every thought, motive, action, and emotion in this life. In spite of my obvious shortcomings and terrible errors, it held me in absolute gentleness, complete forgiveness, and unconditional love as you would a small child. I knew beyond question, cradled in the Light, that love is who we are and what we are becoming.

Scenes of my mother and me together flashed by. Many of these scenes were of difficult times when our hearts were closed to one another and we were not in our best selves. Yet, from the vantage point of the Light, every interaction seemed perfect, calculated to teach us something about loving better. As the scenes went on, life's mysterious circularity came clear. Mom had birthed me into this world, and I had birthed her soul back out. We were one. I was reborn at the moment of her death—bathed in love, forgiveness, and gratitude. I thought of the words of St. Paul, that we see through a glass, darkly. For a moment I was granted the gift of seeing face-to-face.

When I opened my eyes, the entire room was bathed in light. Peace was like a palpable presence, a velvety stillness, the essence of Being. All things appeared to be interconnected, without boundaries. I remembered how my high school chemistry teacher had explained that everything was made of energy, of light. That night I could see it. Everything was part of a whole, pulsing with the Light of Creation. I looked across my mother's dead body and saw my son sitting opposite me. Justin's face was luminous. It looked as though he had a halo. He was weeping softly, tears like diamonds glinting with light. I got up and walked around the bed, pulling a chair up close to him. He looked deep into my eyes and asked softly whether I could see that the room was filled with light. I nodded, and we held hands in the silence. After a few beats, he whispered reverently that the light was his grandma's last gift. "She's holding open the door to eternity so that we can have a glimpse," he told me.

Continuing to look deeply into my eyes, Justin spoke from a well of wisdom deeper than his twenty years. "You must be so grateful to your mother," he said. I knew exactly what he meant. I'd been an ungrateful daughter, holding on to years of grudges against my difficult mom. Now my heart was overflowing with gratitude, which was a completely new emotion with respect to her.

It turned out that Justin had also had a vision, which to this day he's kept to himself. But he told me these things there in the hospital room, where the shell of his beloved grandmother's eighty-one-year-old body lay. My mother, he said, was a great soul, a wise being who had far more wisdom than her role in this lifetime had allowed her to express. She had taken a role much smaller than who she was, he assured me, so that I would have someone to resist. In resisting her, I'd have to become myself. My purpose in life, he explained—a purpose in which she had a vital part—was to share the gift of what I'd learned about healing, compassion, God, and self-discovery.

I looked down at the floor to gather myself, and then back into my son's gentle green eyes. "Can you forgive me, Justin? I know I've made a lot of mistakes as a mother. Do you know how much I love you?"

He took my hand. "Mistakes are made in love's service," he whispered.

AND then the energy in the room shifted, the Light faded, and we hugged for a long time. Finally breaking away, he smiled and laughed, "Hey, Mom, you wounded me in just the right ways." We got up and did a silly little dance together that we had seen Ren and Stimpy, the cartoon characters, do one day on television. "Happy, happy, joy, joy," we chanted as we danced around incongruously in the room of a dead mother, a dead grandmother, whose love we had shared and experienced in very different ways.

"Please remember that you forgive me, sweetheart," I reminded him a little while later. "I'm sure that I'm not done making mistakes yet."

In the eighteen years since we shared my mother's death, Justin and I both made mistakes, and we've both taken responsibility for them and made amends as best we could. But the grace of mother-child forgiveness, and the sense that we're here together because we're learning to love, has made the process much easier. For that alone, I'm so very grateful.

If You See Buddha on the Road, Say Vroooooooom

Patricia Kaplan Madsen

ONE night without thinking, I told my motorcycle-obsessed husband of twenty-six years I was going to a friend's house to talk about a book on spirituality. The "spirituality" word pushed the start button for a familiar conversation.

"So, what is this spirituality stuff, anyway?" he predictably said, in the voice he uses when he does not actually want an answer. After twenty-six years, he has yet to learn that the Don't Really Want Answer voice goes straight to the Must Give Answer center in my brain.

As was necessary every time we had this conversation, I paused. How do you define the ineffable, the untouchable, the invisible? Since we are both lawyers, I thought I would try a new tack: legal precedent.

"It's like obscenity," I told him. "I can't define it, but I know it when I see it. Or I would know it if I could see it, but I can't because spirituality is not something you see. It's something you feel."

"So is obscenity," he said. "Only if I'm feeling it, it feels pretty good. Which must mean it isn't obscene. Anyway, whatever a spiritual experience is, I'm pretty sure I've never had one."

Legal precedent was not working as a path to enlightenment, at least from my point of view as would-be guru. I tried again. "Remember the hike we took in the mountains last week? When we came over a ridge and there, spread out in front of us, was a spectacular view—the little valley filled with wildflowers, purple, red, orange, all at their peak? The creek running through the flowers, wet rocks sparkling like jewels in the sun, sky the color of heaven. What was your first impulse?"

"The view amazed me. I just stood there taking it in," he said.

"You didn't picture it divvied up into five-acre ranchettes with fifteen-room log MacMansion cabins?" I asked.

"No," he said.

"You didn't want to go straight home and call up a developer to see how much it would be worth as an executive golf course?"

"No," he said again.

"You didn't see the site as a nice, out-of-the-way closed basin perfectly suited for toxic waste disposal?"

"Of course not. I just enjoyed the view. Damn it, you were with me!" he fumed.

I thought the time had come to break it to him. With a sweetness only available to a soon-to-be-triumphant spouse, I told him, "You may have had an actual spiritual experience right then and there."

"Wouldn't I notice a spiritual experience if I was having one?" he said. My triumph was making a U-turn. Time to tap dance.

"Maybe you just don't know what to call a spiritual experience when you have one, so you don't think what you are having is a spiritual experience."

"What do I call it?" he asked me.

"How the heck would I know? I'm not the one having your spiritual experience!" I snapped back.

"So who's fuming now?" he cooed sweetly—ominously sweetly.

I sank to the occasion. "Okay. You tell me what you call it when you feel... what's the right word? Transformed, yes, when the edge between you and everything else that exists vanishes and you can't tell where you stop and the universe begins, and not only does it not bother you that you've disappeared, but somehow, it's wonderful?"

He paused. We both knew what the answer would be, but he paused anyway. After a couple of beats he said, "Riding a perfectly tuned dirt-racing motorcycle in upstate New York on a fall day after a rainstorm." Another beat. "Because if there isn't enough mud, it isn't really spiritual."

Did I mention we'd had this conversation before? This was the point at which I always decided he was making fun of me and that there is just no talking about spiritual matters with some people, one of whom I happened to be married to. Only, this time...

This time, I decided to take him at his word. (I know, I know, how long would the institution of marriage last if spouses went around taking each other seriously all the time? But taking your spouse seriously every now and then, what could it hurt?) So, the thunderbolt: what if riding a noisy machine at breakneck speed with mud spraying every which way really *is* a spiritual experience? What if my husband, instead of making fun of me, was telling the truth, the whole truth, and nothing but the truth, as he saw it?

What if there are infinite paths to the heart of the Infinite, and one of them is reserved for dirt bikes?

My husband rides on that dirt bike path, just possibly a true path for him, but because it is not my path, I refused to see his as a true, or even a possible, spiritual path. I spent years being so exasperated by his refusal to acknowledge what spiritual means to me, in my words, that I shut myself off from what it might mean in his words, to him. And that means I spent years cut off from a part of myself, because my best and wisest self believes deeply that openness to other human beings is at the heart of what I mean when I use the word "spiritual."

I'm not buying an extra helmet so I can ride the Dirt Bike Road to Enlightenment, and my husband has yet to join me on the yoga mat. But sometimes I am right there with him, and he with me, like that time we came over the ridge into the breathtaking beauty of the high mountain valley. We connected with the scene, and with each other. For that moment, the edge between him and me and everything else that exists vanished and we could not tell where any of it or us stopped and the universe began, and not only did it not bother us that we'd disappeared together, but somehow, it was wonderful.

Vroom.

A SHORT VISIT IN GOD

Stephen Levine

IN 1965, having escaped from New York via Mexico, I stopped a day's drive away from a sensed new birth awaiting in San Francisco. Having loosed the bonds of the drug-induced haze of the beat poetry scene in Greenwich Village, this felt like the space between births.

I rented a cottage by the Pacific Ocean for a few weeks of purification and reflection on my relationship with the divine; to pow-wow with God before the next big bang in my journey journey.

When I was a child, God was who I prayed to; God was fear, the father, but not divine. Then I denied God as, in an adolescent ear, Nietzsche intoned that there was no God after all, only the Furies and the broken heart. God was dead and I was left alive.

But as I grew older, no matter how I tried, I could not keep God dead. He changed guises from the power above to the power within.

Because I learned early on that "God is Love" in the midst of turmoil, I on occasion interchange these words. I do not mean to imply a Person or personage, Judge or Architect. I simply mean a certain level of mind we refer to as heart, when cultivated to exclude nothing; also stated, its revealed nature in the effortless flow of level-after-level of Creation. With certainty, I can say, whatever we name the unnameable, it belongs to no one and everyone belongs to It.

Now having come to what seemed, on so many levels, a midpoint between destinations, my sitting on the beach reading Buddhist scriptures made it clear that to surrender a devotional heart meant committing to precisely the same process as the letting go inspired by the Buddha mind. It then becomes all heart opening into the mystery.

In a gradually deepening stillness not cluttered by drugs or small talk or appointments or knowing where I was going, I sat for hours at the edge of the continent looking out to sea. Over the next three weeks, each day felt quite remarkably as if weight was lifting while simultaneously a sense of extraordinary lightness increased. A delightful awareness grew, of simply being. I was happy, in a very different way than I could remember ever being.

I was later told that sometimes when people turn wholly toward a spiritual practice and make it part of their daily existence, a kind of "karmic catch-up" or brief period of unusual clarity and open-heartedness can occur, which brings one "up to speed." It may have been where that practice had been left off in a previous incarnation, or just the given grace of what might be available in the practice.

In a very gradual manner, like the paint on an old canvas wearing thinner each day, the original drawing beneath began to appear, and the sacred could be seen peeking through all around me. Everything was a metaphor for God. Even God was a metaphor for God.

God was in the trees and pebbles, in the earth and in the sky and in my eyes. I was filled with a compassion for myself and all else. In near ecstasy, I felt the breath of God pouring over me.

I was absorbed into the ground of being. I could not tell where God ended and I began. My heart quickened with rapture, God was all that was real and I was just an illusion.

Before I left for San Francisco I wrote myself a note.

In timelessness the gods convene
to become molecules and memories
there is only One of which all else is composed
we are consciousness
in all its unconscious forms...

Buddha said it takes eons to be wholly born, for this "purification" to drop the veils, defeat the hindrances, and then enter deeper, the truth.

EMBRACING FEAR, SURRENDERING, AND FINDING NEW TRUST

Christine Hibbard, Ph.D.

SINCE childhood, I have thought about what it means to be human in this world. Through this kind of introspection, I began to feel what I call being healthy; that is, feeling inner peace and "right" in my relationships with others. Most of my insights have come when I have been forced to deal with a life-threatening situation, times when I found myself scared. But as it turns out, that fear was a skewed perception of what was really happening. Whenever I've been able to find peace of mind in the midst of the chaos, my life has miraculously taken a turn for the better. In retrospect, I realize that nature has often held up a mirror so I could see the ongoing process of growth and transformation in my life. The following story is an example.

Some years ago, my husband, David, and I joined a group of friends on a river-rafting trip on the Colorado River, at the beautiful Westwater Canyon. I had a front position on one of the three rafts when we started this three-day journey. The astounding natural beauty of the river and canyon walls was awesome—it took my breath away. The day boasted magnificent clear blue skies and the sun sparkled on the crystal blue water. We were enjoying the languid headwaters of the river while connecting with nature and one another.

Little did we know that we should have been focusing on the rapidly changing conditions of the river. While navigating a series of rapids, my boat was suddenly hit by a rogue wave of white water, and I was quickly thrown out of the boat. At first I thought it was a delightful surprise because I was very hot. Since I was wearing a life jacket, I didn't try to get back on the boat immediately. I had no idea that my relaxed attitude was ill-conceived. The next moment, we hit the start of the dangerous and continually thundering white water.

My fellow rafters began to sense the gravity of the situation but could not keep the boat from moving forward at lightning speed, so my husband jumped into the water to rescue me. Immediately, the guide in charge yelled to David to get back on or they might lose two people. David got back on the raft and seconds later the raft was out of sight around a bend in the narrow canyon.

For the next mile, I was alone and fighting to keep from drowning in the continuous whirlpools of raging water. I was sucked under the water over and over again.

Terrified, I tried to think about surviving. I remembered a story someone had told me, about surrendering to the flow of the river if tossed overboard. But apparently, I was at odds with the river's flow that day because I continued to be thrown into the gauntlet of rocks, whirlpools, and sinkholes. I suppose this was the point where I crossed from survival into acceptance. Then I started praying very hard. After a while, I knew I just didn't have the strength to come up one more time.

At that moment, I realized I was going to die. A small voice inside of me said it would be okay to die and become *a part* of this river rather than *apart* from it and the process. And that's when I experienced true surrender—the last thing I remember feeling was the great peace of not having to struggle anymore.

Then I felt the hot sun upon my freezing skin, and solid rock beneath me. I was on a huge boulder, looking over a falls area—a big drop-off where the river cascades through a chute between two huge boulders. Looking up, all I saw were high, sheer inner canyon sandstone walls.

My first thought was how lucky I was that I had managed to get myself up onto this enormous rock when I had been totally exhausted. In the shock of it all, I must have forgotten how I had accomplished this incredible task. Then I realized that there was no way that I could have gotten up on that huge boulder by myself. But it wasn't until much later that I realized what had happened. I had been helped onto the rock by Divine Grace. I had received a gift of life from God, the deeper mystery in which we are all surrounded and embraced.

The most important lesson that I learned from this amazing experience was basic trust. When I was in the water, and knew I could no longer hold on, I experienced a basic trust in just letting go—an unspoken, implicit trust that what is optimal will happen, and that whatever happens will ultimately be fine—a trust that I hadn't known since I was very young. I learned, very confidently, that life is ultimately good and that nature and all that exists is trustworthy.

This trust was different from what I had known before the rafting incident. The ordinary trust I had based my life on was dependent on the reliability of people and situations. Painful experiences and personal betrayals had disrupted that trust; it was always subject to change. For example, when I was a child, when my father said he would be at one of my school functions, and he did not show up, I was bitterly disappointed. From then on, I relied on a conditional trust.

This new trust that I learned that day in the water was different. It was not a trust in something, some person, or some situation; therefore, it could never be diminished by life circumstances. Now, with that trust behind me, I can be one with all of life's circumstances and relax more. I feel in my bones that I was and will be okay, even if some disastrous event happens. Even if I become frightened in the future, I know it will be okay. That fall in the water changed my life, because it gave me an inherent trust in life.

I had many life changes after this stunning revelation; I became more honest and more grounded in my work and my spirituality. In my work, for example, I trusted in the process of psychotherapy. I took a firm stance that people had their own inner resources and would heal in their own time.

Personally and spiritually, I stopped running away from what I didn't want to feel, and I took the risk of being much more vulnerable. I processed my emotions as they came up, much like riding the white water in the river. Instead of fighting and repressing them, I let my emotions wash over me and then let go of them. I also started working with death and dying at our clinic and prayed daily for direction in my life. I found that I gained more freedom to live and more of an appreciation for the people I love.

And I saw the sacredness and the glory of the world every day.

A feeling of overwhelming awe would wash over me when I would stay in the present moment, and notice the beautiful color of the trees and flowers as I was out doing errands or driving to work. And the more I am finding out who I am through deeper meditation, prayer, and contemplative thought, the more I allow myself to know God. In doing this, I become more whole and less fragmented in my work, my life, and my destiny. I now embrace each day that passes with surrender, mystery, gratitude, and direction.

I will forever feel blessed from my river experience and the lessons that I learned. And I continue to remember to embrace my own fear and surrender to life's changes, trusting that I will be okay no matter what happens, knowing that God's grace is always present.

I would like to offer the following wisdom about the power of the river from the Hopi Elders conference in 2001. Their wise wisdom reminds me of my harrowing experience on the river, which allows me to deeply hear their words. I can rely on a basic inherent trust in life making sense however it turns out.

"To my fellow swimmers—there is a river flowing now very fast. It is so great and swift that there are those who will be afraid. They will try to hold on to the shore and they may be torn apart and suffer greatly. Know that the river has its destination."

The elders say, "We must let go of the shore. Push off into the middle of the river and keep our eyes open and our heads above the water." They say, "See who is there with you and celebrate that this time in history we are to take nothing personally, least of all, ourselves. For the moment that we do, our spiritual growth, the journey, comes to a halt. The time of the lone wolf is over—gather yourselves. Banish the word 'struggle' from your attitude and even from your vocabulary. All that we do now must be done in a sacred manner and in celebration for we are the ones we have been waiting for."

Finally, I would like to add that we are living in an age of enormous change. The lessons are coming more quickly as our souls and the universe push us into new growth. Familiar water suddenly seems perilous, with uncharted obstacles that shift with the changing river sands. We now require new navigational aids. The more we make contact with our inner knowing, the more we will begin to hear and trust truly profound and useful messages. My deepest wish is that we all learn to swim with courage and God's grace in the amazing flow of the twenty-first century.

MY GURU

Paramahamsa Prajnanananda

EVERY individual needs to grow in every aspect of life. Physical and intellectual growth are essential requirements, but without spiritual growth, the real beauty of a person remains unmanifested.

We develop skills and talents through the love and care of our parents, the sincerity of our teachers, and the discipline that we acquire in schools and universities. But to cultivate timeless spiritual values like love, calmness, and peace, to learn to live without stress, in a balanced way, in spite of the turmoil of life, we need to build a strong spiritual foundation.

For spiritual growth and to manifest our divine qualities, we need a teacher, a guide, a guru, a preceptor, or a master, who through his or her exemplary behavior, strong spiritual foundation, deep scriptural knowledge, and realization can mold and shape the life of the student and open the way to the path of self-realization. That spiritual guide will help the sincere seeker eradicate stumbling stones like ego, jealousy, and hatred, and transforms his or her life to fill it with love, purity, and devotion. Once the chosen guru is found, a sincere student will blossom under his care.

A guru, in the holy scriptures, is described as the mystical philosopher's stone that is able to turn ordinary metal (the student) into gold. But a guru's power goes beyond that; he or she can transform ordinary metal into another philosopher's stone. A true teacher knows, through divine insight, the mind and thought pattern of his disciples. With these tools, he or she guides them to achieve their true potential.

I share stories of my life and spiritual journey with my master, Paramahamsa Hariharananda. I call him Gurudev; he passed in December 2002. Personal experiences are hard to portray in a written form; life's picture is far too complex to be depicted in black and white. But this story needs to be told, as a tribute to my divine master and as a source of inspiration to all travelers in search of truth.

The guru-disciple relationship is not easy. The disciple needs to make many sacrifices to grow in the spiritual path. Meeting my master was the turning point in my life. My master represents the essence of spirituality to me. For more than twenty years of close association, I have struggled to serve him.

In return, my guru has given me the biggest blessing: he has helped me to accelerate my spiritual evolution. Our bond is complete; he is my father, I am his child, we walk together as father and son. I have grown through his love and wisdom. Here are two stories about my guru.

The Divine Gardener

Gurudev was a gifted gardener. He loved his garden, and gave careful attention to the flowers and the fruits in all his different ashrams, both in India and in the West. When he came to each ashram, he moved from one corner to the other, looking at the garden, taking note of how the plants had grown and guiding his disciples on how to make the garden even more beautiful.

Gurudev was not only a gardener in the outside world; he wanted us to cultivate our inner garden, too. He believed that the Garden of God should bloom with beautiful human beings that are filled with love, peace, and purity. Gurudev was not only a gardener externally; he was a gardener spiritually. He created a parallel between the inner and outer spheres. And his admiration for God's creation was manifested in his own garden.

Years ago, when we lived in the Karar ashram (a yoga ashram in India), with its sandy soil, it was very important to water the plants every evening. There was no pipe connection, so we had to carry water in buckets from the hand pump. Gurudev would look on the whole procedure with a beatific smile, full of encouragement. It was truly a beautiful experience.

While at the ashram in Homestead, Florida, Gurudev took care of the garden. He loved the fruits, trees, and flowering plants. He had a whole team of devoted disciples that listened carefully to his instructions.

Gurudev was fond of comparing a spiritual person with the fruit of a tree. If the fruit was small, it was useless. When it dropped from the tree, still unripe, it was lost and wasted. But if the fruit remained attached to the tree, slowly it would grow, ripen, and its color, smell, and taste would evolve and change. When the fruit was really ripe, it detached itself gently from the tree. People turn toward a tree full of ripe fruit. Once he told me that if a tree can give neither fruit nor flower, it is of less value. So also each spiritual person should try to give as much as he can to the rest of humanity.

A guru is like such a tree, and the disciple is the fruit. A tree is known by the fruit it bears.

A Guru Kills Ego

Gurudev wanted to crush our ego. One day I was serving Gurudev, sitting in his room in the Puri ashram (in India) taking dictation. I had a cold and a runny nose, so I held a handkerchief to my nose with one hand and I wrote with the other. Baba was aware of my difficulty and said to me, "If I tell you to do something, will you follow me?" This was really a difficult question to answer without knowing what he would ask. I looked at him. He repeated, "Tell me if you want to follow me or not." Hesitantly I said, "Yes." Then he told me to open his bag and take out some cold medicine. Finally, he instructed me to take two tablets immediately. I took the tablets but kept them in my pocket. This is where my ego came up. I had been very sick in my childhood and I was always dependent on medicines, but since 1979, I had taken no medicines. I thought I did not need any medicine since I was a yogi. Gurudev knew about this and wanted to remove my ego. I wanted to leave the room on the pretext of getting some water, so I could come back without taking the medicine. As though he read my mind, Gurudev said to me, "No need to go out," and gave me his glass of water. I swallowed the medicine for my cold and for my ego. A guru knows not only our mind, he knows the cause of our ego and he wants to remove it, to help us grow spiritually. I learned a valuable lesson.

SUKKOT: LEARNING TO LIVE IN SECURITY AND WITHOUT SAFETY

Ellyn Hutt

SUKKOT is a wonderful Jewish holiday that is celebrated in the fall. One of the central ways to observe Sukkot is to build and spend time in a temporary "booth" outside called a sukkah. Being in a sukkah feels almost childlike—somewhat like being in a tree house, but on the ground. The sukkah, with its wood-slatted roof open to the sky and dappled sunlight peeking through the pine boughs that loosely cover the slats, invites you to come in and bask in the unique experience of being both in the sun and in the shade, inside and outside, sheltered and exposed. And at night, when you go into the sukkah, you can often see stars and the moon.

The sukkah isn't always a comfortable place, though. On some days it is cold and windy, possibly even snowing or raining; and on occasion, the whole roof collapses and the sukkah needs to be built all over again. This holiday is a little strange!

Sukkot commemorates the visible divine protection that the Jewish people lived with during the forty years in the Midbar (Wilderness). We don't know whether the sukkahs that the Jewish people lived in were actual structures, such as the ones we build and dwell in during the seven-day festival of Sukkot, or if they refer to the Clouds of Glory that God sheltered the people with during their wanderings that protected them from heat and cold. In either case, the sukkah that we build allows us to live for at least one week of the year with a clearer sense that God is the source of our protection and security.

The Torah teaches us that we are to observe the holiday of Sukkot because "God caused the Jewish people to dwell in sukkahs." When we dwell in the sukkah—eating, sleeping, and spending time there—we have an opportunity to demonstrate our trust in God's protection. Interestingly, the mitzvah (commandment) is not to just go outdoors and be completely exposed to the elements and "nature," but rather to actively build a sukkah, which does provide some sort of protection, albeit fragile. Why is this?

The sukkah, which must have a roof of natural substance and be partially open to the sky and exposed to the elements, reinforces the truth that nothing we can construct in the physical world can provide us with true safety. Security only exists in the spiritual realm, and that security comes from God alone. The sukkah reminds us that the physical world is fragile, despite all of our efforts to make ourselves "safe." Physical things such as houses, buildings, cars, and possessions are ultimately fragile. So, too, are our circumstances. Jobs, health, financial situations, physical abilities, and so much more can change in an instant.

So, what is the attitude that we're trying to cultivate toward the physical world that we clearly inhabit? The sukkah tells us to be involved in the physical world. Build your sukkah, but don't rely on it or trust it as the source of your safety, your well-being, or your identity. When we put our trust in things and in circumstances, as we are tempted to do by our nature and by our cultural conditioning, it only encourages us to believe that we can have protection in the physical world. Some of us trust bank accounts, some security systems, and some trust exercise programs for safety. But if we trust these things, we are stepping into a world of illusion.

The sukkah, with all of its required temporariness and fragility, is a more "real" place to dwell. And if and when our sukkah occasionally collapses, then we can forge ahead and rebuild without the anger, angst, and anxiety that usually accompanies situations when what we have relied on falls apart. Many people who build a sukkah for Sukkot have a very different attitude toward their sukkah than their homes. If, after the week of Sukkot, their sukkah hasn't fallen apart, they're happy! How often do you come home at the end of the day and rejoice that your home is still in one piece and that you are, too?

Building a sukkah, and more importantly, keeping a sukkah mentality for the entire year, creates space for joy and happiness. Perhaps this is one reason why Sukkot is called Z'man Simchateinu, meaning the holiday of our joy. Deep joy comes from knowing what is real in this world, what can be trusted, or what might be a fragile illusion. As we enter the sukkah, we can leave worry and fear at the door. Worry and fear can kick us out of the present moment. The sukkah is the place and space that speaks to us about trust, security, and what is real. The sukkah is said to hold the Shechinah, the Divine Presence. Allowing Her to engulf us is the source of our security in this world and helps us to dwell in the Present Moment.

Building this sukkah mentality, however, isn't easy. This mentality seems to need constant attention and repair. But, I've noticed that the more I practice building it and living in it with the small situations in life, the more easily I can enter into it for the bigger, more challenging moments. The truth is I have always been a worrier—trying at all costs to be "safe." I have spent most of my life being overprotective of myself, and now my two children. I have the tendency to see danger lurking everywhere, which can be very draining. My mind goes into a state of preemptive worrying, thinking in some crazy way that if I can anticipate the danger, name it, and worry about it, it won't ever happen. Let me tell you, this is a full-time job!

So, imagine my maternal fright when in the summer of 2003, at Denver's Coors Field baseball stadium, an escalator, overloaded with fans leaving after the game, sped up and hurled hundreds of people on top of each other, seriously injuring more than thirty of them. What, I wondered, was wrong with me? I'd never worried about this particular problem whenever I attended games with my family. I had only worried about things like elevator cables snapping and plummeting to the ground or shoelaces getting caught in escalator steps, trapping me or my kids in the machinery, destined for terrible injury. I also had other typical baseball game worries: What if one of us was injured by a fly ball or a thrown bat? I had not even considered worrying about an escalator speeding up and dumping my kids or me down the stairs into a pile of people at the bottom.

Even though I did not attend the game where this incident took place, somehow, through this event at Coors Field, I realized that life really *is* a sukkah. Everything in the physical world is fragile, temporary, and imperfect. I cannot find or create perfect safety

for my children or the rest of the world. There is no way to anticipate, worry about, or fend off every possible problem. In a way, this
realization is a relief! If I really, really accept in my heart of hearts
that what I seek is *impossible*, then I can, in a way, let myself off
the hook.

I can reconsider what it is that I can actually have; and what I
can have is a sukkah. I cannot have guaranteed physical safety, but
I can have spiritual security. I can trust that God has and will continue to equip me with everything that I need to deal with whatever happens in my life. I can trust that God is there to strengthen
and support me and that I can face life with courage. Since I am
not expecting my sukkah to be sturdy or permanent, nor am I relying on it to give me safety, I can sit in it, not knowing if or when it
might collapse, and feel spiritually secure and happy. It is enough
to be surrounded by God's Presence.

This perspective, however, is always being put to the test. Right
now, I am really working hard to keep my sukkah mentality. My
son recently left for Israel to study at a yeshiva (seminary) for the
year. He was in the air, on his way to Israel, at the time of one of
the many suicide bombings in Jerusalem. My stomach churned. My
instinct to protect my child and keep him safe was overwhelming
me. But truly, a vision of my sukkah intervened into my frightening images and worries. Remember, I told and keep telling myself,
he is going to the land of Israel to study Torah—holy work in a
holy land. What he is building is spiritual and can never be taken
away or destroyed. He is strengthening the space within himself to
hold the Divine Presence. What could possibly make me feel more
secure than that?

When well-meaning friends grimace after I tell them that my
son is in Israel, and I think they are wondering what kind of mother

I am for letting him go, I then picture my sukkah and feel calm. I know that I cannot make him safe in Israel or anywhere else, but I do feel that both of us are secure. My son and I are relying on the spiritual while maintaining cautious optimism about the physical. We pray that the sukkah won't collapse; at the same time we know that what is inside the sukkah is what counts.

My maternal instinct is still alive and well and ready to assert itself at any moment, but my spiritual instinct is growing day by day. I make many trips into my mental sukkah. On some days it is warm and sunny and on other days the cold wind blows. But in it I sit and bask in the pleasure that comes from knowing that all of us are in God's sukkah surrounded by the Divine Presence. And I feel secure.

RESOURCES: SPIRITUALITY

Books

Anatomy of the Spirit, by Caroline Myss (Random House, 1997)

Anger: Wisdom for Cooling the Flames, by Thich Nhat Hanh (Riverhead, 2002)

The Art of Happiness: A Handbook for Living, by the Dalai Lama (Riverhead, 1998)

Autobiography of a Yogi, by Paramahansa Yogananda (Self-Realization Fellowship, 1998)

Broken Open: How Difficult Times Can Make Us Grow, by Elizabeth Lesser (Villard, 2004)

Call Me by My True Names: The Collected Poems of Thich Nhat Hanh, by Thich Nhat Hanh (Parallax Press, 1999)

Fire in the Soul, by Joan Borysenko (Warner, 1993)

The Four Agreements, by Don Miguel Ruiz (Amber-Allen, 1997)

Handbook for the Soul, by Richard Carlson and Benjamin Shield (Little, Brown, 1995)

The Heart and Science of Yoga, by Leonard Perlmutter with Jenness Cortez Perlmutter (AMI, 2005)

Inspiration: Your Ultimate Calling, by Wayne Dyer (Hay House, 2006)

Meditation from the Heart of Judaism, by Avram Davis, ed. (Jewish Lights, 1997)

My Time with the Master, by Paramahamsa Prajnanananda (Prajna, 2001)

The New American Spirituality, by Elizabeth Lesser (Random
    House, 1999)
A New Earth: Awakening to Your Life's Purpose, by Eckhart Tolle
    (Dutton, 2005)
An Open Heart, by the Dalai Lama (Little, Brown, 2001)
The Seat of the Soul, by Gary Zukav (Fireside, 1990)
The 72 Names of God, by Yehuda Berg (Kabbalah, 2003)
Simple Meditation and Relaxation, by Joel Levey and Michelle Levey
    (Castle, 2002)
What Happy People Know, by Dan Baker (St. Martin's Griffin, 2003)
A Woman's Journey to God, by Joan Borysenko (Riverhead, 1999)
Yoga Pathway to the Divine, by Paramahamsa Prajnanananda
    (Prajna, 1999)

Spiritual Music, Books, and Meditation Aids

Joan Borysenko guided imagery and meditation CDs:
www.joanborysenko.com

Deva Premal music CDs:
Love Is Space (White Swan, 2000)
The Essence (White Swan, 1998)
Embrace (White Swan, 2002)
www.devapremalmiten.com

Sri Karunamayi mantra CDs:
www.karunamayi.org

Paramahamsa Prajnanananda books and CDs:
www.kriya.org

Etherean Music
www.ethereanmusic.com

Sounds True
www.soundstrue.com
800-333-9185

Penguin Group (USA)
http://us.penguingroup.com

Hay House
www.hayhouse.com

Help Line

24-hour alcohol and drug help line:
800-448-3000

Conferences and Classes

Omega Institute
260 Lake Drive
Rhinebeck, NY 12572
www.eomega.org

Kripalu Center for Yoga and Health
P.O. Box 309
Stockbridge, MA 01262
www.kripalu.org

American Meditation Institute for Yoga Science and Philosophy
60 Garner Road
Averill Park, NY 12018
www.americanmeditation.org

Satyananda Yoga
www.satyananda.net

Kriya Yoga
www.kriya.org
305-247-1960

Plum Village
Zen master Thich Nhat Hahn
www.plumvillage.org

Family, Love, and Relationships

In the end these things matter most:
How well did you love?
How fully did you love?
How deeply did you learn to let go?

—THE BUDDHA

. . .

Your children are not your children.
They are sons and daughters of life's longing for itself.
They come through you but not from you.
And though they are with you, yet they belong not to you.
You may give them your love but not your thoughts
For they have their own thoughts.
You may house their bodies but not their souls,
For their souls dwell in the house of tomorrow, which you
cannot visit, not even in your dreams.
You may strive to be like them, but seek not to
make them like you.
For life goes not backward nor tarries with yesterday.

—KAHLIL GIBRAN

Love Is the Only Thing
That Matters

Like a song
Carooning my soul like strings
   on a harp
entraining all the hidden parts
   of me
O love maybe you have found me
although I have hidden from you
   at times
you have been patient
and bidden your time
till
I was ready to see your truth and
   beauty
Never far away

From my heart and my soul
You have me wrapped around
   your light
Believing in truth
I have unwrapped my layers
And peeled away my defenses
That bind me
And isolate me
They say Time can heal
With grace
And Love is the only thing that
   matters

Andrea Joy Cohen, M.D.

MATTHEW'S STORY

Matthew Scala

I am a man, forty-two years old, with a story to tell.

I grew up on the East Coast. For most of my life, I've lived very close to the ocean. Living in this moist, humid environment, I never gave any thought to cacti or deserts and had no direct experience of dry, arid environments. As moist as this outer world was, though, my inner world was dry and barren. As a boy, I never cried. The fertility and lushness of the soil did not translate to a fertility of my soul.

I have been terrified for most of my life and am only recently coming to terms with my lifelong depression. Growing up, I experienced horrific times with my parents' mental illnesses. My mother was in and out of mental institutions from just after my birth until I was a teenager. She'd either be raging and manic, or like a zombie on Stelazine and virtually comatose on the couch. In the early 1960s, women were still being brutalized by a mental health system that provided neither health nor sanity. No one seemed to understand the profound effect this had on the entire family system. To this day, I wonder who my mother was attempting to become.

Meanwhile, my dad held on to his rage and somehow kept my three siblings and me alive, but barely.

I taught myself to contract, to withhold, to collapse. Never knowing when the raging would begin, I hid inside, yet outwardly I strove to succeed. I became an accomplished runner and tennis player and excelled at school. My deep fear led to developing an angry, unapproachable persona as my armor in life. When I was around people, my guardedness would not allow for any authentic emotional connection. I would withdraw into the background, afraid to open my mouth. It was as if I was all blocked up, closed in, shut down.

I did not see the world as friendly. And I certainly did not experience myself as friendly. Over the course of three decades, I somehow managed to survive. I severely limited any human contact and certainly had no spiritual contact. Being Catholic, even being an altar boy, did not instill in me a sense of the divine. I went to Mass because that's what we had to do, yet I had no sense of God or love. You'd think that after eighteen years of churchgoing I'd have some notion of what God was all about. No, none whatsoever! And serving as an altar boy, standing on that altar for six years, brought me no closer to heaven, either. My only refuge in life was distance running.

After getting my architectural training in New York, I left the state. For the next fifteen years, I hid in rural Maine, trying to find a version of myself that made sense, while looking for a woman to grow with. I floundered with one woman for seven years during my twenties. I don't know what we did. We certainly weren't happy. We just coexisted, with no idea of how to live with or love another human being. She left me.

Somehow I was fortunate enough to meet and recognize some

men who were also searching for themselves. I became an avid self-searcher. For five years, I diligently studied, learned, sang, thera-pized, body-worked, danced, gardened, and made ceramic vessels. I continued to construct other aspects of who I could be, without ever knowing who I was.

During my early thirties, a relatively new woman in my town, who I'll call "M," became pregnant. She and the father of the child didn't share much time together; conception was the final straw. They broke up. I was friends with some of the men she'd been in relationships with before this time and could never understand the rapid changing of the guard. I was very judgmental. I watched her belly grow from afar.

When M was four and a half months pregnant I had the oppor-tunity to witness her in a moment of personal pain due to not hav-ing her unborn child's father in her life. Seeing her vulnerability in this moment, my heart began to open a little toward her.

At the seven-month mark of her pregnancy, I was at a party that she attended as well. Eventually there were just two married couples left, and M and myself. It was New Year's Eve. I couldn't help but think, "Why is she here, why am I here?"

At the time of the birth of her daughter, I was not happy. Her delivery was difficult, culminating in a cesarean section. When I heard that she had been released from the hospital, I was not emit-ting peace. Why did I feel such anger? During her pregnancy, much was said about her power being a single woman and rais-ing this child on her own. I always believed that fathers were vital and here was M outwardly flaunting her belief to the contrary. This was occurring at a time when women were in the news for wanting to become pregnant and raise children by themselves, while men were being bashed and ridiculed. I fumed. Of course, fuming was nothing new to me as I'm only recently getting a handle on my use of seething negativity.

When her daughter was six weeks old, I attended a friend's fortieth birthday celebration. There was only one seat left at the meal when M and her baby arrived. It was right next to me, so over they came. I couldn't believe they'd have to sit right next to me. Yes, here they were, mother and baby.

What I didn't know was that my life was about to change.

When M needed to use the bathroom she asked if I would hold six-week-old Iris. I couldn't believe she'd actually ask me this—me, the one who had been spewing bile in her direction for months. How could she? Didn't she know what I felt or thought? I guess I didn't really know either. How could I say no?

I remember holding Iris for the first time. At thirty-three, I had never held a baby before. Iris locked in to my eyes and stayed that way, beaming at me. I was transfixed, spellbound, taken over. I didn't fully comprehend what was happening. She was calling out to me through her eyes and her touch.

When her mom returned, I managed to say that I would like to hold Iris again; perhaps I could visit and give her a hand with chores around the house or garden? What was I saying? I had been captivated. A week later, I traveled a long country dirt road to visit these two fragile souls. Who was really the fragile soul? One afternoon I held Iris for two hours during blackfly season in Maine. We walked around gardens while her mom hauled manure and compost. The black flies were ferocious, yet I held this small person and gazed into the eyes of God. This I knew for certain.

I talked to her and I talked to God. I sang songs to her of the extraordinary life that she'd have; I sang of God and splendor. Those two hours of divinity were spectacular. The black flies enjoyed their feast, leaving my neck bleeding and bloated. M and I shared some supper, then I left.

For the next seven months, I only saw them in passing. A monumental moment and an awakening had occurred; I don't know why I stayed away. I went back to sleep again or perhaps I was gestating. I suppose with all of the anger that I had felt, I still couldn't make sense of the conflicting and powerful feelings arising in me.

In midwinter, M and Iris arrived at another intimate gathering, this time a baby shower for a pregnant friend of mine. Once again M eventually needed to use the bathroom and she asked me to do the holding. This time I had no reservations. The magic of the moment was apparent to all; I glowed and was awestruck at Iris's growth and light. A third wondrous moment had occurred. A small voice in me spoke up, and invited them to visit me in my sacred space, my "crybaby shack."

This shack was actually a small cabin that was unused and had sunk into the Maine soil. Toward the end of one winter I jacked it up out of the ground and renovated it. This space and the surrounding gardens that I designed and developed became my sanctuary. I filled it with love and beauty. Most of my very personal inner work of self-discovery occurred here and in the gardens. I cried and grieved so much over my life in this place that I named it my "crybaby shack."

Moisture was coming into my life.

One week later they arrived. I tried not to look as nervous as I felt. M and I sat on the floor and watched Iris playing with my cats' food, then plopping it into their water. I was completely enamored and scared, as were my cats, Tubby Dumpster and Other One. For the next few weeks, we all got together a couple of times. The magic continued to occur.

I was becoming a dad.

Through becoming a dad, I was opening and becoming human. All the while M and I were discovering many common joys and inspirations. My delight, joy, and radiance had seemingly come from nowhere.

All of a sudden, I was alive and proud. All of a sudden, I felt like a grown-up. All of a sudden, I felt like I belonged. I knew exactly what to do with Iris. I had more fun, wonder, joy, and gratitude than I knew possible. I was simultaneously growing into adulthood, while awakening and parenting the very small little Matty in me. I was present in ways that no one ever was with me. I had not ever seen or really felt love, but here it was emanating out of every pore of my body, with Iris.

I cherished every minute with her. Carrying her on my back for walks and doing all of the parent chores gave me such satisfaction. I loved holding her, singing to her, reading to her, showing her our new, wonderful world. I loved clipping her nails with those minis-cule fingernail clippers. Oh, I was so happy.

M and I married quickly. But we struggled with our marriage from the very beginning. We both became seized by the idea and the vision of a family. We thought that we loved each other, but really, the driving force behind the union was this: she wanted a father for her child, as well as help raising her, and I sure wanted to be that dad. But what had opened between us couldn't be held. Our dreams and visions vanished.

For three and a half years we mostly battled. I still don't fully comprehend why. We both loved Iris so very much, yet our times as husband and wife were filled with gut-wrenching despair. The dichotomy of all the love for Iris and so little for one another was just too much for us. Perhaps we adults were really still infants ourselves.

I endured the best that I could because I wanted us to make it as a family. But it was never right. I did what I could to stay in the flow of parenthood. Iris and I would go to parades and performances, where she'd paint my toenails green. We fished for mackerel and planted gardens, lots of garlic, irises, and sugar snap peas. We loved to drum and dance. I adored every minute of my time with Iris for those three and a half years.

M and I agreed to divorce. While in this process, she and a new man took Iris and moved to the opposite coast. It seemed that they moved as far from me as they could go. My daughter was stolen from me and I didn't know why, nor did I know exactly where they were.

This all came about during the Christmas season. I was in Maine; it was cold and bleak. My heart, which had opened so miraculously, was crushed. I had just lost my wife and my child. I cried and cried. I screamed, despaired, prayed, and raged. I hurt so badly. I was such a good dad in every way except that I couldn't keep my marriage together. So I lost it all and was humiliated.

And I lost many so-called friends. It was as if my family had died and no one had the guts to ask me about them. My own parents said they didn't want to make me upset. Couldn't anyone see that I was already upset? I felt so alone and lonely. I'd wander around my house looking at all the signs of love, all of Iris's toys, books, clothes, drawings, photos, and little kid's collections of objects. But no Iris. This was a winter of crying. I'd awaken in the mornings and sit on my cushion to pray and cry.

I had become a father but with no legal rights. All of the cells in my body had been awakened to being a dad, but without my blood being present there was nothing I could do.

A store clerk once said to me, "This is your daughter? Matthew, she doesn't look like you." That might've been true, but it mattered not. All of me was with her, and now she wasn't here.

Eventually, months later, M called to tell me where they had gone. I began making cards and sending letters to Iris. Every week I would do this, sending my love for her on paper with words and silly drawings. Sending, sending, and sending, never knowing if her mom showed her, read them to her, or threw them away.

Since I lived in rural Maine, where the closest Xerox machine was miles away, I'd always make another original as a copy. That way if I ever saw her again, I could show her that I had loved her all this time, that I didn't abandon her. Very rarely would a photo appear. I'd send birthday gifts and Christmas presents out into the ether.

As the years passed, I prayed even more, never knowing if this small child would remember her dad and never knowing if she'd look for me. Never knowing who or what her mom would set in the path before her.

As my grieving continued, my friend Sally, whom I had known for six years, was experiencing her own grief over a betrayal and the breakup of her marriage. Living in a small community, we knew a great deal about each other. We soon embarked on a partnership that led to marriage after four years. All through this, though, my grief over my lost child weighed heavily upon me. I loved and trusted Sally completely, yet a fog moved with me wherever I went.

We moved to Colorado, where I began to learn about the high plains. Here moisture was scarce. Cacti, yucca, and other succulents hold what little moisture there is and can thrive in aridity. As lush as my life was with Sally, I felt all dried up.

During these years, I would write to Iris, perhaps every other week and sometimes every third week. It was so painful all the time, to never have a dialogue, nothing coming back to me, except for my own painful love. My heart had opened with a small child, not even my own blood, and had gotten crushed. I became a very pale shadow of what I once was as Iris's dad.

Four and a half years after M and Iris's disappearance, I received a legal-sized envelope with a very small item in it. The envelope had my name on it in a child's writing. My heart raced as I opened the envelope. In it, I found a tiny piece of paper folded up really, really teensy-weensy. As I unfolded it I saw that it said, "Matthew, it's me Iris."

I cried my eyes out then, as I am now, recollecting.

"Thank you for all those things you sent me. The shirt, the books...I really love you. I can't remember what else. Oh yeah, the hairclips. Love Iris."

Oh...I cried and cried for joy. I could not believe it.

I had not been forgotten. My own moisture was returning.

I would call friends to tell them of this wonderful letter. I'd read it; in fact it was etched in my mind and voice. With delight I'd express my joy, yet I always wondered, what now? As the days went by my euphoria came to be replaced with my ever-present depressive mood. I never knew to call it anything; it seemed to be just me: quiet, removed, agitated.

The summer passed with my sending letters to Iris, but for some reason my energy just wasn't as it used to be. Even with this precious note, I was still putting my love into a void. I was still afraid. Sometimes I found it very difficult to write; what do I say with nothing coming back? I had begun cultivating cacti, intrigued with their multitude of shapes and forms. I bought one to share with Iris, but I just couldn't seem to send it for the longest time. Why?

In the early autumn of 2002 the phone rang. Sally answered it and told me that it was M, my ex-wife. I must've gone white; I was stunned. I heard her voice asking me for my input into helping her see some patterns at work in her life, which was currently in upheaval. And I heard myself saying, "Of course." I'd offer what I could. No anger and nastiness, no sarcastic passive-aggressive remarks. Just of course, it is time.

Our conversation ended with me asking to be able to resume talking with Iris. It had been almost five years; she was now eight and a half years old. M said yes, it is time. I never asked why she had had to run and take Iris. It didn't really matter at this point, now that I'd be able to talk to Iris again. Over the course of this conversation everything changed. Everything I'd been holding on to vanished, everything holding me back. Our civil conversation allowed me to be released from an awful captivity of fear and unexpressed anger.

Everything about how I related to my wonderful, loving part-ner, Sally, changed. The crippled me was beginning to walk again, maybe for the first time. I was able to begin feeling a level of love and admiration, joy and appreciation for her that was no longer locked away. I had been released from my prison.

I took all of this in for one week, then called Iris. She came on the phone and the first thing she said was, "I love my cactus!" Just like that, no hesitation, no nonsense. No "Where the hell have you been?" No "Who are you?" Just a lovely voice saying, "I love my cactus!" Then we were off and running, talking as if we had seen each other yesterday, not five years ago. I listened to her voice with awe and wonder. Is this really happening?

We ended with "I love you" and "You hang up first," "No you," games. I was filled with utter joy. Sweet tears rolled down my face as I collapsed in a chair. Sally's lovely, radiant face beamed with joy at me.

Iris and I now had a plan that I'd call her each week before she watched Disney on TV, Sunday evenings. What a wonderful time this has been to get to know my not-so-small daughter and to hear what she likes and does not like. How wonderful to hear about wolves, gymnastics, her little brother, her city and to ask her all of the questions that I've been writing and wondering about. At one of my questionings about her loves, she asked me, "Are you asking...so you can get me presents?" Awed and feeling found out, I said, "Well, uh, maybe." Then we both giggled.

One day while tending to my cactus garden, I glanced at another version of the miraculous. One of my cacti with the tightest, most intricate weaving of thorns had sprouted flowers, beautiful violet and pinkish flowers coming through these dense thorns. What a surprise. I can't claim to know anything substantial about cacti. I never would have thought that this one would flower. Sally was very quick to point out, lovingly, all of the metaphorical similarities between myself and this cactus.

In January 2003, I asked if I could come to see Iris. To my amazement and joy, I heard her mom say, "Yes, of course." When I told Iris that I would be flying out to see her, her immediate delight was music to my ears. As she was taking this in she said, "You promise? You promise? Do you really promise? If you don't, you'll be in trouble." As I heard this, my heart ached once again for all that she must've gone through as a child who had lost her dad.

In the two weeks prior to my visit, Iris kept telling me how she couldn't wait. She told me about the places she wanted to show me in "her town." She was so excited! Her class was going to have a pajama party at school the day that I was to visit. She asked if I'd come to her school and wear pajamas as well. Sally had gotten me a pair of J.Crew drawstring pants that would be just the ticket. I told Iris that I'd sure dress the part and that she'd be surprised!

On February thirteenth, Sally and I flew to Seattle to see my daughter, Iris. Oh, my! I was a bundle of nerves and excitement. I met M at the elementary school. After signing in, I walked down the hallway to a movement class. We stood at the glass door looking in, with me scanning the students in the room. Looking and looking. Where is she? Will I recognize her?

We saw each other simultaneously. Iris came running and jumped up into my arms! Again, she showed no hesitation. I hugged her, thinking, "I am actually here." Hugging her "hello" and saying, "I love you so much!" This being the day of her school pajama party, she giggled and giggled when she saw my pants, which are red and white and completely covered with hundreds of hearts.

Her look of joy and wonder that I was actually there with her was so precious. As I met her friends, she beamed such happiness and excitement while introducing me as her dad. And I could hardly keep from completely breaking down as tears rolled down my face. Here she was, tall and lean, with long hair and utter radiance, smiling as she told her mom that she had five years to make up for. We're doing just that!

As I finish sharing with you these parts of my life, so many "life lessons" become apparent to me:

- Being open to the love of a child will certainly heal our heart and soul, and show us so much more about ourselves than could ever be imagined.
- Once connected deeply to another, that connection endures through space and time.
- People can be drawn to one another for a multitude of reasons, some of which may take a very long time to become apparent.

- The children of our planet give us so many opportunities to grow up ourselves.
- Mothers, fathers, and all caregivers have such a profound responsibility to heal and forgive the hurts between each other.
- Childhood hurts and wounds, as tragic as they may appear at various points in our lives, when viewed from a much larger perspective, can actually be seen as the lessons of our soul's desire for transformation.
- So much joy can occur with all of this.

So here we are, Iris and me after five long years, as if no time had passed.

WHY THROW YOUR LIFE AWAY?

Martha Beck, Ph.D.

"IF you want to become straight," says Lao-tzu in the *Tao Te Ching*, "let yourself be crooked. If you want to be reborn, let yourself die. If you would be given everything, give everything up."

I encountered this counterintuitive philosophy as an Asian studies major at Harvard. I would begin to understand it a few years later, halfway through my Ph.D. program, when, six months into my second pregnancy, doctors discovered that the fetus I was carrying had an extra twenty-first chromosome: Down syndrome.

Already bonded to my unborn son, I refused what would have been a very late-term therapeutic abortion. Doctors, advisers, and peers told me I was "throwing my life away." They were right. What no one told me was that the life I would throw away was utterly wretched compared to the life I would get in exchange. A decade and a half later, I think we'd all do well to throw away our lives, when and if our hearts encourage it.

I named my son Adam, partly to remind myself that he is

Everyman, a prototype of the person who cannot quite measure up to social expectations—in other words, you, me, and every other human being who ever lived. Even if you were born "perfect," beautiful, brilliant, healthy, and strong, the fate of Adam will eventually befall you: accident or illness could snatch your perfection from you at any moment, and should you *be* lucky enough to avoid these catastrophes, their friends—old age and death—will be along before you know it.

Having an "imperfect" child forces these uncomfortable thoughts into one's awareness—but strangely enough, it makes them comfortable. A thirteenth-century Buddhist master wrote that "to be enlightened is to be without anxiety over imperfection." Adam embodies this enlightenment, embracing his identity and his differences without complaint or self-doubt. By having the chance to accept him (even before he was born), I found to my own surprise that I could accept myself, imperfect as I am.

All my desperate efforts to achieve academic success had been in pursuit of this acceptance. The anxious pursuit of perfection was the first thing I threw away when I opted to bear and raise Adam. In return, I found more peace and lasting happiness than I had ever felt before.

Another part of the life I threw away was the striving summed up in the modern Olympic motto: "higher, faster, stronger." I doubt that Adam will ever make the regular Olympic team in any sport. He loves the Special Olympics, and as a participant has learned the motto recited by the ancient Greek athletes in the original Olympics: "Let me win, but if I cannot win, let me be brave in the attempt."

It was a huge relief for me to stop lunging after higher, faster, stronger; to occasionally be lower, slower, and weaker—and brave enough to enjoy it. "Enjoy" is the operative word here, and enjoyment, like beauty, is its own excuse for being. Adam has taught me to find joy in the comedy of real life, rather than seeking it in the realm of superhuman strength and speed.

An example of Adam finding enjoyment in life came when he was seven. The dentist told me that he wasn't getting his molars clean enough; his genetically low muscle tone and coordination made it difficult for him to brush thoroughly. Coincidentally, the dentist just happened to be selling a fantastically expensive electric toothbrush, right out of the office! So I shelled out a hundred bucks, took the toothbrush home, and taught Adam to use it. Then I sent him to the bathroom with his sisters to do his morning ablutions.

A few seconds later, I heard strangled whoops and yells emerging from the bathroom, as though someone had shoved an unwilling chimpanzee into the shower. I ran down the hall, terrified that Adam had lost control of the toothbrush, that it was crawling down his throat, or that it was electrocuting him with its pricey little buttons.

I bumped into Adam's five-year-old sister, Elizabeth, as she emerged from the bathroom.

"Lizzy!" I yelled. "What's wrong with Adam?"

She cocked an eyebrow. "There's nothing wrong with him," she told me calmly. "He's just overwhelmed by joy again."

And so he was. The tickle of the expensive bristles on his gums and the buzz of the brand-new handle in his palm were so delightful to Adam that he was emitting banshee whoops of enthusiasm as he brushed. So now we all have hundred-dollar toothbrushes in our house—and let me tell you, there are worse things than being overwhelmed by joy every time you brush your teeth.

This is just one of infinite gifts, from the tiniest to the most enormous, that Adam has given me by being lower, slower, and weaker than a typical child.

By bringing me closer to the ground, to the foundations of life, he has made me more aware of the roots of things, the basic components of wisdom and solidity.

By slowing me down, he has reminded me that this moment, and not some remembered past or imagined future, is the only life we have.

By approaching tasks through yielding, asking for help, and accepting confusion, as well as force and independence, Adam has given me permission to use the whole range of my true abilities, rather than having to pretend I am always strong.

"All streams flow to the sea," says Lao-tzu, "because it is lower than they are. Humility gives it its strength." I shudder to think how neurotic I'd be by now if Adam didn't demonstrate this every day.

Another part of the life I threw away was the pretense of omniscience, the effort to appear intelligent. Growing up in a professor's family, spending my early adult life at Harvard, I learned to speak in lofty, esoteric terms. I learned how to make others feel slightly stupid, uncertain, and self-critical—the way I myself felt inside—as a means of feeding and protecting my ego.

Raising Adam has taught me that trying to sound smart is really very stupid; anything that can't be communicated in simple terms is probably not important, and the things that make life worth living—the recognition of beauty, truth, love, happiness—come from beyond the mind, and are obscured, or even lost, by too much thinking.

When Adam started school in Arizona, where we live, teachers and administrators seemed universally reluctant to include him in their schools. He was subjected to endless, repetitive intelligence tests, all of which had the same structure: they'd start with easy conceptual tasks, then increase the difficulty level gradually. The final score is assessed by the level at which the test-taker (in this case, Adam) could no longer answer the questions. Over and over, Adam completed the same boring tasks, answered the same boring questions. When he'd been sufficiently assessed, the testers would send him out to the playground or give him a can of Sprite.

After a couple of weeks of this, Adam started performing dramatically worse on his intelligence tests. He no longer seemed capable of answering even the simplest queries; his language skills had dropped to an apparent zero; he was unable to identify even the most rudimentary images.

I was horrified until I figured out what was going on: Adam had learned to game the system. He was playing dumb, topping out on the very first questions, so that he could get to the swing set and the Sprite.

I remember the moment I finally got it. I was thirty, and I'd been passing academic tests all my life. I still hadn't finished my third Harvard degree. I'd been struggling to pass test after test, leap through hoop after hoop, ever since I was five years old, and I'd never finished. Where was my swing set? Where was my Sprite? What on earth had I been doing, obsessing over narrow tests of intellect when I could have been actually *living*? What kind of "intelligence" was that?

Once I'd put in a few obstreperous calls to my local school board, Adam was finally allowed to enter school, where he has thrived. As for me, I started taking time away from tests and putting those hours into play. I started having fun. I started taking it easy.

I stopped writing academic articles and began turning out pages that, as one of my writing buddies put it, were "down where the goats could get it." I began to teach my business school students how to enjoy life, instead of how to master theoretical concepts.

Publishers liked my new way of putting words together, and students began hiring me outside of class to "coach" them, a process I love. After all those years of trying to act intelligent, I finally learned to play it smart, thanks to my "retarded" son.

Here again, Adam agrees with the wisdom I learned in my Asian studies classes long before I really understood it.

"In the beginner's mind, there are many possibilities," said the Zen master Suzuki Roshi. "In the expert's, there are few."

Buddhist texts refer to the ideal mental state as "don't know mind," the openness to experience that allows true understanding to dawn and grow. When I threw away the life I'd built at Harvard, with its obsessive focus on intellect and competition, I made room for the life I'd always wanted.

Plato said that we gain our first measure of intelligence on the day we first admit to our own ignorance. Maybe he knew someone with Down syndrome, too.

Of all the things Adam has taught me, perhaps the most crucial is the ability to let go of life as I know it—not just once, but over and over again. Acceptance and commitment therapists like Stephen Hayes call this a "continual conceptual suicide." It is the willingness to kill off our beliefs about what is proper and desirable, opening instead to the ever-changing, ever-surprising reality of actual experience.

Many people who have interacted with Adam tell me about moments when his unexpected view of life "kills" their expectations, their way of looking at the world, and brings a fresh perspective to life. Zen Buddhists call this experience *satori,* a moment of insight when concepts die and comprehension is born.

Such moments are rare in most people's lives because they require a gift for letting go of preconceptions, rather than clinging to them. Sometimes this happens slowly, like a sunrise. Other times it flashes like a bolt of lightning, quick, brilliant, and illuminating.

One of Adam's teachers, whom I'll call Mrs. Simons, had a moment of *satori* with Adam just the other day. Adam had worn a new sports watch to art class that morning. It was a large, elaborate watch, with several buttons and a snazzy band. Adam loved it. So did one of his classmates, Scotty, who also has Down syndrome. Scotty begged for a chance to put it on his own wrist, and Adam was glad to comply. Mrs. Simons helped negotiate the transfer, taking the band off Adam's wrist and buckling it around Scotty's. Not thirty seconds later, Scotty dipped his entire hand into a bucket of paint, giving the watch a whole new look, which was a good thing since it could no longer tell time.

Two days later, Mrs. Simons had not even begun to recover from this experience. Because she'd helped Adam hand over his watch, she blamed herself for the destruction. She apologized repeatedly, begging Adam's pardon for failing to supervise the watch-lending experience. As she later reported to me, Mrs. Simons felt that Scotty had not been sufficiently contrite, and she couldn't keep herself from riding him about it.

"Tell Adam you're sorry!" she told Scotty, several times. "No, you can't borrow his pen—remember what you did to that watch?"

Halfway through the class period, Mrs. Simons looked up to find Adam standing by her desk.

"Mrs. Simons," he said, "Scotty broke my watch."

"I know!" Mrs. Simons exclaimed. "It was terrible! He shouldn't have done that!"

"No," said Adam patiently, "he broke *my* watch."

He looked at her intently, to see if she got it. "It was *mine*," he repeated.

Mrs. Simons was confused. "Yes, but—"

"Mrs. Simons," said Adam, "let...it...go."

"Oh," said the teacher.

And there it was: *satori.*

In that moment, Mrs. Simons was reminded of a skill few "normal" people really comprehend, let alone develop: the ability to let things go, to release the tight hold we keep on our possessions and our stories and the way we want things to be.

Adam seems to do this naturally, and it is the most freeing lesson he has taught me. The moment I learned his diagnosis, I had to let go of many expectations, hopes, ambitions, goals, and desires that I had mistaken for the promise of happiness. In reality, they were only shackles that kept me bound to things that had never nourished my true self.

Living with Adam has allowed me to soak up lessons like these through the osmosis that comes with hanging out. I consider him my handy home Zen master, a small blond guru whose laughing eyes and sly smile are always ready to confound my preconceptions.

I know that not everyone is lucky enough to have such a teacher nearby, or to accidentally concoct one, as Adam's dad and I did, with a few simple tools we found around the house. But whether or not you have children, or a Zen master, or friends with genetic anomalies, I guarantee you have an Adam somewhere. Today it may be a kitten that shows up insisting that you are its human;

tomorrow a parent with Alzheimer's; or next week, a financial loss. There is no end to the supply of Adams in this world, no end to losses that make room for unimagined gains, disasters that open the door to opportunities.

I'm still not sure what it was that made me defy my doctors and academic advisers back when I was twenty-five and my world had just been shattered by the test results from an amniocentesis. It wasn't politics or ethics. (I would politically and ethically support any woman who made a different choice.)

No, it was something wilder and stranger; love, yes, but mixed with the paradoxical intuition that sometimes leads us away from our expected paths, squarely into our right lives. Lao-tzu might have called it the voice of my awareness, the One Who Knows, the true self that lives at the core of consciousness, far deeper than the mind.

I don't know when the voice of your true self may speak to you, but when it does, *listen.* Take the un-traveled road, the one that may seem to lead toward crookedness and death, to giving everything up. If and when your heart demands it, throw your life away. You never know what lovely and delicious life you're going to get in return.

THE GREAT MOVEMENT
OF THE COUCH

Elizabeth Lesser

Normal is someone you don't know very well.
—ANONYMOUS

ONE of my son Rahm's childhood friends, Jonah, began
directing and shooting films when he was still in elementary school. This was fortunate, because I have an aversion to using
cameras. My picture albums are filled with photos taken by my
mother, and the only video footage I have of my children was made
by Jonah—fully scripted theatrical pieces involving large casts and
well-rehearsed scenes. At a recent Thanksgiving gathering, my
whole family watched a couple of these videos. One in particular
helped me retrieve some lost memories from an important time
in my parenting journey—the three years between my first and
second marriages when I was a single mother. The film, entitled
Slam Ball, is a hilarious how-to sports documentary about a complex and wildly imaginative game that the boys had invented. Slam

ball had its heyday during a long and snowy winter, when my kids and their friends would congregate almost every afternoon in my living room.

When we watched the slam ball instructional video, my sisters were astonished by the mess I had allowed to overtake the house. "I never let my kids be so wild in my house," one of my sisters said. "Or rearrange the living room into a sports arena," said another. Looking around the same house now—at the carefully arranged furniture and objects of art—it is hard to believe that I ever let a gang of boys shanghai the living room, push the couch against the French doors, duct-tape the boundaries of the court on the wide-board pine floor, and use the center pattern of a Persian rug as the circle from which a large rubber ball would be slammed with great force by the server's fist.

The video features my sons and their friends playing a rousing game of slam ball, which is a cross between squash and professional wrestling. At one point, as the players hurl themselves at each other, the ball ricochets off the ceiling and smashes into the television set. But while it shocked my sisters, watching the film was a nostalgic experience for me. It brought me back to a few months christened the Winter of Slam Ball by Jonah and Rahm. During that entire winter I left the slam ball arena intact. I was too overwhelmed by single motherhood, work, and life in general even to remember that living rooms can also be used for lounging quietly on a couch or entertaining people who prefer talking to slamming into each other.

I look back on the Winter of Slam Ball with a certain sense of pride. Pride that this girl raised in a family of girls acquired a taste for the wildness of boys, and took pleasure in hosting their wacky experiments. I was genuinely happy to be sharing my life with a whole village of kids—feeding them, listening to them, hitching a ride on their exuberant energy. But I also see in my permissiveness a desperation to make a happy home for my sons. As a single mother I lived with a nagging sense of shame—shame that my family wasn't a "real" family, and that I wasn't providing for my kids the normal life they were supposed to have. And since I had destroyed the possibility of normalcy, I was going to knock myself out making sure they were happy. If they wanted to use the living room as a gym I'd let them, and so I allowed my house to double as a slam ball arena week after week as the winter dragged on.

The video does not include an important slam ball moment, dubbed by Rahm and Jonah as the Great Movement of the Couch. Toward the end of the winter, when the melting snow and heavy mud of March were being brought into the living room on the kids' boots, I had an epiphany about slam ball, parenting, and families. It began in the late afternoon, as I stood in the kitchen watching my boys and their friends troop through the woods from the school bus, laughing and shoving each other, getting louder as they approached the house. I had the sudden urge to lock all the doors. The prospect of another afternoon of slam ball had lost any appeal. I hated slam ball. Things had gone too far. I wanted my living room back. It was as simple as that. If not, I wanted these boys to go away; all of them, even my own kids. My heart sank. I was mortified to feel like this, but there was no denying it: something had to change.

As the kids descended on the house, kicking off their muddy boots in the living room, draping their coats and bags wherever they wanted, raiding the refrigerator, and bringing food and drinks into the slam ball arena, I secretly decided that this was the last time I would allow the game to be played in my living room. If I didn't put an end to slam ball, I would have to bar the players from the house, and that wouldn't do, since two of them belonged to me. As I watched them clear away stray items from the court and set up for another raucous game, I knew that it was time for me to step back into the role of the adult and set some guidelines for civilization.

The afternoon dragged on; the slam ball volleys were as wild as ever, but I was calm. I had made up my mind. The game came to its natural end as it was getting dark. Several kids left; others put on their coats and boots and waited for their parents to pick them up. Finally, only Rahm and Daniel and Jonah were left.

"Boys," I said, coming into the living room, "I want you to help me rearrange the room."

"But, Mom," Rahm said, "we're just going to have to put it back the same way tomorrow."

"No," I said, with a sad firmness in my voice. "I don't think so. I don't want you to use the living room for slam ball anymore."

The three kids looked at me as if I had announced the end of the world. "I want to move the couch here," I said, pointing to the middle of the room.

"But, Elizabeth," Jonah protested, "that's the *middle* of the slam ball court!"

"I know, Jonah," I said, putting my arm around his shoulder. "I just cannot have slam ball in my living room anymore. It's time for you guys to invent a different game, in a different room, or go outside, or find another house where the parents are as crazy as I am."

"You're not crazy, Mom," said Daniel. "You're nice." Being the little brother, Daniel had never been allowed to participate fully in slam ball games and so had less to lose, but I took it as a compliment anyway.

"Thank you, sweetie," I said, choking up. "But I think I've been a little too nice. Let's move the couch, okay?"

So the two older boys got on one side of the couch, complaining and bargaining with me as they lifted and pushed, and I took the other side with Daniel, and we placed the heavy piece of furniture smack in the middle of the slam ball court. Later, when Jonah had gone home and the boys had gone to bed, I vacuumed the rug, unstacked the chairs, and arranged the room to look like the kind of place where people chat and read. I lit a fire in the fireplace, sat on the rug with a glass of wine, and tried to pretend that everything was normal, now that the couch was back in place and order had been restored.

But who was I fooling? My life was *not* normal; things were seriously out of order. I was divorced. My kids went back and forth between my house and their father's. This was not the way things were supposed to be. During the divorce I had hung on to Carl Jung's words that "nothing has a more disturbing influence psychologically on children than the unlived life of the parent." That sounded right to me: I hoped the divorce could bestow on the boys the gift of parents with full and happy lives. But now I was so racked with guilt that I was unable to really believe anything.

I sat there, letting these cold facts chill my heart as the fire warmed my face. In the stillness, with nothing to distract me, an all too familiar feeling of despair descended and hijacked my heart. But instead of getting up, washing the dishes, or calling a friend, I let myself sink into the thick soup of shame and sadness. Tears pooled in my eyes and fell down my cheeks. "How long do I have to feel like this?" I asked the flames. "How long does it take to get back to normal?"

As the fire crackled and I cried and sipped my wine, I remembered a funny thing someone had recently said to me, and I said it out loud: *"Normal is someone you don't know very well."* And then, staring at the flames, I laughed, and I threw my hands up and announced, "I give up. I am not normal. I'll never be normal again."

Was it the wine? The flames? The end of slam ball? I don't know. But in that moment I sensed it was time to let normal die. I saw clearly how some of my freewheeling mothering style came from a respect for the natural spunkiness of children. I liked that part of the way I mothered. I decided to hold on to that part. But some of my leniency came from my guilt over the divorce, and from my mistaken notion that normal homes are always happy homes. It was time to let that part go.

"May I toss my yearning for normal into the flames?" I asked the Phoenix in the fire. "Will you burn it to bits and show me a new way?" I thought of my boys asleep upstairs, of Jonah at his house up the road, of children everywhere in all kinds of families. And I said a prayer to the Phoenix, to the goddesses and gods of all parents, to whoever was listening: "Please help us raise our children with grace and wisdom and pleasure. Please remind us that our kids are just goofy little humans—junior bozos on the bus—who will not, under any circumstances, always be happy, no matter how hard we try. Please watch over all of us sleeping and waking in this imperfect world."

After my prayer I thought I heard the furniture heave a sigh of gratitude, sensing that the days of slam ball and backpacks and wet shoes were over. I patted the couch and assured it that, although it would never enjoy the prim isolation of couches in childless homes, I was ready to set some limits. Then I went upstairs to bed and fell into a hopeful sleep, certain that in the morning something good would arise from the ashes.

The next day the same group of kids got off the school bus and headed toward our house. When they reached the front door, I steeled myself for an uprising, but instead Jonah explained to them, in a dramatic voice, that the evening before he and Rahm had witnessed the Great Movement of the Couch, and the tragic and untimely end of slam ball. They then convinced me to allow them to move the couch one more time, so that slam ball could live on, preserved forever on videotape. Impressed by their inventiveness, I conceded, and for one more deranged afternoon, the sounds of slam ball resounded through the house.

I sat in the viewing stands (the couch), watching the last game with glee as Jonah and Rahm took turns filming. My heart filled with a poignant sense of love toward my sons and their friends, and toward myself. I had taken a stand, and the kids had responded with creativity. Sure, there were a few grumbles, but they all seemed to understand the logic of my decision and accepted my authority with surprising goodwill. After the final match, they retired to my office to type up a slam ball instructional manual. Then they put their coats back on and went into the woods to shoot a movie about an FBI raid.

The Great Movement of the Couch was significant to the kids in that it essentially ended slam ball, since no other parents were interested in hosting the game. But along with their disappointment, I sensed relief in my sons—relief that I had resumed the role of boss. Children do not want to be in charge of family life. They may act like they do, but they don't. Not when they're toddlers, and not when they're kids, and not when they're teenagers. Children need their parents to lead the way, to show them how to navigate the waters of real life. I also was relieved by something revealed to me through the Great Movement of the Couch: I saw how resilient children are—how much better able they are than adults to accept and work with what is. They are interested in making the most of each moment, while we are trying to string the moments together into a preconceived picture of life. They're alive in the moment; we're stuck in normal.

After the Great Movement of the Couch, my quest for normalcy mellowed. I'd be dishonest to say it disappeared overnight, but I took new vows and began to put them into action. I vowed to honor the flawed authenticity of real life. Instead of expending wasted energy longing for the way it was supposed to be, I vowed to make what *was* as harmonious and vibrant as I could. I vowed to honor the family we already had, and to include and respect every member—me and my kids, their father, and later their stepfather and stepbrother, and their stepmother and her family, and their new brother who would come along a few years later. The full catastrophe! I renew my vows every day, and thank slam ball for bouncing such a big lesson into center court.

INTIMACY

Dean Ornish, M.D.

ON my fortieth birthday, I thought my dreams were coming
true. During that week:

- My third book reached number one on the *New York Times*
  bestseller list.
- My colleagues and I received a letter from the American
  Heart Association informing us that they accepted our latest research findings for their annual scientific meeting: we
  had found even more reversal of heart disease after five years
  than after one year in our research patients. They planned a
  press conference to announce our results.
- I was invited to spend the night at the White House.

Two weeks before my birthday, our research was featured on
the front page of the *New York Times* and on all of the evening
news shows. That is when Mutual of Omaha announced it would
pay for our program for reversing heart disease, the first time a

major insurance company paid for an alternative medicine treatment. Later, *USA Today* ran a front-page headline, "Patient Calls Ornish Program 'Miraculous.' "

I went to my twenty-fifth high school reunion. The former captain of the football team—who wouldn't give me the time of day when we were in high school together—came up to me, gave me a big hug, and boomed, "Gee, Dean, I should have been nicer to you in high school but I didn't know you were going to be so successful!"

So...why was I feeling so lonely, unsatisfied, and discontented?

Unhappiness was no stranger to me. When I was nineteen, I became profoundly depressed and almost committed suicide. I wrote about this time in my life in an earlier book, *Dr. Dean Ornish's Program for Reversing Heart Disease*, published in 1990. It was a little scary to be that self-disclosing. After all, like most people, I usually want to show my best side, not my darkest moments.

Since the publication of that book, I have received letters from many people who wrote to say that this chapter was the most meaningful and useful to them. Having a greater understanding of the process I went through often gave them more insight into their own lives. Also, my willingness to reveal myself made it easier for them to do the same.

In that spirit, I want to share with you the process of what I have been learning in recent years. Part of me hesitates to do so because I do not want to seem either self-aggrandizing or foolish, although there are times when I am each of these. Nevertheless, I decided to write this in hopes that this phase of my journey may be of some value to you. Of course, this is still an ongoing process. Perhaps these experiences may help you avoid some of my mistakes. (You can make new ones!)

A few months after I recovered from depression, I went back to college. Meditation and yoga helped me stay so much calmer and focused that I was able to graduate summa cum laude and gave the commencement address. During the next twenty years, I had many accomplishments.

Yet I was no freer than when I was profoundly depressed in college and thought I would never amount to anything. I was in a golden cage rather than a steel one, but a cage nonetheless. I was still looking in the wrong places for happiness and peace, even though I knew better.

The loneliness could not be fed for long by external accomplishments and activities, no matter how interesting or exciting. Not that I didn't try; I worked at least eighty hours a week, sometimes more, which was a good distraction from these feelings.

On my fortieth birthday, the contrast between what I was achieving and what I was feeling was so great that I could no longer pretend to myself that external accomplishments would bring happiness. I could no longer continue as I had been. I couldn't continue to tell myself, "Gee, maybe if I accomplished more, then I'd be happy."

The extremes of worldly success and inner turmoil were impossible to ignore—as if the universe were saying, "Hey, Dean—listen up! Pay attention! Can I make it any clearer for you?"

I had moments of satisfaction and joy, of course, but not with any continuity. I was missing what was the most meaningful. I didn't have the depth of love and intimacy I desired in the relationship that was most important to me. I was afraid to open my heart.

Physician, Heal Thyself

The disconnect between how much I was able to help others and how little I was able to help myself in this area became a catalyst and a crucible for the next phase in my journey.

Over time, years of meditation gave me glimpses of the interconnectedness and interdependence of all life. I experienced that on one level, we are alone, separate, apart from everyone and everything; on another level, we are the Self in different disguises, different names and forms, a part of everyone and everything. Many religions proclaim as a fundamental truth, "The Lord is One."

This experience of interconnectedness is part of spiritual traditions and the perennial wisdom in virtually all religions and cultures. Although these glimpses of transcendent experiences gave me hope and awareness, they did not last. I could feel the peace of experiencing this oneness, but, like a visitor in someone else's home, I couldn't stay there for very long. I know now that I first needed to learn how to more fully be human. Trying to skip that stage was like trying to pretend I was not feeling angry and going straight to forgiveness without first allowing myself to be human and to acknowledge the feelings of anger. I needed to get out of my head and into my heart.

From Passion to Compassion

I dated a lot in high school and college, like many people in my generation. At first, it seemed liberating to go out with different people. After a while, though, I began to realize that what I thought was bringing me the most freedom was exactly what was most limiting and binding me. I later learned that what seemed to be the most confining—commitment, discipline, and monogamy—were actually the most liberating and joyful. In high school and college, though, these words sounded dry, boring, confining, and limiting. I wanted to feel free and enjoy life.

I am learning that I had it backwards. Consciously choosing commitment, discipline, and monogamy can be liberating. There is great freedom in these words. Why? Freely choosing discipline gives more power—power to create, to express, to enjoy. Freely choosing commitment and monogamy creates safety and make intimacy possible.

Intimacy is liberating and healing, but only if you feel safe. You can only be intimate to the degree you can be vulnerable. You can be vulnerable and open your heart only to the degree you feel safe—because if you make yourself vulnerable, you might get hurt.

Dating more than one woman helped buffer intimacy. If I got too close to one person and thus became too vulnerable, then I could go back to another one. Push—pull. I was neither alone nor too intimate. It was usually fun in the moment, but often left me feeling even more empty and lonely.

I found myself caught in a vicious cycle. The temporary relief from emotional pain and loneliness that an evening out, an award, or an accomplishment could provide was what made these so seductive. In a strange way, I found it easier to be open and intimate with someone I didn't know very well than being in a long-term relationship. I didn't have a history with a new person; we hadn't spent years hurting each other and closing down parts of ourselves to protect those soft spots. But the intimacy was limited and without continuity.

Why was I so afraid of the intimacy that I most desired?

Like many people, I grew up in a loving family without many personal or emotional boundaries—what I affectionately call "the Ornish Blob." In every family there is a process of how each person individuates and separates from the rest of the family. This was my form of the task, which was not unique to me.

In one sense, the lack of personal boundaries felt warm, fuzzy, and comfortable. In another, though, it went beyond that. As in many families, I began to realize that I did not have a very well-formed sense of having a separate self. Over time, I learned that in order to be in an intimate relationship with someone I first had to learn to be separate and to have a well-developed sense of self. Otherwise, I could not let someone in without feeling overwhelmed.

Not having a well-formed sense of self can be terrifying, for it can feel like nonexistence or death. In psychology, this is referred to as narcissism. The word "narcissism" often brings to mind self-centered, self-absorbed, or self-aggrandizing, when it really means that a person has a very poorly defined sense of self and self-worth. It often goes along with a deep sense of sadness and loneliness, and it is very common in our culture, especially in people who have heart disease.

Growing up in my family, as in many families, the unspoken yet heard message from my parents was this: "You don't exist as a separate person; you are an extension of us. Therefore, you have a great capacity to cause us joy or pain. If you act right, we will be so proud of you. If you don't, we will suffer. If you really mess up, we will really suffer—and if we suffer enough, we will die and leave you all alone. Since you don't exist separate from us, then if we die, you'll die, too."

Every family has its own version of these. I'm not blaming my parents; I love them dearly. I am deeply grateful for all they have given and done for me and the many sacrifices they have made on my behalf. They had parents and grandparents and great-grandparents who unknowingly may have given them similar messages which they unwittingly passed on to me. Each generation takes on the emotional work that wasn't completed by the previous ones.

There are many different paths to autonomy. Some are healthier than others. One of the time-honored ways of differentiating from one's parents is to rebel, to do that which they do not approve of. I found ways of rebelling that were socially constructive—for example, taking a year off from medical school to do my first research project.

"Isn't it ironic?" my parents once told me in one of their more memorable moments. "You want to drop out of medical school to do research on stress and the heart and you're giving us heart attacks!" Since they didn't see me as a separate person, my behavior was often unfathomable to them.

How does this relate to intimacy? I wanted to be in an intimate relationship, but I was afraid to be. When there are no boundaries, intimacy can feel dangerous. If you become too open to someone, you can become controlled, hurt, or even annihilated by them— often without awareness.

Being unmindful, I tended to choose relationships with women who also had similar issues about intimacy at that time, so we often became unhealthy mirrors for each other. Then, I could blame them for not being more open or intimate without having to face my own limited capacity for intimacy then. If only they would change, I told myself....

I remember a conversation I had twenty-five years ago with Swami Satchidananda about a woman I was in love with then when I was in college:

"She's driving me crazy!"

"Good!"

"What do you mean, 'Good!' It's not good, it's horrible."

"Why is it horrible?"

"She's doing this, she's not doing that…how can I get her to do that and not do this? If only she would change, then I'd be happy and everything would be wonderful."

"Look here, boy," he said, laughing compassionately, "it's not her, it's you. As long as you think the problem is with her, then you're setting yourself up for more suffering."

He went on to explain that it would be empowering if I could understand that the problem was with me, because then I could do something about it. I couldn't really grasp what he meant. It took a while, but I finally began to comprehend.

This simple idea—taking responsibility and examining my own issues—was the foundation of a powerful motivational shift that began transforming my life. Before, when problems arose in a relationship, I focused on finding evidence of what the other person was doing wrong to justify and to rationalize my own habitual actions and patterns of behavior. Later, I began taking a hard look at myself and finding my own authentic response and responsibility.

When a person begins to feel accountable for his or her own actions rather than blaming the other person in the relationship, then the relationship transforms. Either the relationship may grow and become more authentic and intimate, or one person or both may decide to end a destructive relationship and choose another person who is more compatible with them or who has a greater capacity for intimacy.

As I became more aware of these patterns, I examined how

I related to some people in the past. I began to feel very sorry for whatever pain I caused along the way. I had made some unwise choices years before that I sincerely regretted. I knew I couldn't change the past, but I became determined not to keep reliving and repeating it.

I think there is great value in living fully and making mistakes, if you survive and learn from them, because then your knowledge is authentic: it comes from your own experience. Great mistakes can lead to great wisdom, if we pay attention, learn, and stop repeating the mistakes. I learned to define a separate self and to live with the terrors of facing loneliness without running from it. As a result, I could choose to be in one intimate relationship without the compulsion of distracting myself from real intimacy by being in several.

What had seemed liberating—going out with different people—became increasingly frustrating. I knew that I needed to make some significant changes. The same drive that was causing these problems was now getting my attention to begin addressing them. I wanted more intimacy in my life.

I began to realize that an important part of my healing was that I needed to learn to be alone without distractions. If I wanted intimacy and love, then I first needed to learn to coexist with this pain without trying to numb it or run from it in the ways that had been most familiar to me.

I spent increasing amounts of time by myself. The hardest times were when I would travel somewhere to attend a meeting or to give a lecture; afterwards, I would end up in a hotel room, alone. Unlike before, I tried not to call anyone, spend time with anyone, or even watch television or read a book; instead I would stay with whatever feelings arose. I discovered that when I was alone, I felt as if I disappeared.

In one sense, I did. I was experiencing my self—more precisely, my lack of self—without distractions. That frightening realization helped me to begin constructing a real sense of self and self-worth.

Although it was very painful, it was also very healing. This same pain that I had been avoiding began cutting through some of the layers and walls that had protected my heart yet isolated it for so many years. I began to realize that I didn't need to be with people in order to feel I existed. Slowly, little by little, my heart began to open.

While it was important for me to define a separate self as part of my own growth, it was equally important for me to go beyond separation. So much of psychotherapy tends to focus on the first half—helping people develop an autonomous, independent, separate self—at the expense of learning how to be in an intimate, sharing relationship and finding community. I am finding that real freedom comes from choosing interdependence rather than the false choice between codependence and independence.

I learned that the capacity for love and intimacy—an open heart—is so important to having a joyful life as well as to survival. This is true in all relationships, not just romantic ones.

In the past, being involved with women whose capacity for intimacy was as limited as my own had felt safe. At least I wouldn't be controlled and consumed, even if it was frustrating because it wasn't very close. As my capability for intimacy grew as a result of working on these issues, I was able to make different choices in relationships. As I began to heal, I found myself in a committed relationships with a wonderful person.

I am not saying that the key to happiness is finding the right Cinderella or Prince Charming, getting married, and living happily ever after. Until I had done enough work on my own obstacles to intimacy, I was incapable of being in an intimate relationship with anyone, no matter who they were. It was not about finding the right person; it was about being the right person. I knew my beloved for a long time before we got into a relationship, but I couldn't even see her fully until I had done the work to be the right person.

Often we don't see people for who they really are. Sometimes when you "fall in love," it is with your illusion, your projection. We imagine an idealized image of a person and fall in love with that, projecting that image onto the other person. As we get to know them better, we become disillusioned—quite literally—that they did not live up to our illusion of who we wanted them to be. When I was younger, I thought I was in intimate relationships only because I didn't know that intimacy really meant seeing, feeling, hearing, and processing the inner world of another person instead of just projecting onto her images of who I thought she was and who I wanted her to be.

When my sweetheart and I made a commitment to the process of taking responsibility for our own behavior rather than project-ing idealized images upon each other, then the possibility of real intimacy was greatly enhanced.

I began to see and to love how exquisite she really is.

This relationship is transforming my life in ways that are amaz-ing to me. It feels like grace. Through it, I have learned how to experience happiness on a different level. Not all the time, of course, but with much greater continuity and depth than before. The more whole I feel within myself, the greater the capacity I have for intimacy with someone else.

When two people commit themselves to each other, magical things can begin to happen. Instead of repeating the same superficial experience with different people, I am having different, extraordinary experiences with the same person.

I had realized long before that great sex is no substitute for an open heart. What I began learning is that an open heart can lead to the most joyful and ecstatic sex. Every day, my beloved and I are learning to trust each other a little more so the walls around our hearts begin opening a little further. I realize how wonderful it feels to be truly relaxed and comfortable with another person.

In a similar way, I am finding that being in a committed, monogamous relationship has given me more joy and freedom than ever. The act of making a commitment itself has value, in relationships.

In other words, we may choose to follow the restrictions of our own religion or tradition not to please God but rather to experience God. We begin to heal our separation from God and from each other. Also, choosing not to do something helps us define who we are. A person without a separate self has no real choice. Freedom comes from choosing not to do something as well as from choosing to do something. Only when we can say "no" are we free to say "yes."

In a committed relationship, saying "no" to everyone but your beloved sanctifies the relationship. Not in the dry, boring sense—rather, sacred is just another way of saying the most special, which, in turn, makes it the most fun, the most joyful, the most wonderful.

Of course, relationships can be stultifying and oppressive. Whether discipline, monogamy, and commitment are liberating or confining is in part a function of whether or not you feel free to choose or whether these are imposed on you.

When I can see and love God in my beloved, and then in myself, I can begin to love and see and experience God in everyone and everything. I am learning that the sacred is found not just in altars of churches and synagogues, not just by looking for the extraordinary, but rather by finding the extraordinary in the ordinary—thereby removing barriers that separate us from each other and from ourselves.

Sitting on the couch watching a movie, eating popcorn, going for a walk together, holding hands, watching her sleep, kissing, or sharing a meal together; somehow, these simple moments are far more meaningful to me than any award or accomplishment.

For so much of my life, I felt as if I had to show that I was special by doing extraordinary things in order to be loved. This approach was self-defeating, for to be special in that way was to be isolated, different—setting myself apart from others in hopes that would help me feel close to them. I began to learn that those who really loved me did so despite what I've done, not because of it. Others may have become envious, causing even more separation and isolation.

I used to feel loved because I was special. Now, I feel special because I am loved and because I can love. We all have the ability to love, to be loved, and, thus, to feel special.

I'm learning that the real grace is not just being loved; it is learning how to love. I have needed trust, commitment, and complete honesty in order to feel safe enough to make myself vulnerable to love someone else without holding back. In this context, commitment can be liberating.

As I learn how to open my heart to my beloved, I have moments when I actually feel love for myself. Not in a narcissistic way (it's hard to love yourself if you don't have a self), but in a way that feels whole, holy, and healing. The more love I feel for myself, the more love I have to give others.

As I feel more compassion for myself, I have a greater capacity to view others with more compassion and with less judgment. At times, I can experience the transcendent interconnectedness—the universal Self, which goes by many names and forms—without getting lost in it, maintaining a "double vision" of the oneness and the diversity.

From that perspective, we can begin to love our neighbor as our Self in different forms—which is the essence of empathy and compassion.

I am learning that the key to our survival is love. When we love someone and feel loved by them, somehow along the way our suffering subsides, our deepest wounds begin healing, our hearts start to feel safe enough to open a little wider. We begin feeling our own emotions and the emotions of those around us.

HALF LIFE

Stephen Levine

We walk through half our life
as if it were a fever dream.

barely touching the ground,

our eyes half open
our heart half closed

Not half knowing who we are
we watch the ghost of us drift
from room to room
through friends and lovers
never quite as real as advertised.

Not saying half we mean
or meaning half we say
we dream ourselves

from birth to birth
seeking some true self.

Until the fever breaks
and the heart can not abide
a moment longer
as
the rest of us awakens,
summoned from the dream,
not half caring for anything but love.

PREGNANCY: A CRASH COURSE IN VULNERABILITY

Harriet Lerner, Ph.D.

I think that kids are the best teachers of life's most profound spiritual lessons; that pain and suffering are as much a part of life as happiness and joy; that change and impermanence are all we can count on for sure; that we don't really run the show; and that if we can't find the maturity to surrender to these difficult truths we'll always be unhappy that our lives—and our children's—aren't turning out the way we expected or planned. Life doesn't go the way we expect or plan—a lesson I learned most vividly during my first pregnancy.

I was thirty when I became pregnant for the first time. Before conceiving, I had not experienced even one maternal twinge. In fact, to say that I wasn't maternal is an understatement of vast proportions. I enjoyed adult company; my idea of a good time did not

include hanging out with babies who were unable to dress themselves, use the toilet, or make interesting conversation.

But as soon as I got the news that I was pregnant, I was bursting
with self-importance and pride. I wanted to grab strangers in the
supermarket and say, "Hey, I may look like a regular person, but
I'm pregnant, you know!" My confidence inflated even more when I
sailed through my first trimester without a flicker of discomfort. I
took credit for the fact things were moving along so swimmingly,
and concluded that maybe I was suited to motherhood after all.

But in the beginning of my second trimester I began spotting,
then bleeding. Sometimes I wouldn't bleed at all and I'd be filled
with hope, and sometimes I'd really bleed and think that I—or the
baby—was dying. I felt panic-stricken, filled with a mixture of terror for our dual survival and of utter humiliation at the prospect of
ruining someone's expensive couch.

The whole thing was a gamble. I didn't know whether enough of
the placenta would stay attached because it had become implanted
too low and was shearing off as the pregnancy progressed, increasing the risk of brain damage or fetal death. There is probably a more
medically accurate way to describe what was happening, but this is
how I understood my situation at the time. I had a healthy fetus in
utero, and I thought that the medical profession, as advanced as it
was, should know how to make a placenta stay put. It seemed like a
minor technicality that needn't have life-or-death consequences.

I had my first panic attack during this time, forcing my husband, Steve, to awaken my doctor at midnight to tell him I was having a heart attack or perhaps dying.

"It sounds like you're hyperventilating, doesn't it?" the doctor
said when I had composed myself enough to describe my symptoms. I should have put my head in a paper bag instead of calling

my doctor. Now that I knew I would live, I was embarrassed that we had awakened him at midnight. My husband and I were two psychologists who had failed to recognize the ordinary symptoms of anxiety.

Having this baby was now almost all I cared about. I wanted this baby with a fierceness I had not known was possible, so much that I would burst into tears if I found myself in line at the supermarket with a mother and her infant. I'm not sentimental about fetuses or motherhood, so there was no way I could have anticipated the searing intensity of this bond and the devastation I felt at the prospect of my loss. I desperately, desperately wanted this baby, but what I got was a crash course in feeling totally vulnerable and helpless.

Up until the time my pregnancy became prefixed by the word *complicated*, I assumed that my adult life would go as I planned, that nothing really bad would ever happen to me. Intellectually, I knew this wasn't so, because bad things happen to everyone, and indeed, some bad things had already happened to me. But I secretly believed that I could surely get pregnancy right, if I only put my mind to it.

It's the American Way to believe that every problem has a solution and that every obstacle can be overcome. We believe that we're in charge of our own destiny, that we get what we deserve. When things get rough, we can try harder, make a new plan, think positively, and pull ourselves up by the bootstraps to success. Everything that goes wrong can be fixed, if not by us, then surely by the doctor (or therapist, rabbi, priest, or healer). I believe that much of the pain and grief that mothers feel stems from the belief that we should have control over our children, when it's hard enough to have control over ourselves.

Pregnancy, no matter how it goes, is a lesson in surrender and vulnerability. Your body is inhabited; you live with the realization that childbirth is a wild card. You know at some level that your life will soon be altered in ways you can't even begin to imagine. You can't run the show, and dramatic change is the only thing you can count on for sure.

With so much anxiety about the pregnancy itself, I had almost forgotten that the end result might be a baby. But on June 5, 1975, I woke up in the middle of the night with menstrual cramps. I racked my brain to figure out how I could possibly be having menstrual cramps since I was pregnant. Then I figured that everything was going wrong anyway, so here was just one more bit of weirdness from my untrustworthy body. I considered searching for Midol, but remembering the no-drug rule, I simply lay in bed figuring that surely the menstrual cramps would go away, since it was inappropriate for them to be there in the first place.

It was an amazing bit of denial. My due date was in August, so going into labor in June was unthinkable. I fell back to sleep with my menstrual cramps, only to be awakened minutes later by something gushing out of me that I took to be blood, which meant I would be dead in a matter of minutes since there was no way to get to the hospital fast enough to save my life.

I pounded Steve awake, and he flew out of bed to switch on the light. We saw, to our most incredible relief, that whatever had poured out of me was definitely not blood because it was colorless. Steve suggested that I was in labor, that my water had broken. Yes, it was early, but it was happening, and that was why the bed was soaked.

I refused to accept this reality. Obviously the baby had kicked my bladder and knocked all the pee out of me, because I had recently heard of this very thing happening to some extremely pregnant person while she was grocery shopping. So I crouched on the bed on all fours, put my nose to the wet sheet, and insisted that Steve get down and sniff it with me. I was quite positive that I detected a definite urine-like odor.

It's said that comedy is tragedy plus time. If I had been a fly on the wall, I would have observed a scene of great hilarity; the two of us crouched like dogs on our bed, noses to the sheet, coming up for air only long enough to fight with each other about whether we were, or were not, smelling pee. We called the doctor, who said he would meet us at the hospital right away.

Standing under the moon, outside the hospital door, all fear left me to be replaced by the most ineffable sadness I've ever known. I turned to Steve and said, "I am so sorry." He hugged me and said he loved me and that nothing was my fault, but I knew it was. I knew I had just committed the biggest screwup in the world. The stakes had never been so high, and I couldn't even get pregnancy right.

Labor is a well-named, all-consuming experience. When it was determined that I could go ahead with natural childbirth, I was entirely immersed in getting through it. My obstetrician said that a helicopter was available to fly the baby to the intensive care unit at the medical center in Kansas City, if need be. Everyone was predicting a small, premature infant, of, say, four pounds. I imagined one even smaller because, as I lay on my back and looked down, I didn't even look pregnant anymore.

There was nothing I could do but have this baby. I was taken over by the pure physicality of the event, and now everything went by the book. Soon I was being wheeled from a small, dark room into a large room flooded with sunlight. I remember my body pushing

for me, how struck I was with the mammalian nature of it all, and then out slid the most beautiful baby that you could ever imagine seeing in your entire life, meaning a normal-appearing *big* baby.

I didn't trust my eyes. It occurred to me that maybe he was only the size of a hamster but that, in my psychotic denial, my mind was blowing him up into a normal-sized baby. So I held my breath and waited for someone to speak. And then my doctor said, "He's *big*!" and someone else said, "Well, look at this perfect baby boy!" Steve was beside himself with joy, and if I have ever in my life known perfect happiness, it was then.

Matthew Rubin Lerner was 20 inches long and weighed 7 pounds 4 ounces. Three years later when his brother, Ben, weighed in at 9 pounds 13 ounces, we realized that Matthew at 7 pounds showed some signs of prematurity, but he wasn't nearly as early as we had all calculated. Most importantly, he was here.

My first pregnancy taught me all the basics about mother-hood. I learned that we are not in control of what happens to our children. But this fact needn't stop us from feeling totally guilty and responsible. I also learned that matters of life and death turn on a dime, and that most of what we worry about doesn't happen (although bad things that we fail to anticipate do happen). These are the essential lessons of motherhood that were repeated again and again as my boys were growing up, and the universe taught them to me right up front.

RESOURCES: FAMILY, LOVE, AND RELATIONSHIPS

Books

Are You the One for Me? by Barbara De Angelis (Island, 1993)

Broken Open: How Difficult Times Can Make Us Grow, by Elizabeth Lesser (Villard, 2004)

Closing the Gap: A Strategy for Bringing Parents and Teens Together, by Jay McGraw (Fireside, 2001)

Codependent No More, by Melody Beattie (Hazelden, 2001)

The Dance of Connection, by Harriet Lerner (Quill, 2002)

Embracing the Beloved, by Stephen and Ondrea Levine (Anchor, 1996)

Expecting Adam, by Martha Beck (Berkley, 1999)

Feeling at Home: Defining Who You Are and How You Want to Live, by Alexandra Stoddard (Harper Resource, 2001)

Finding True Love, by Daphne Rose Kingma (Conari Press, 2001)

Forgiveness: A Bold Choice for a Peaceful Heart, by Robin Casarjian (Bantam, 1992)

Guilt Is the Teacher, Love Is the Lesson, by Joan Borysenko (Warner, 1990)

If Love Is a Game, These Are the Rules, by Cherie Carter-Scott (Broadway, 1999)

In Love and in Danger: A Teen's Guide to Breaking Free of Abusive Relationships, by Barrie Levy (Seal Press, 1998)

Love Poems from God: 12 Sacred Voices from the East and West, by Daniel
    Ladinsky (Penguin, 2002)
Love and Survival: The Scientific Basis for the Healing Power of Intimacy,
    by Dean Ornish, M.D. (HarperCollins, 1998)
The Mastery of Love, by Don Miguel Ruiz (Amber-Allen, 1999)
Teachings on Love, by Thich Nhat Hanh (Parallax Press, 1998)

Organizations

Big Brothers and Big Sisters of America
215-567-7000

For teens in an emotionally or physically abusive relationship:
Break the Cycle
P.O. Box 1797
Santa Monica, CA 90406-1797
E-mail: btc@pacificnet.net
888-988-TEEN

Down Syndrome
National Association for Down Syndrome
www.nads.org

Special Olympics:
Sports training for people with intellectual disabilities in more than
    165 countries
www.specialolympics.org

Living Authentically

What is real?
What is not?

What has meaning?
What is taught?
Guideposts everywhere,
Yet no real path.

Smiling faces
Light the way
If you can find them
And push darkness away,
All the way laughing at what fate
   has handed
you.

Trust is a must
For the warrior
on the path.

As you strip away
Layers that you no longer need
Layers upon layers
of old.
Blocking
Getting between you
and your truth

Let it go.
Let it go.

It will find a home
And you will have
Made room for the new.

Your truth will arrive
When you are ready to
hear it—not before

Make room
Prepare the Space
Let out the darkness
Only then can light move in

Trust
Trust yourself
Trust the universe
Let the truth be known

Andrea Joy Cohen, M.D.

DISCUSSION QUESTIONS FOR PERSONAL TRANSFORMATION

I have listed some provocative questions for discussion. If answering these questions appeals to you, you can approach them in any order. You might want to journal the answers, think about them, verbalize, draw them, or discuss them with friends, family, or your therapist. These questions can also be used to spark group discussions, but please take note—you may want to select safe people for discussions. You might find that some of the questions are challenging to answer, or bring up feelings of sadness or discomfort. You can choose to skip those questions, and return to them at a later time when you feel more able to think about them with the support of others. Since some of these are challenging questions, you may choose to do one at a time.

Overcoming Challenges

1. What is the biggest challenge in your life right now? Why?

2. Who are the friends, relatives, and supporters who can be with you during this challenge?

3. Who are your heroes—in this life, and in general? Why?

4. What person or persons did you emulate as a young person?

5. Who challenges you in your life to do your best, reach higher, and stretch further?

6. Have you ever had a life-threatening accident, illness, or situation that broke you down and really made you take stock of your life? How did your life change afterward?

7. Have you taken care of someone with great challenges, e.g., development disorders, paralysis, terminal illness, or mental illness? What have you learned from that experience?

8. Did you ever have to work hard at something that came easier to others? What did you learn from having to put in that extra, often frustrating effort?

9. If you could change one thing in your life, what would it be? How would you change it? How would changing that make your life better?

10. What emotions in your life would you like to release (anger, rage, sadness, fear, anxiety, resentment, mistrust, jealousy)?

11. Do you have an issue with chronic pain? How do you cope?

12. Have you been in therapy, coaching, or counseling? Write about what you have learned about yourself.

13. Have you ever suffered from major depression, grief, anger, or other emotional problems (anxiety, obsession, compulsive behavior, anorexia, bulimia, bipolar disorder)? Have

you survived a "meltdown" or a "breakdown"? Have these experiences helped you see your soul's path more clearly?

14. Do you have any secrets that you haven't ever shared with another human being? How has keeping this secret impacted your life?

15. Are you stuck in your life, by a relationship, a job, a house, or some other way that you just can't get out of it? Write or talk about this. What do you think is holding you back from moving on?

16. Do you express your emotions or do you "stuff" them or numb out so that you don't have to deal with them? Do you cry regularly?

17. Have you ever used alternative medicine for healing, like acupuncture, massage, natural products, or homeopathy? What was your experience?

18. How do you relax?

19. Can you be yourself and show your vulnerabilities to your friends and family (such as your anxiety, shame, and perceived failures)?

Soul Expression

1. What is your greatest dream in this life? If you are not pursuing it yet, what is keeping you from pursuing this dream?

2. Name ten things you would like to learn or accomplish or see in your life.

3. Talk about your current prosperity in all aspects of your life (e.g., health, money, career, spirituality, and creativity).

4. What do you think are the main lessons that your soul has learned in your life thus far?

5. What is your main form of creative expression (painting, drawing, photography, crafts, woodworking, love, animals, children, cooking, work)?

6. Who has supported your creative expression? Who has blocked it? How have these people influenced you?

7. How did your parents affect your expression? What effect has that had on you as an adult?

8. Where does your inspiration come from? Do you have a muse? What is the role of nature in your inspiration?

9. What type of creative endeavor or hobby thrills you to the core?

10. Which artist has inspired you the most? (It could be a visual artist, a sculptor, a musician, a speaker, or anyone.)

11. What is your primary creative goal for the next twelve months?

12. Think about your ideal career. What is different about this ideal that's not present in your current career? Is this dream attainable for you? Why or why not?

13. Where do you live? Does your home express your creativity? Do you love your home? If not, why not? What

keeps you from moving to or creating a home that you do love?

14. Do you make up your own mind on most things, or do you let others influence you?

15. Is there an accomplishment that you are especially proud of? Talk about it, and describe why.

16. What is your problem-solving style? Give an example.

17. What activity or skill would you like to master? What is stopping you from taking steps to doing that? What has kept you from it to date? Do you or others place limits on your capabilities?

18. What are the most important things in your life right now? What about the most important people—who are they and why?

19. Do you have fear of success or failure? What would be the downside of success for you? Do you ever sabotage or punish yourself? Why do you think that could be?

20. Are you great at manifesting what you want? If so, to what do you attribute your success?

21. Are you comfortable speaking up for yourself and standing in your power?

22. What are the "stories" of your life? Are you ready to let go of some of these stories?

23. Would you rather be right or happy?

Death and Dying

1. Has a close friend or family member died? What was the passage experience like for you?

2. Think about or share your grieving process. What do you think happens to a person after they die? Do you believe in heaven or another realm?

3. Have you or a close friend or relative ever had a near-death experience? Please describe. How did this experience change your view of the world?

4. Did one or both of your parents or grandparents die before you became an adult? Write about that experience and that loss. How did that affect your childhood, and your current life?

5. Have you had a pet die? What was that grieving process like for you?

6. What would you like to happen on your deathbed or at your funeral?

7. How would you comfort a child or a teen that was grieving?

8. If you had six months to live, how would you live your life?

9. If you had two weeks to live, how would you live your life?

10. What three things do you want to do before you "die"?

Life's Everyday Lessons

1. Are you a good listener? What are the qualities of a good listener?

2. Do you hold any grudges against anyone?

3. Do you apologize when you hurt someone's feelings or make an inadvertent mistake? If not, what holds you back from that?

4. Has anyone's apology ever impacted you?

5. What lessons did you learn from your parents when they took the moral high ground?

6. Have there been episodes in your life where there were hidden lessons, like in Bernie Siegel's story "Understanding Why," or lessons that were blessings in disguise?

7. What do you know about bullies and victims?

8. Have you ever been bullied by or bullied someone else?

9. What do you do for fun? How do you nourish the child in you?

10. How do you deal with your anger? Is it a healthy management style? What would you like to change about the way you deal with anger—with yourself, with a partner, with friends, with family, at work?

11. Do you think your feminine and masculine sides (yin and yang) are balanced?

12. What is your greatest fear? Describe a time when you overcame a specific fear and took action.

13. Are you a workaholic? Why do you think that is?

14. Is there anything you feel bitter or resentful about? What do you do when you feel bitter? How could you or how have you healed bitterness in your life, so that you can release it and move on?

15. Do you focus on positive things most of the time? If you are feeling down or negative, how do you shift yourself?

Spirituality

1. Do you believe in God or a greater power of some kind? What is your concept of God? If you have no belief like this or are undecided, write or share why.

2. Have you ever had an adverse religious or spiritual experience? Write about that experience, and how you felt about it. How has it affected your current beliefs?

3. Have you ever experienced a miracle or synchronicity, or a mystical experience?

4. How do you connect with your higher power? Does nature play a role in how you live your life?

5. What was your parents' concept of religion or spirituality? How did their beliefs or actions affect you? How have your friends' or partner's concepts of religion or spirituality affected you?

6. How have some of your life lessons affected your spiritual views and/or practices?

7. Have you ever taken a leap of faith in your life? Talk about it. What was it, and how did you do it?

8. Do you have a spiritual practice? Describe what these terms mean in your life. How has this practice affected your day-to-day life? Is it a comfort to you, and if so, how?

9. As Oprah would say, what do you know for sure?

10. Do you pray? Have your specific prayers been answered?

11. Do you feel that God has ever let you down? Are you currently angry at God or hold resentment? Do you completely trust God? How much do you trust yourself, from 0 to 100 percent?

12. Do you believe that everything you need will be provided, or do you fear that you will be abandoned in this life?

13. What do you think makes a person happy or unhappy?

14. What does forgiveness mean to you? What is your way of going about forgiveness?

Family, Love, and Relationships

1. Who has touched your soul the most? Why?

2. Have you ever been in love in a romantic way? If so or if not, how has this affected you?

3. Do you have issues with fear of rejection, abandonment, or annihilation?

4. Have you ever had a relationship you completely regretted? What was the effect of that?

5. Have you ever been through a divorce or a painful breakup with a partner? What did you learn from that experience? What is your relationship with that person now? How do you feel about that status? Is there anything that you would do differently that would have made that process easier for you?

6. Have you ever been betrayed by a friend/family member/significant other? How did you heal from that betrayal? How did this scenario affect you?

7. Write about forgiveness, and the struggles this concept can bring.

8. Have you parented children or mentored younger people? Share how becoming a parent or a mentor has changed you as a person. Were these conscious decisions to change or a gradual process?

9. What is your favorite movie romance? Why? What makes it special to you?

10. Have you ever had an "illicit" romantic encounter? How did this experience make you feel? What emotions did this bring up for you? Would you do it again if you had the chance? Why or why not?

11. Describe what codependence means to you. Have you ever been involved in a codependent relationship? If yes, how did that relationship feel?

12. Describe the main things you remember about your childhood.

13. How does your childhood experience affect your present adult relationship with your parents or caregivers?

14. Think about how you feel about romance, both currently and in your past?

15. What was your most memorable romantic experience? Why?

16. Have there been painful experiences that have wounded you and affected you negatively? Think about how you can heal those, and release them from you.

17. If you wanted to share a big piece of news (positive or negative), who would you call or e-mail? Why? What makes that person special to you?

18. Do you love yourself?

19. Do you love yourself first? If so, give examples. If not, explain why you think this is.

CONTRIBUTORS

Peter Amato

Acknowledged as a visionary, luminary, and distinguished teacher of spiritual inquiry, Peter Amato is the president and founder of Inner Harmony Wellness Centers. As a pioneer in the field of medicine, Amato has developed and designed the nation's first true center for integrative medicine, complete with protocols and business acumen. In addition, he lectures and gives workshops on the spiritual journey. The scope of his work ranges from children to corporations. Amato achieved worldwide success in the automotive and parts industry then turned his attention inward. As a recovering society member, Amato continues to spread his message in the health-care field, in corporate America, and in the corrections and drug and alcohol fields. He has recently retreated again to listen in on the next chapter of his soul's journey. His website is www.peteramato.com.

Angeles Arrien, Ph.D.

Angeles Arrien, Ph.D., is a cultural anthropologist who researched, created, and synthesized the Four-Fold Way educational program.

Medical, academic, and corporate companies currently use the program. Angeles is also an award-winning author, educator, and consultant to many organizations and businesses. She lectures and conducts workshops worldwide, bridging cultural anthropology, psychology, and comparative religions. Her work shows how perennial wisdoms relate to our families, professions, and our relationship to the Earth. Arrien is the president of the Foundation for Cross-Cultural Education and Research and a fellow at the Institute of Noetic Sciences. There is more information at www .angelesarrien.com.

Martha Beck, Ph.D.

Martha Beck, Ph.D., is an innovator in life design and a monthly columnist at *O, The Oprah Magazine*. She founded Martha Beck, Inc., a life-coaching firm that helps clients redirect their careers and lifestyles, and North Star. Beck was a business consultant, a researcher at the Harvard Business School, and a professor at the International School of Business before becoming a life coach. She earned a B.A., M.A., and Ph.D. in sociology from Harvard University. Beck left the academic environment and embraced change with the birth of her son Adam, who has Down syndrome. This experience inspired her *New York Times* bestselling book, *Expecting Adam*. Beck also wrote *Finding Your Own North Star: Claiming the Life You Were Meant to Live*. Her most recent book is *The Joy Diet: 10 Daily Practices for a Happier Life*. The mother of three children, Martha Beck lectures and conducts seminars for a diverse clientele that includes medical professionals, magazine sales forces, boards of education, and business executives. See her website at www.marthabeck.com, and www.liveyournorthstar.com.

Joan Borysenko, Ph.D.

Joan Borysenko, Ph.D., has been described as "a rare jewel: respected scientist, gifted therapist and unabashed mystic." Truly a woman for our times, her brilliance, sense of humor, and compassion have thrilled hundreds of thousands of people worldwide. A powerful and articulate writer and speaker, Borysenko has a clear personal vision—to bring science, medicine, and spirituality together in the service of healing. Borysenko completed both her doctoral and postdoctoral work at the Harvard Medical School in cancer cell biology and behavioral medicine, returning later in her career as an instructor in medicine. She is a licensed clinical psychologist, and cofounder and former director of the mind-body clinical programs at the Beth Israel Deaconess Medical Center, on which her breakthrough *New York Times* bestseller, *Minding the Body, Mending the Mind*, was based. Borysenko has written thirteen books on integrative medicine, psychology, spirituality, and women's studies. Her latest books include *Inner Peace for Busy Women* and *Your Soul's Compass*. Her website is www.joanborysenko.com.

Don Campbell

Don Campbell is a recognized authority on the transformative power of music, listening, and the Mozart Effect. He's a leading lecturer and consultant to health-care organizations, corporations, parenting groups, and educational groups. Author of eighteen books, including *Music: Physician for Times to Come* and the 1997 bestseller *The Mozart Effect*, he has also produced sixteen albums including the accompanying music for the Mozart Effect series for adults and children, which dominated the classical *Billboard* charts for two years. His latest book is *The Harmony of Health*. Don is the acoustic and musical director of Aesthetic Audio Systems, an innovative company that provides quality music to health-care facilities, and is on the board of the American Music Research Center at the University of Colorado, Boulder. For more information see www.mozarteffect.com.

Stephen Fulder, Ph.D.

Dr. Stephen Fulder is a British scientist, lecturer, and author who has written many books on herbal and complementary medicine. He was a lecturer at London University and at the Hadassah Medical School, Jerusalem. Fulder has been involved in creating a medicinal plant industry in Israel, and is now working on a Jewish/Arab medicinal plant garden and cultural site in Galilee. He also practices and teaches Buddhist meditation in Israel. He can be reached at fulder@zahav.net.il. Many of his articles are published at the site www.eolife.org; view his teaching schedule at www.tovana.org.il.

Christine Hibbard, Ph.D.

Dr. Christine Hibbard has been a clinical psychotherapist and psychophysiologist in Boulder County, Colorado, for twenty-two years. In 1980, she cofounded the Family Medical Center with her husband, David Hibbard, M.D. In addition, Hibbard has been the director of the Louisville Biofeedback Clinic since 1982. She is on the faculty of the Transpersonal Psychology Department at Naropa University, where she teaches graduate-level courses. In addition to being a noted lecturer and author, Hibbard is published in professional journals and has edited book chapters on mind/body health. Hibbard received a master's degree in science education and a Ph.D. in clinical psychology. She is a nationally certified biofeedback therapist, a master neuro-linguistic programming practitioner, an advanced certified bereavement counselor, and a graduate of conflict dispute resolution mediation. Hibbard has traveled to East Africa, Venezuela, India, and Israel to share her knowledge. Working with the Healing the Wounds of War project, she taught a training program on postwar trauma to Albanian health-care professionals in Kosovo, Yugoslavia. Hibbard lives in Boulder with her husband and has raised three children. You can visit her web page at www.christinehibbard.org.

Ellyn Hutt

Ellyn Hutt is a longtime educator and teacher of Jewish studies in Denver. She prepares Jewish children for their bar and bat mitzvah coming-of-age ceremonies and teaches adults in both formal and informal settings. Hutt offers classes and programs on various aspects of Judaism, all focused on enhancing the understanding and relevance of Jewish life and rituals from a traditional Torah perspective. Her primary goal is to increase Jewish knowledge and share the joy and spirituality that Torah life offers. Hutt is working on her first book, *Dwelling in the Present Moment*, which focuses on how to use the spiritual wealth of Jewish wisdom, tradition, and ritual as a guide for transformative living. She can be reached at Ellyn40@aol.com.

Susan Jeffers, Ph.D.

Susan Jeffers, Ph.D., is an internationally renowned author who has helped millions of people overcome their fears and heal the pain in their lives. Her books include *Dare to Connect*; *Embracing Uncertainty*; *End the Struggle and Dance with Life*; *Feel the Fear Power Planner*; *Feel the Fear...and Do It Anyway*; *Feel the Fear...and Beyond*; *Freeing Ourselves from the Mad Myths of Parenthood*; *I Can Handle It!*; *I'm OKAY...You're a Brat!*; *Losing a Love...Finding a Life*; *Opening Our Hearts to Men*; *The "Fear-Less" Series That Works*; *Peace of Mind: The Little Book of Confidence*; *The Little Book of Peace*; and *Thoughts of Power and Love*. Jeffers is also a public speaker, workshop leader, and media personality who specializes in the areas of personal growth and relationships. She lives with her husband in Los Angeles. See her website at www.susanjeffers.com. Dr. Jeffers founded The Jeffers Publishing Company. You can visit the website at www.jefferspress.com.

Barry Neil Kaufman

Barry Neil Kaufman has spent the last thirty years doing what most people say is impossible. As a young child, Kaufman's son Raun was diagnosed by professionals with the "incurable" disorder of autism. With his wife, Samahria, Kaufman created an innovative technique that brought their son from a mute, withdrawn, "functionally retarded," under-thirty IQ state to a highly verbal, extroverted, happy young man who tested at a near genius IQ. Drawing on this experience, the Kaufmans established the Option Institute International Learning and Training Center as a nonprofit organization where they share their work with individuals, couples, families, businesses, and groups. In addition to their three biological children, the Kaufmans adopted three other children from desperate situations. They now have three grandchildren as well. Barry Neil Kaufman wears many hats. While directing and teaching at the institute, he also works with individuals, families, groups, businesses, and corporations as well as presenting motivational talks internationally. Kaufman is currently at work on his thirteenth book. His other published works include *No Regrets*; *To Love Is to Be Happy With*; *Happiness Is a Choice*; and *A Sacred Dying*. See the website for the Option Institute at www.option.org.

Dharma Singh Khalsa, M.D.

Born in Ohio and raised in Florida, Dharma Singh Khalsa, M.D., is the founding president and medical director of the Alzheimer's Prevention Foundation International in Tucson, Arizona. He is the only doctor ever invited to testify before the U.S. Congress about using an integrated medical approach to prevent Alzheimer's disease.

Dr. Khalsa is the author of many bestselling and critically

acclaimed books: *Brain Longevity*; *The Pain Cure*; *Meditation as Medicine*; *Food as Medicine*; *The Better Memory Kit*; *The New Golden Rules*; and *The End of Karma*. He has also created ten meditation CDs and a spiritual pop CD called *Love Is in You* by his group, Bliss.

After meeting his spiritual teacher, Yogi Bhajan, in 1981, Dr. Dharma adopted the Sikh faith. He has since donned the full beard and turban of an American yogi. He lives in Tucson, Arizona, with his wife, Kirti, originally from Rome, Italy. Dr. Dharma lectures and consults worldwide. You can contact him through his website, www.drdharma.com.

Tama J. Kieves

Tama J. Kieves, an honors graduate of Harvard Law School, left her law practice with one of Denver's largest law firms to write and to embolden others to live and breathe their most meaningful self-expression. She is a national creativity coach and life/work coach and the bestselling author of *This Time I Dance! Trusting the Journey of Creating the Work You Love*. Kieves's work has been featured on television, radio, and in national publications. Learn more about Tama's workshops and work at www.awakeningartistry.com.

Daphne Rose Kingma, M.A.

Daphne Rose Kingma, M.A., is a poet, psychoanalyst, and writer. An undisputed expert on matters of the heart, Kingma has appeared six times on *Oprah,* and on many other television shows, including *Sally Jesse Raphael*, *Leeza*, and on CNN. She has also been interviewed on over three hundred radio shows. Kingma's books have been featured in numerous magazines and newspapers such as *Glamour, Cosmopolitan, Mademoiselle, Redbook,* the *Los Angeles Times,* and the *Dallas Morning News.* Dubbed the "Love Doctor" by the *San Francisco Chronicle,* she is the author of ten books, including the bestsellers *Finding True Love* and *Coming Apart.* Kingma also wrote the foreword for the book *Random Acts of Kindness.* See her website at www.daphnekingma.com.

Phyllis R. Koch-Sheras, Ph.D.

Phyllis R. Koch-Sheras, Ph.D., is a practicing clinical psychotherapist and coauthor of several books on dreams and couples, including *The Dream Sourcebook* and *Dream On: A Dream Interpretation and Exploration Guide for Women.* She is founder and president of the Creative and Healing Arts Institute, a nonprofit organization in Charlottesville, Virginia, that promotes healing in the community, past president of the Virginia Applied Psychology Academy, and president of the Virginia Psychological Association. Koch-Sheras received her doctorate from the University of Texas and has worked in state hospitals, university counseling centers, and private practice. She is an adjunct faculty member at the University of Virginia's Curry School of Education. See her website at www.couplepower.com.

Linda Schierse Leonard, Ph.D.

Dr. Linda Schierse Leonard is a philosopher and a Jungian analyst trained at the C. G. Jung Institute in Zurich, Switzerland. She is the author of the bestselling books *The Wounded Woman*, *On the Way to the Wedding*, *Witness to the Fire*, and *Meeting the Madwoman*. Her books have been published in twelve languages. She has been the recipient of an American Council of Learned Societies postdoctoral fellowship, and in 1994 she was chosen Distinguished Visiting Scholar at the College of Notre Dame in Belmont, California. She has taught at the University of Colorado, Denver, and at San Diego State University. Currently she is a consultant on creative issues and gives lectures and workshops worldwide. She is a founding member of the Inter-Regional Society of Jungian Analysts and a member of the C. G. Jung Institute of San Francisco.

Harriet Lerner, Ph.D.

Harriet Lerner, Ph.D., born in Brooklyn, New York, in 1944, is the second of two daughters of Rose and Archie Goldhor. Her parents were first-generation Americans, both born to Russian Jewish immigrant parents. Lerner is a prolific scholar as well as a nationally acclaimed expert on the psychology of women. She has a remarkable ability to translate complex theory into accessible prose. Lerner's books have been published in more than thirty foreign editions with sales of over 3 million. Her ever-popular trilogy *The Dance of Anger* (1985), *The Dance of Intimacy* (1989), and *The Dance of Deception* (1993) challenges and changes readers in fundamental ways. In addition, Lerner is the author of *Life Preserves: Good Advice When You Need It Most*; *The Mother Dance: How Children Change Your Life*; and *The Dance of Connection: How to Talk to Someone When You're Mad, Hurt, Scared, Frustrated, Insulted, Betrayed, or Desperate*. In addition to writing, Lerner travels nationally to lecture, consult, and present workshops. She is in private practice in Topeka, Kansas. For more information, see her website, www .harrietlerner.com.

Elizabeth Lesser

Elizabeth Lesser is the cofounder and senior adviser of Omega Institute, located in Rhinebeck, New York. The Omega Institute is recognized internationally for its workshops and professional training in holistic health, psychology, and cross-cultural arts and religion. Since 1977, when Omega was founded, she has helped direct the institute's organization, research and develop its programs, and train its staff. She has also been privileged to study and teach with leading thinkers and practitioners in the fields of human development and spiritual growth. Prior to her work at Omega, Lesser was a midwife and childbirth educator. She attended Barnard College and San Francisco State University. Lesser lives in the Hudson River Valley with her family. For contact information, see www .eomega.org

Joel Levey, Ph.D., and Michelle Levey, M.A.

The Leveys' work offers a unique synthesis of insights woven from contemporary disciplines and enduring wisdom traditions, including systems thinking; mind-body medicine; social architecture and organization design; community building; peacemaking; quality communications and high-performance teamwork; peak performance training; comparative religion and contemplative traditions; and global travel and cross-cultural study. Their publications include their newest books, *Wisdom at Work: A Treasury of Tools for Cultivating Clarity, Kindness and Resilience* and *Living in Balance: A Dynamic Approach to Creating Harmony and Wholeness in a Chaotic World.* In addition, *Quality of Mind: Tools for Self Mastery and Enhanced Performance* speaks to the profound synergy between personal and organizational learning and transformation. Their first book, *The Fine Arts of Relaxation, Concentration, and Meditation: Ancient Skills for Modern Minds*, is a classic that has been used widely in mind-body medicine education and peak performance programs around the globe.

Joel Levey, Ph.D., has also served as graduate faculty and adviser for Antioch University; director of psychophysiological therapy and stress management for the Group Health Cooperative in Seattle; director of corporate education for American Biotec Corporation; and director of mindbody fitness training for SportsMind, Inc. Michelle Levey, M.A., has also served as senior consultant for SportsMind, Inc., and as lead clinician for the Biofeedback and Stress Management Clinic at Children's Hospital in Seattle. The Leveys are based in Seattle and offer services to organizations around the globe. For further information, visit their websites at www.wisdomatwork.com and www.kohalasanctuary.com.

Stephen Levine

Writer and poet Stephen Levine has devoted more than eighteen years to investigating the mind/body relationship, particularly as it relates to the states of healing, dying, and grieving. His work has affected healing and medical practices worldwide. He has written many classic bestsellers such as *Embracing the Beloved* and *A Year to Live*. Having raised three children, he and his wife, Ondrea, moved into the deep woods, where they have been involved in a relationship experiment of considerable song and intensity. His website is www.stephenlevine.com.

Patricia Kaplan Madsen

Patricia Kaplan Madsen received her education at Brandeis University, Loretto Heights College, the University of Denver College of Law and Judaic Studies Program. She is a judge and practices law in Denver, Colorado. She is also a writer, yogini, and devoted spouse. She manipulates concepts (air) related to water law (water) to earn a living (earth) with a passion (fire). Deep down, she suspects astrology is a bunch of hooey, but she'd like it to be real because it is so elegant. Which would you rather have: Saturn in Virgo at the top of your chart with Moon in trine, or an Adlerian death wish? You can contact her at Patsact@yahoo.com.

Belleruth Naparstek, M.A., L.I.S.W., B.C.D.

Clinical social worker, author, and guided-imagery pioneer Belleruth Naparstek, M.A., L.I.S.W., B.C.D., has practiced psychotherapy for more than thirty years. She is best known as the creator of Time Warner's fifty-two-title Health Journeys guided-imagery audio series. Naparstek's first book, *Staying Well with Guided Imagery*, first published in 1993, continues to be a widely used primer for medical professionals and health consumers. Her second book,

Your Sixth Sense, first published in 1997, has been translated into nine languages and is considered one of the more thoughtful examinations of the nature of intuition. Naparstek is currently completing her third book on imagery and trauma. She has helped to make guided imagery part of mainstream health care by persuading corporations such as Aetna U.S. Healthcare, the U.S. Veteran's Administration, GlaxoSmithKline, the Red Cross, Blue Shield of California, OrthoBiotech, Roche Laboratories, Medical Mutual of Ohio, Kaiser Permanente, and nearly two thousand hospitals, clinics, and worksite health venues to distribute her guided-imagery recordings. For more information, see www.healthjourneys.com.

Thich Nhat Hanh

Thich Nhat Hanh has lived an extraordinary life in an extraordinary time. Since age sixteen, he has been a Buddhist monk, a peace activist, and a seeker of the way. He has survived persecution, three wars, and more than thirty years of exile. He is the master of one of the most prominent temples in Vietnam, and his lineage is traceable directly to the Buddha himself. Thich Nhat Hanh has also written more than one hundred books of poetry, fiction, and philosophy, including the national bestsellers *Anger, Living Buddha, Living Christ*, and *The Art of Power*. He has founded universities and social services organizations; rescued boat people; and led the Buddhist delegation at the Paris Peace Talks. The Rev. Martin Luther King, Jr., nominated him for the Nobel Peace Prize. Thich Nhat Hanh makes his home in France and Vermont. For more information on his programs, teaching, and giving opportunities, please see the website www.plumvillage.org.

Dani Noble (Danielle Joy Noble)

Dani is a sensitive, talented seventeen-year-old young woman (who participates in multiple theater productions in school) with a great sense of humor, who is beautiful inside and out. She wrote this piece when she was fourteen. Not only does she excel at everything she does, but she is a compassionate and highly conscious human being who easily connects with people of all ages. She has made significant contributions to her school, her community, and in the political arena.

She is the editor-in-chief of the school newspaper and community service director for her high school. This includes volunteerships at local homeless shelters and clothing drives. She planned and executed a charity banquet benefiting the Kelly Anne Dolan Memorial Fund, an organization that financially assists local families with children who have terminal illnesses. Dani has also tutored and mentored first graders and peers, and volunteers at a local senior center.

In addition, she is active politically—she was a precinct organizer in the last federal election, an intern for a Pennsylvania senate campaign, and is president and founder of the Springfield Township High School Human Rights Club. Dani was the co-organizer for the first ever Philadelphia Youth Conference on Darfur. Dani was recently nominated for the Young Hero Award in Philadelphia. Her e-mail address is noble_dani@yahoo.com.

Dean Ornish, M.D.

Dean Ornish, M.D., is the founder, president, and director of the nonprofit Preventive Medicine Research Institute in Sausalito,

California, where he holds the Bucksbaum Chair. He is a clinical professor of medicine at the University of California, San Francisco. Ornish received his medical training from the Baylor College of Medicine, Harvard Medical School, and Massachusetts General Hospital. He received a B.A. in humanities summa cum laude from the University of Texas in Austin, where he gave the baccalaureate address. For the past twenty-four years, Ornish has directed clinical research demonstrating for the first time that comprehensive lifestyle changes may begin to reverse even severe coronary heart disease, without drugs or surgery. He is the author of five bestselling books, including *New York Times* bestsellers *Dr. Dean Ornish's Program for Reversing Heart Disease*; *Eat More, Weigh Less*; and *Love and Survival*. Ornish's research and writings have been published in *The Journal of the American Medical Association*, *The Lancet*, *Circulation*, *The New England Journal of Medicine*, *The American Journal of Cardiology*, and elsewhere. A one-hour documentary of his work was broadcast on the PBS science series *Nova* and was featured on Bill Moyers's PBS series *Healing and the Mind*. His work has been featured in virtually all major media, including cover stories in *Newsweek*, *Time*, and *U.S. News & World Report*. Learn more about him at www.pmri.org.

Paramahamsa Prajnanananda

Paramahamsa Prajnanananda, leader of Kriya Yoga and the disciple and designated successor of Paramahamsa Hariharananda, has taken on the mission of bringing the ancient secret teachings within the reach of common people who are thirsting for spiritual knowledge. Paramahamsa Prajnanananda was born in 1960 in the village of Pattamundai in Orissa, India. He has always been a sincere seeker of truth. After a childhood filled with prayer and a youth enriched by education joined with meditation, the former Triloki Dash (his birth name) became a caring teacher as a professor of economics and guided and inspired many of his students spiritually.

A truly powerful and extremely loving teacher, author, and speaker on world religion, well versed in the scriptures of the East and West, he combines a divine compassion for humanity with his love for God and his mastery of complex philosophical thoughts. His vast knowledge and his oratory and intellectual skills are fully utilized in interpreting deep philosophical thoughts in the light of modern science and psychology. His metaphorical interpretation of the scriptures is unique. Using Kriya Yoga as a reference point and an interpretative tool, Prajnananandaji manages to reveal the hidden truth contained in the most complex passages of the sacred texts in ways that make the meanings relevant and helpful in our daily lives. He has written many inspiring books. His website is www.kriya.org.

Rachel Naomi Remen, M.D.

Dr. Remen is one of the earliest pioneers of integrative medicine. She is clinical professor of family and community medicine at the University of California, San Francisco, School of Medicine. Remen is director of the innovative UCSF course The Healer's Art, presently taught in twenty-one medical schools nationwide. She is cofounder and medical director of the Commonweal Cancer

Help Program featured in the groundbreaking 1993 Bill Moyers PBS series *Healing and the Mind*. She is founder and director of the Institute for the Study of Health and Illness at Commonweal, a postgraduate and undergraduate program for physicians who wish to reclaim their calling and integrate holistic approaches into their work. Remen has a fifty-year personal history of Crohn's disease, and her work is a unique blend of the viewpoint of physician and patient. Remen wrote one of the first books on complementary and integrative medicine, *The Human Patient*, published in 1981. In addition, she wrote the *New York Times* bestseller *Kitchen Table Wisdom: Stories That Heal* and *My Grandfather's Blessings: Stories of Strength, Refuge, and Belonging*. Remen is the author of over fifty papers and articles on integrative medicine, and her books are used as teaching texts in medical and nursing schools nationwide. She has been the invited speaker at several medical school graduations and holds three honorary degrees. Her website is www .rachelremen.com.

Matthew Scala

Matthew Scala says, "I am one person who has been incredibly blessed with many experiences apparently designed to teach me about transformation. My strength has been in developing a life's work that embodies these learned lessons. While working with couples and men in transition, I've gained a deeper satisfaction for life. Love and joy have become the essence of this.

"I enjoy curling, weight training, landscape sculpting, and most any sport that involves moving my body in Taurean fashion, close to the earth, at reasonable speeds on the coasts of Maine and Washington and in the central mountains of Colorado.

"I am available for speaking engagements in which to share more of this transformative journey. I can be reached at matthew scala@yahoo.com."

Anne Wilson Schaef, Ph.D.

Anne Wilson Schaef has a Ph.D. in clinical psychology and an honorary doctorate in humane letters from Kenyon College in Ohio. She left the field of psychology and psychotherapy in 1984. Schaef has since conducted intensives and training sessions in the United States and throughout the world in an approach to healing that she has developed called Living in Process, which is an alternative approach to healing that comes out of ancient teachings. Schaef is internationally known as a speaker, consultant, and seminar leader. She has published thirteen books and numerous articles. For more information see www.livinginprocess.com.

Peter L. Sheras, Ph.D., ABPP

Dr. Peter Sheras is a clinical psychologist who has coauthored several publications on couples, dreamwork, brief therapy, and youth violence and adolescent development, including *Your Child and Clinical Psychology: A Social Psychological Approach* (1979). He has a diplomate in clinical psychology, is a fellow of the American Academy of Clinical Sexologists and past president of the

Virginia Psychological Association, and has presented more than thirty workshops in the past five years. He appears frequently as an expert in the media on topics of couples, adolescents, and families. He received his doctorate from Princeton University and is a professor in the University of Virginia's Curry Programs in Clinical and School Psychology. See his website at www.couplepower.com.

Bernie Siegel, M.D.

Bernie Siegel, M.D., is one of the world's foremost physicians, authors, motivational speakers, and advocates for individuals facing the challenges of all chronic illnesses.

His many articles, bestselling books, tapes, and videos serve as a testimony to his loving commitment to those who choose to take an active role in their own healing. He and his wife, Bobbie, have introduced the concept of individual and group therapy based on "carefrontation," a loving, safe, therapeutic confrontation enabling everyone to understand his or her healing potential. Bernie (as he prefers to be called) attended Colgate University and Cornell University Medical College. He holds membership in two scholastic honor societies, Phi Beta Kappa and Alpha Omega Alpha, and graduated with honors. His surgical training was at Yale New Haven Hospital and the Children's Hospital of Pittsburgh. He is a retired pediatric and general surgeon. Today, Bernie lectures extensively around the world, sharing his message of peace, love, and healing.

In 1978, Bernie began talking about patient empowerment and the choice to live fully and die in peace. The same year, he founded the nonprofit Exceptional Cancer Patients based upon his loving philosophy of creating awareness for using one's healing potential to overcome the challenges of difficult times. As a physician who has cared for and counseled innumerable people whose lives have been threatened by an illness, Bernie embraces a philosophy of living and dying that stands at the forefront of the medical ethics and spiritual issues that our society grapples with today. His pioneering efforts in the field of mind-body interaction and healing, patient empowerment, and the humanizing of medical education and care are making a significant difference today. Never before has there been a better opportunity to offer his message of love, hope, and healing. Visit his website at www.berniesiegelmd.com.

David Whyte

Poet David Whyte grew up among the hills and valleys of Yorkshire, England. The author of four books of poetry, he is one of the few poets to take his perspectives on creativity into the field of organizational development, where he works with many American and international companies. Whyte holds a degree in marine zoology and has traveled extensively, including working as a naturalist guide leading anthropological and natural history expeditions. He brings this wealth of experiences to his poetry, lectures, and workshops. In organizational settings, using poetry and thoughtful commentary, Whyte illustrates how we can foster qualities of courage and engagement—qualities needed if we are to respond to today's call for increased creativity and adaptability in the workplace. He brings a unique and important contribution to our understanding of the nature of individual and organizational change. Whyte is also the author of *The Heart Aroused: Poetry and the Preservation of the Soul in Corporate America*, an audiocassette lecture series, and an album of poetry and music. His new book of prose, *Crossing the Unknown Sea: Work as a Pilgrimage of Identity*, was published in March 2001. He lives with his family in the Pacific Northwest. His website is http://davidwhyte.bigmindcatalyst.com.

ABOUT ANDREA JOY COHEN, M.D.

Andrea Joy Cohen, M.D., is a physician, writer, and cancer researcher. As an international speaker, she is well known for her wisdom, warmth, and sense of humor. Board certified in internal and pulmonary medicine as well as holistic medicine, Dr. Cohen's vision for the future of wellness is an integrative medical system where conventional medicine merges with complementary medicine, and the arts, psychology, and spirituality are woven together in a personalized fashion bringing health and prosperity to the individual.

Dr. Cohen is also an inspirational writer and a prolific poet. In addition to her numerous scientific writings, she has compiled two anthologies about psychological and spiritual topics and penned over a hundred poems. *A Blessing in Disguise* includes luminaries from the fields of medicine, psychology, religion, and literature writing of the lessons learned (their "blessings in disguise"), gleaned from challenging life events.

In addition, Dr. Cohen has just completed a book with teens and young adults describing their life lessons and how these challenges can be responded to with faith, wisdom, and courage. Her writings are a bridge between her scientific endeavors and her vision for society.

One of Dr. Andrea Joy Cohen's great passions is teaching about how to claim prosperity while learning about, and transforming, ourselves. To provide information and inspiration, Dr. Cohen delivers lectures worldwide on integrative medicine, wellness, and cancer research. Her innovative workshops, seminars, and teleclasses have been met with great enthusiasm. She has given keynotes, seminars, and workshops worldwide in locations such as Singapore, India, and Tokyo.

The media often turns to Dr. Cohen as a reliable source on integrative medicine. She has appeared in or been interviewed for many newspapers, television and radio broadcasts, and magazines, including *Oprah, Arthritis Today, Yoga Life*, the *Boulder Daily Camera*, and *National Public Radio*. Dr. Cohen was featured in *Self* magazine on the healing power of poetry.

A traditional lung cancer molecular biologist for many years, Dr. Cohen founded the Complementary and Alternative Medicine Research Program in Cancer at the University of Colorado Health Sciences Center. In 2002, the National Cancer Institute awarded Dr. Cohen a program grant to study the efficacy of complementary and alternative medicines such as innovative natural products in cancer. Dr. Cohen has contributed many chapters to medical textbooks and has been published in multiple journals such as *Cancer Research* and the *American Journal of Respiratory and Critical Care Medicine.*

As a physician, professor, researcher, writer, and lecturer during these past twenty years, Dr. Cohen's visionary approach and energy have put her on the cutting edge of those in traditional medicine who are now creating the medicine of the future. Read more about her work and get inspired at her website, www.DrAndreaJoyCohen.com.

SELECTED WORKS BY
CONTRIBUTING AUTHORS

Arrien, Angeles, *The Four-Fold Way: Walking the Paths of Warrior, Teacher, Healer, and Visionary* (HarperSanFrancisco, 1993)

———, *The Nine Muses: A Mythological Path to Creativity* (Jeremy P. Tarcher, 2000)

———, ed., *Working Together: Diversity as Opportunity* (Berrett-Koehler, 2001)

———, *Gathering Medicine: Stories, Songs, and Methods for Soul Retrieval*, CD (Sounds True, 2006)

Beck, Martha, *Expecting Adam* (Berkley, 1999)

———, *Finding Your Own North Star* (Three Rivers Press, 2001)

———, *The Joy Diet: 10 Daily Practices for a Happier Life* (Crown, 2003)

———, *Leaving the Saints: How I Lost the Mormons and Found My Faith* (Crown, 2005)

———, *Wisdom from Finding Your Own North Star* (Peter Pauper Press, 2005)

———, *The Four Day Win: End Your Diet War and Achieve Thinner Peace* (Rodale, 2006)

———, monthly column in *O, The Oprah Magazine*

Borysenko, Joan, *Minding the Body, Mending the Mind* (Bantam, 1988)

———, *A Woman's Journey to God* (Riverhead, 1999)

———, *Inner Peace for Busy Women* (Hay House, 2005)

Borysenko, Joan, and Gordon F. Dveirin, *Saying Yes to Change* (Hay House, 2005)

———, *Your Soul's Compass* (Hay House, 2007)

Campbell, Don, *Music: Physician for Times to Come* (Quest, 1995)

———, *Music for the Mozart Effect, Vol. 2, Heal the Body*, audio CD (Spring Hill Music, 1998)

———, *The Harmony of Health* (Hay House, 2006)

Fulder, Stephen, *The Book of Ginseng and Other Chinese Herbs for Vitality* (Inner Traditions, 1993)

———, *The Handbook of Complementary Medicine* (Oxford Medical, 1996)

Jeffers, Susan, *Feel the Fear . . . and Do It Anyway* (Ballantine, 1988)

———, *End the Struggle and Dance with Life* (St. Martin's Press, 1996)

———, *Embracing Uncertainty* (St. Martin's Press, 2003)

———, *The Feel the Fear Guide to Lasting Love* (Jeffers Press, 2005)

Kaufman, Barry Neil, *A Sacred Dying* (Epic Century, 1996)

———, *Power Dialogues* (Epic Century, 2001)

———, *No Regrets* (H. J. Kramer, 2003)

Khalsa, Dharma Singh, *Brain Longevity: The Breakthrough Medical Program That Improves Your Mind and Memory* (Warner, 1999)

———, *Meditation as Medicine: Activate the Power of Your Natural Healing Force* (Atria, 2002)

———, *The Better Memory Kit* (Hay House, 2004)

———, *Food as Medicine* (Atria, 2004)

———, *The End of Karma* (Hay House, 2005)

———, *The New Golden Rules* (Hay House, 2005)

Kieves, Tama J., *Dreams Come True When You Do* (Awakening Artistry, 2002)

———, *This Time I Dance! Trusting the Journey of Creating the Work You Love* (Jeremy P. Tarcher, 2003)

Kingma, Daphne Rose, *The Book of Love* (Conari Press, 2001)

———, *Finding True Love* (Conari Press, 2001)

———, *Loving Yourself: Four Steps to a Happier You* (Conari Press, 2004)

———, *101 Ways to Have True Love in Your Life* (Conari Press, 2006)

Koch-Sheras, Phyllis R., and Amy Lemley, *The Dream Sourcebook: A Guide to the Theory and Interpretation of Dreams* (Lowell House, 1999)

Koch-Sheras, Phyllis R., and Peter L. Sheras, *The Dream Sharing Sourcebook: A Practical Guide to Enhancing Your Personal Relationships* (McGraw-Hill/Contemporary Books, 1998)

Lafaille, Robert, and Stephen Fulder, *Toward a New Science of Health* (Routledge, 2005)

Leonard, Linda Schierse, *The Wounded Woman* (Shambhala, 1998)

————, *Witness to the Fire* (Random House, 2001)

————, *Following the Reindeer Woman: Path of Peace and Harmony* (Spring Journal, 2005)

Lerner, Harriet, *The Dance of Intimacy: A Woman's Guide to Courageous Acts of Change in Key Relationships* (HarperCollins, 1989)

————, *The Dance of Connection: How to Talk to Someone When You're Mad, Hurt, Scared, Frustrated, Insulted, Betrayed, or Desperate* (Quill, 2002)

————, *The Dance of Anger: A Woman's Guide to Changing the Patterns of Intimate Relationships* (HarperCollins, 2005)

————, *The Dance of Fear: Rising above Anxiety, Fear, and Shame to Be Your Best and Bravest Self* (HarperCollins, 2005)

Lesser, Elizabeth, *The New American Spirituality* (Random House, 1999)

————, *The Seeker's Guide* (Villard, 2000)

————, *Broken Open: How Difficult Times Can Make Us Grow* (Villard, 2004)

Levey, Joel, and Michelle Levey, *Living in Balance: A Dynamic Approach for Creative Harmony and Wholeness in a Chaotic World* (Gift, 2007)

————, *Simple Meditation and Relaxation* (Castle, 2002)

————, *A Moment to Relax: Stress Relief in Minutes* (Chronicle, 2003)

————, *Fine Arts of Relaxation, Concentration, and Meditation: Ancient Skills for Modern Minds* (Wisdom Publications, 2005)

————, *Luminous Mind: Meditation and Mind Fitness* (Conari Press, 2006)

Levine, Stephen, *A Year to Live: How to Live This Year as if It Were Your Last* (Random House, 1997)

————, *Unattended Sorrow: Recovering Your Loss and Reviving the Heart* (Rodale, 2005)

Levine, Stephen, and Ondrea Levine, *Embracing the Beloved: Relationship as a Path of Awakening* (Anchor, 1996)

————, *The Grief Process: Meditations for Healing* (Sounds True, 2006)

Naparstek, Belleruth, *Health Journeys: A Meditation to Ease Grief*, audio CD (Image Paths, 1992)

————, *Staying Well with Guided Imagery* (Warner, 1995)

————, *Invisible Heroes: Survivors of Trauma and How They Heal* (Bantam, 2005)

————, *Health Journeys: 4 Meditations for Unlocking Intuition,* audio CD (Health Journeys, 2006)

Nhat Hanh, Thich, *Anger: Wisdom for Cooling the Flames* (Riverhead, 2002)

————, *No Death, No Fear* (Riverhead, 2002)

————, *Taming the Tiger Within* (Riverhead, 2002)

————, *Teachings on Love* (Parallax Press, 2006)

————, *Understanding Our Mind: Fifty Verses on Buddhist Psychology* (Parallax Press, 2006)

Ornish, Dean, *Dr. Dean Ornish's Program for Reversing Heart Disease: The Only System Scientifically Proven to Reverse Heart Disease without Drugs or Surgery* (Ivy, 1995)

————, *Love and Survival: The Scientific Basis for the Healing Power of Intimacy* (HarperCollins, 1998)

————, *Eat More, Weigh Less: Dr. Dean Ornish's Life Choice Program for Losing Weight Safely while Eating Abundantly* (HarperCollins, 2000)

Prajnanananda, Paramahamsa, *Yoga Pathway to the Divine* (Prajna, 1999)

————, *My Time with the Master* (Prajna, 2001)

————, *The Last Decade* (Sai Towers, 2005)

————, *Rama Katha* (Sai Towers, 2005)

Remen, Rachel Naomi, *Kitchen Table Wisdom* (Riverhead, 1996, 2006)

————, *My Grandfather's Blessings* (Riverhead, 2000)

————, *The Little Book of Kitchen Table Wisdom* (Riverhead, 2007)

Schaef, Anne Wilson, *Beyond Therapy, Beyond Science: A New Model for Healing the Whole Person* (HarperSanFrancisco, 1992)

————, *Women's Reality: An Emerging Female System in a White Male Society* (HarperSanFrancisco, 1992)

———, *Meditations for People Who (May) Worry Too Much* (Ballantine, 1996)

———, *Meditations for Living in Balance: Daily Solutions for People Who Do Too Much* (HarperSanFrancisco, 2000)

Sheras, Peter L., *Your Child: Bully or Victim? Understanding and Ending Schoolyard Tyranny* (Fireside, 2002)

———, *I Can't Believe You Went Through My Stuff: How to Give Your Teens the Privacy They Crave and the Guidance They Need* (Fireside, 2004)

Sheras, Peter L., and Phyllis Koch-Sheras, *Couple Power Therapy: Building Commitment, Cooperation, Communication, and Community in Relationships* (American Psychological Association, 2006)

Siegel, Bernie, *How to Live between Office Visits* (HarperCollins, 1993)

———, *Love, Medicine and Miracles: Lessons Learned about Self-Healing from a Surgeon's Experience with Exceptional Patients* (Harper, 1998)

———, *Getting Ready* (Hay House, 2004)

———, *Love, Magic and Mudpies: Raising Your Kids to Feel Loved, Be Kind, and Make a Difference* (Rodale, 2006)

Whyte, David, *Crossing the Unknown Sea* (Riverhead, 2001)

———, *The House of Belonging* (Many Rivers Press, 2002)

———, *Everything Is Waiting for You* (Many Rivers Press, 2003)

JOIN US

Contribute to *A Blessing in Disguise*

I hope you enjoyed this copy of *A Blessing in Disguise*. I invite you to send stories, essays, poems, and photographs that you would like to be considered for future publications of *A Blessing in Disguise* or similar books. I would also like to hear your reaction to the stories in the book, or any worthy resources for future resources sections in the book or on the web page.

Please send your original stories and correspondence information to Dr. Andrea Joy Cohen at stories@drandreajoycohen.com. Please include an attachment using Word, as well as inserting the story into the e-mail. Or mail the stories on CD to Dr. Andrea Joy Cohen, PO Box 6488, Denver, CO, 80206.

Unfortunately, we will not be able to return stories, poems, pictures, or photographs that we do not include in future editions of *A Blessing in Disguise* so please keep a copy of your work for yourself. Visit my website, www.DrAndreaJoyCohen.com, for more details on submitting your piece.

Visit the Website

For more information, inspiration, and activities about *A Blessing in Disguise*, or to contribute a story or feedback, please go to **www.DrAndreaJoyCohen.com**, where you can join our community and read about upcoming teleclasses, conferences, and media events.

In addition, you will find information and resources about topics in medicine, as well as integrative medicine and complementary therapies, cancer research, prosperity, emotional and spiritual issues, and much more. See you there!

Help Others

Here are a few philanthropic giving opportunities you might enjoy learning more about. For more information on philanthropy, visit my website, www.DrAndreaJoyCohen.com.

Hand in Hand USA Paramahamsa Prajnanananda founded Hand in Hand, a nonprofit organization, to provide humanitarian aid to victims of natural calamities and free medical treatment and education for the poor. For more information, please see www.handinhandusa.org.

Karunamayi Foundation This modern-day saint assists the underserved in India with a free hospital, handicap clinic, opthamology clinics, and mobile medical vans as well as free schools. For more information, see www.karunamayi.org.

Plum Village Program on Love and Understanding Thich Nhat Hanh's program to provide food, water, and education to children, the poor, and the elderly. For more information, see www.plumvillage.org.

PERMISSIONS

Section Two: Soul Expression

Section Three: Death and Dying

"The Final Gift: Honesty." from *No Regrets: Last Chance for a Father and a Son* by Barry Neil Kaufman © 2003 by Barry Neil Kaufman. Reprinted with permission of HJ Kramer/New World Library, Novato, CA (800-972-6657 ext. 52 or www.newworldlibrary.com).

"Waking Up within Life's Mashugana Dream" by Joel Levey, Ph.D., and Michelle Levey, M.A. © 2003. Printed with permission of Joel Levey, Ph.D., and Michelle Levey, M.A.

"Death and Dying" by Thich Nhat Hanh © 2003 by Thich Nhat Hanh. Printed with permission of Thich Nhat Hanh.

Section Four: Life's Everyday Lessons

"Jewel" by Andrea Joy Cohen, M.D. © 2001 by Andrea Joy Cohen, M.D. Printed with permission of Andrea Joy Cohen, M.D.

"Understanding Why" by Bernie Siegel, M.D. © 2003 by Bernie Siegel, M.D. Printed with permission of Bernie Siegel, M.D.

"You Are the Gift" by Daphne Rose Kingma © 2003 by Daphne Rose Kingma. Printed with permission of Daphne Rose Kingma.

"Patience Pays—Wait: Life Lessons Learned from Being a Medical Pioneer" by Dharma Singh Khalsa, M.D. © 2003 by Dharma Singh Khalsa, M.D. Printed with permission of Dharma Singh Khalsa, M.D.

"We Are Never Too Young for Life's Lessons" by Anne Wilson Schaef, Ph.D. © 2003 by Anne Wilson Schaef, Ph.D. Printed with permission of Anne Wilson Schaef, Ph.D.

"The Power of Genuine Apology: A Shape-Shifting Tool" by Angeles Arrien, Ph.D. © 2003 by Angeles Arrien, Ph.D. Printed with permission of Angeles Arrien, Ph.D.

Section Five: Spirituality

"Earth and Sky" by Andrea Joy Cohen, M.D. © 2001 by Andrea Joy Cohen, M.D. Printed with permission of Andrea Joy Cohen, M.D.

Section Six: Family, Love, and Relationships